DOPE AND TROUBLE

Also by Elliott Currie

Confronting Crime:
An American Challenge

DOPE AND TROUBLE

Portraits of Delinquent Youth

Elliott Currie

Pantheon Books   New York

Grateful acknowledgment is made to the following for permission to reprint previously published material:

Screen Gems-EMI Music Inc.: Excerpt from the song lyrics "Mary Jane" by Dave Mustaine and Dave Ellefson. Copyright © 1988 by Mustaine Music/Elfson Music/ Theory Music. All rights controlled and administered by Screen Gems-EMI Music Inc. and Theory Music. All rights reserved. International Copyright Secured. Used by permission.

Willesden Music: Excerpt from the song lyrics "City of Dope" written by Todd Shaw/Al Eaton. Copyright © 1989 by Willesden Music/Strand Music/One Little Indian Music. All rights controlled by Willesden Music. Reprinted by permission. All rights reserved.

Library of Congress Cataloging-in-Publication Data
Currie, Elliott.
Dope and trouble : portraits of delinquent youth / by Elliott
Currie.
p.   cm.
ISBN 0-394-56151-1
1. Juvenile delinquents—United States—Interviews.   I. Title.
HV9104.C85   1992   90-52577
364.3'6'0973—dc20

Book Design by Anne Scatto
Manufactured in the United States of America
First Edition

Contents

PART 3 · The Intermittent Blaze of Folly · 179

Acknowledgments

I am deeply grateful to the twenty young men and women who appear in this book, and to all the others I talked with in "the Hall," for their enthusiasm, honesty, and willingness to talk openly and freely to a complete stranger. Because their identities must be kept confidential, I cannot, unfortunately, thank them by name; nor can I name the many people working in the juvenile justice system of "River County" who generously provided access, advice, and friendship. In a world and a time too often hostile or indifferent to the welfare of the young, the dedication and old-fashioned concern of many of the youth workers I met in the course of this project were encouraging and gratifying.

Thanks, too, to all the staff, past and present, at Pantheon Books—to Sara Bershtel for support at the start, to Frances Jalet-Miller for timely enthusiasm and commitment to the project as well as expert editorial advice, and to Dan Frank and Alan Turkus for following through. And thanks, once again, to John Brockman and Katinka Matson for helping to make the book a reality, and to Susannah Currie and Rachael Peltz for support and encouragement on the home front.

E.C.

Introduction

On any given day in the United States, around half a million children and adolescents are locked away out of sight—in juvenile detention facilities, adolescent mental wards, residential drug-rehabilitation programs, and group homes. Vastly more pass through those institutions at some point in their lives; every year over a million are admitted to juvenile institutions alone. And their numbers are growing: between 1985 and 1989 alone, the proportion of our adolescent population held in public juvenile facilities rose by 20 percent. In the 1970s, we passed national legislation designed to keep as many youths as possible out of the juvenile justice system. But in the past few years, that system has increasingly become our social service agency of first resort for many of the troubled and discarded young—not just for the violent and the predatory, but for the parentless, the abused, the homeless, and the addicted.

In this book, twenty of those young people "at risk" speak about their lives; about their fears and hopes, families and friends, frustrations and dreams. They talk about drugs and violence and the terrors and lures of the street, and, perhaps most importantly, about how they came to be where they are. They are drug dealers, gang fighters, runaways and throwaways, the strung-out and the exploited. They are young men and young women, white, black, and Hispanic: serious juvenile offenders, and others for whom the juvenile justice system is likely to be a temporary detour along the road to a brighter life. They are representative of that much larger army of children and adolescents who now flow through our child welfare and youth control systems in rising numbers. What they have to say can tell us much about what is happening to all too many youths and families today—and about our failure to deal seriously or humanely with the growing tragedy that besets them.

These twenty young people are drawn from a larger group of several dozen I interviewed in the late 1980s in a public juvenile facility that I will call "the Hall." I went to the Hall in the first place because I wanted to learn something about the reasons why growing numbers of young people were appearing in the child welfare, juvenile justice, and mental health systems across the country—in an era generally considered to be one of prosperity, of "good times." At the time of the interviews, both the local and national economies were still enjoying what was often described as the longest economic expansion since the 1960s. Yet in the county served by the Hall—I'll call it "River County"—as throughout the United States, a wave of young people were washing into the public and private agencies of control and confinement. And it was widely agreed among River County's social service professionals and juvenile authorities that they were coming at younger ages and with deeper and more stubborn problems—problems that were overwhelming the system's ability to cope.

I wanted to understand why—and I will report on that research more extensively in another book. But I also came to feel that, in addition to a more conventional and analytical treatment of the issues, I wanted to give some of the young people I talked with the opportunity to speak for themselves, and this book is the result.

I did so with some hesitation. Who would want to read about the lives of a bunch of delinquent kids—many of them poor, few of them articulate in conventional ways—from an obscure, dreary juvenile hall in an unremarkable American community? But I knew that listening to them had moved and educated *me*, and I believed others would feel the same. And I was also convinced that what the kids had to say was important and should be heard.

For one thing, I felt that it was only by hearing their own stories that we could appreciate the complexity and uniqueness of each of their lives. And I came to believe that getting across that complexity and individuality was crucially important. Too often, we stereotype troubled and delinquent youth as thugs, or, less often nowadays, as damaged goods, as social wreckage. Like most stereotypes, those are not always entirely wrong. In any juvenile institution in the United States, you can find thugs, and you can find some who are emotionally damaged beyond hope of repair. But the stereotypes also mislead us and hobble a rational approach to the problems of troubled kids. They obscure the complexity of the forces that influence the paths young people take for better or for worse, and, even more importantly, the considerable strengths and constructive potentials most of them possess.

At worst, we assume that they are uniformly brutal predators without hope of reclamation—the people who have turned our cities into places of fear. By lumping them in that category, we dehumanize them (as we complain they do us), and we encourage a social response to youthful delinquency that is simultaneously vindictive, neglectful, and—as is increasingly obvious—often futile. As will be clear over and over again in the pages that follow, our typical approach to delinquent youth is reactive and punitive, not preventive and constructive; we wait until they have endured considerable damage, and probably caused some of their own, and then we cycle them into and out of a swollen and stagnant system that does little to alter the problems that have brought them there in the first place. We then justify that course of action, or inaction, with the argument that the kids can't be helped and, perhaps, shouldn't be.

At best, today we often use a language of "risk" and "vulnerability" in speaking of troubled kids, and I believe the choice of terms is well-meaning. We want to help, to protect the young from forces that are threatening and hurtful and beyond their capacity to control. But in doing so we run the risk of losing sight of their resiliency and their capability.

Many of the young people in this book have suffered from extraordinary neglect, some from fearsome brutality; but they are also capable of extraordinary attachments to others, deep loyalties, and stubborn optimism. Many have been culturally as well as materially deprived, but some are very savvy indeed, keenly aware—in a way many experts on the problems of youth are not—of the strength of the forces in the real world that are arrayed against them. Many have serious problems with drugs or alcohol or have dropped out of school, but many also demonstrate an impressive ability to manage their lives and preserve their dignity virtually on their own, against great odds and with very little help. The failure to recognize those capacities—to think in terms of strengths rather than deficiencies, of potentials rather than limits, of options and opportunities rather than control and "treatment"—is the single biggest obstacle to dealing more effectively with delinquent and troubled youth today, as I'll argue further at the end of this book; and it continues in part because we fail to understand them as real people with distinct backgrounds, values, and capabilities. And no one can give us that understanding more effectively than the kids themselves.

There is also a more personal, visceral reason why I wanted to put together a book about delinquent youth based largely on their own words. The kids in this book, like most of the vastly larger army of "discarded" children and youths in the United States, have been, for the most part, conveniently hidden from view and denied the chance to be heard respectfully and seriously. We are familiar with the media image of the flamboyant drug dealer or the inner-city gang leader, but we know little about how they interpret their own lives and the world around them. And we know next to nothing about the kids who are more typical of the mass of American youth who move in and out of the juvenile justice and child welfare systems—the runaways and the abused, the car thieves and vandals, the ones who have gone over the edge on drugs or alcohol.

The Latin American writer Eduardo Galeano has said that literature should "make audible the voice of the voiceless"; and that description fits the young men and women in this book like a glove. The fact that they are very young, in our society, already undercuts their claim to have something important to say; worse, they are also officially "delinquent," which compounds their "voicelessness." For those who are not just young and delinquent but young, delinquent, and poor, the chance for a hearing is even slimmer; and for those who are young, delinquent, poor, and female, the deprivation of "voice" is almost total. (That accounts for an overrepresentation of young women in the pages that follow, relative to their proportion in the population of young people behind bars in America.) I wanted to give them voice in part simply because I felt they had a right to be heard, and in part because I believed that depriving them of a voice is not only unjust but also self-defeating; when we block their capacity to speak and be heard, we ensure that they will find other, more destructive or self-destructive ways of getting their point across.

And finally, I believe it is terribly important, for our sake as well as theirs, to pay attention to what they have to say. For it's only when you have heard their stories that you can really comprehend the depth and meaning of the disaster that has struck youth and families in the United States in their lifetimes. We do now talk a great deal about the crisis of children and families, and we have even begun, haltingly and with only intermittent success, to promote legislation to do something about it. But I am convinced that most Americans simply do not yet understand how bad things have become for the kinds of people whose lives are described in this book (I know I didn't). Some of the stories here portray lives that are precarious and threatening beyond most people's experience or imagination. And as long as we keep those lives hidden, we will continue to fail these young people; and we will continue to jeopardize their futures —and ours.

All of the adolescents who speak in this book are emphatically distinct individuals, but their stories reveal several common themes that are crucial to understanding the condition of youth and families in America today. They show, in particular, that the larger social tragedy that has shaped the experience of these twenty kids goes beyond the deepening poverty and economic insecurity that has afflicted the country during their life- times, engulfing not only the urban "underclass" but many "ordinary" American families. That economic disaster figures powerfully in most of their histories; it shows up in the looming problems of unaffordable hous- ing, of parental poverty, job loss, and overwork, and in the shrinking economic opportunities many see in their own futures. But the crisis of families and children in America is also a crisis of culture and purpose: the crisis of a society savaged by a growing social Darwinism, increasingly content to leave many children—and their parents—adrift, thrown back on their own resources; a society that routinely shrugs off even the most rudimentary responsibility for the healthy growth and development of its young. That attitude—as is all too apparent in these stories—runs through much of the juvenile justice system and the schools in River County, and, sadly, permeates many of the families of these young people as well.

Tragically, but not surprisingly, the kids have often bought into these values themselves. The saddest and most angering revelation I took from these interviews is that by the age of fourteen or fifteen many have already come to understand and accept that the world is a place where you must scramble relentlessly to survive, harden yourself against emotions of sol- idarity or dependency, and be constantly on guard—against violence, exploitation, and thwarted hope. As you will see, however, many of the kids, to their great credit, have resisted that acceptance, countering the pervasive neglect and self-absorption of the adult society around them with a surprising and impressive capacity for engagement and concern.

The Hall is a closed institution that holds youths, aged anywhere from ten to seventeen, who are sent there from all parts of River County. I cannot reveal River County's location, but it could be anywhere in the United States: I chose it, in fact, because it is so much like so many other places, and because it is sufficiently diverse that it can stand as a kind of microcosm of America. The entire social and economic spectrum is here: there are comfortable suburbs and deteriorating ghettos, older working-class communities and sprouting middle-class bedroom developments, substantial enclaves of the wealthy and struggling communities of the rural poor. The young people in this book are drawn primarily from three communities in the county—"Iron City," "Rivertown," and "Cherry Grove." All are within twenty miles of each other, but the social and economic distance between them is great.

Iron City is a hard, decaying industrial town, struck brutally by the decline of traditional blue-collar industry since the early seventies—during the lifetimes of my interviewees. A small, out-of-the-way town in the early part of the century, Iron City boomed during and after World War Two, when first the war effort and then the years of postwar industrial prosperity drove its steel mills, shipyards, oil refineries, and chemical plants. The refineries are still there, but the steel and shipbuilding are mostly gone, and many smaller industries have also shriveled. Iron City was always a tough, raw place, even in better times; but through the sixties it was a modestly prosperous one. Today much of it is a bleak and volatile slum, racked by violent crime and a flourishing drug trade—a loose collection of scruffy, low-rise neighborhoods adrift in a surrounding industrial waste-land of factories (many now abandoned), scrap-metal yards, and gas flares.

Iron City was thrown together hastily and haphazardly, without any unifying concept or plan: and it looks it. The long, ticky-tacky main streets that run for miles and link its scattered neighborhoods are cluttered with the small enterprises of the poor and near-poor: auto body shops and beauty parlors, adult bookstores, palm readers and thrift shops, places offering "low-fee check cashing," countless bars and liquor stores. Graffiti marking the territory of Hispanic and black youth gangs cover the walls and fences. Along some of the side streets, there are vacant lots lined with racks of dresses and caps and other items for sale: the scene looks much like the markets on the outskirts of many Third World cities. Indeed, much of Iron City looks as though it could have been transplanted whole from a developing country.

Iron City has been only lightly touched by the spread of the "postin-dustrial" sprawl of sleek shopping malls and tidy bedroom housing that has transformed some other parts of River County; but here and there small housing developments have sprung up, modest islands of fresh stucco and paint surrounded by some of the worst housing in the urban United

States. Incongruously, a billboard above a main boulevard, advertising the services of a major bank, advises passersby to "master the mechanics of money." Down the street, a sign above a dingy trailer park crammed with tiny, ancient mobile homes with peeling paint and sagging porches proclaims, with some understatement, "affordable housing." On some corners the signs on the groceries, delicatessens, and liquor shops are now in Vietnamese; a billboard in Spanish pleads NUESTROS NIÑOS NECESSITAN HOGARES—"Our children need homes." Other signs reveal the southern origins of much of the city's population: the carryouts still claim to offer "genuine Louisiana barbecue" or "Texas chili."

Iron City isn't all poverty and deterioration. Some of its outer neighborhoods—well-kept, multiracial enclaves of solid working people —have largely withstood the forces that have eaten away at the city's heart. But hard up against them are some of the poorest white communities in the state. Here men in tank tops, torn jeans, and caps work on the ubiquitous battered Camaros, pickups, and campers that clutter the driveways and many of the front yards; small children with the pinched faces of a Dust Bowl portrait from the thirties zoom around on beat-up Schwinns.

Deeper into the poorest black neighborhoods in Iron City, the level of urban devastation approaches the surreal; it does not get much worse than this anywhere in the United States. Virtually every block has its abandoned and plywooded homes, some in the early stages of collapse. Elaborate iron grillwork covers the doors and windows of those still intact and inhabited: many of them are also ringed by heavy wire fencing, giving whole blocks the peculiar look of a minimum-security prison or work camp. Adding to the sense of the surreal are the religious curios scattered about a few front lawns, and the occasional wildly painted house starkly positioned among others whose paint has peeled down to bare wood. In front of a few homes, people are selling their furniture: they're moving, they've been evicted, or they need the money to buy crack cocaine. Old mattresses, decrepit overstuffed chairs, and various odds and ends clutter the front yards; clothes for sale are displayed forlornly across weathered porches. Stripped and demolished cars, trucks, and old buses dot the side streets and litter the vacant lots. Knots of dispirited men of all ages hang out in front of carryouts and restaurants with names like the Gospel Chicken or stand silently in front of the big soup kitchen down the block.

These are neighborhoods of odd contrasts: some streets are eerily quiet, nearly deserted, while in the next block everyone's out on the street, or in the yards and driveways; black teenagers in baseball caps worn backwards hawk dope on the corners, or race up and down the street in battered Chevys and Buicks, tires squealing, mufflers dragging on the asphalt. Smaller children run up and down the sidewalk laughing and pestering the dealers, while older men and women chat animatedly on the lawns. Around the corner from storefront churches with names such as the Greater Harmony Temple of Deliverance, young men in scruffy sneakers and expensive lettered jackets man the pay phones day and night in front of the barbecue carryout, or patrol the streets in twos and threes sizing up likely customers in passing cars.

Twenty miles from Iron City is Rivertown, an older industrial community, its once solidly working-class neighborhoods now coexisting somewhat uneasily with newer developments for lower-level white-collar people looking for less expensive housing. Rivertown has also been buffeted by the decline of traditional industry, but it is holding on—so far —to its identity as a stable blue-collar town.

There are poor neighborhoods here, too—pockets of sagging frame bungalows scattered along a several-mile string of industrial plants that still pour smoke and fumes into the air day and night, and rows of dusty mobile-home parks. But most of Rivertown's neighborhoods are well kept, if modest, occupied by the people who work in its paper and steel mills, chemical plants, and warehouses. After three o'clock, when many blue-collar day shifts are over, these streets come alive with young men out working on their trucks and cars or tinkering with the small boats that fill many driveways. Across the freeway that splits the town are acres of low concrete warehouses and downscale shopping malls built around a Target or K Mart store, along with block-long dealerships selling row after row of Japanese cars and trucks. The parking lot at Rivertown High School is jammed with high-wheeled pickup trucks and chopped Camaros and Mustangs, modified Volkswagen bugs with flames painted on the hoods; young men with long hair and T-shirts bearing the logos of heavy-metal groups—Slayer, Metallica, Megadeth—banter with girls in tight skirts, teased hair, and running shoes.

Downtown a few spruced-up storefronts, new restaurants, and cute shops testify to the city's effort to revitalize the old business district, which like many in these older towns has been depleted by the rise of shopping malls on the outskirts of town. But there's little life here, even at midday;

for every new shop, there's an empty storefront, and an almost eerie quiet suffuses the downtown for most of the day. Across the top of a stone monument to the town's founding families someone has spray-painted two small swastikas and the letters SWP, for Supreme White Power.

Cherry Grove is a largely middle-class community about fifteen miles from Iron City and ten from Rivertown. Until the seventies, it was mainly a placid suburb; it is still a "bedroom" community, even more so as rising housing prices have pushed families farther and farther out from the larger cities in the region in search of affordable housing. But beginning in the late seventies, Cherry Grove was transformed by a boom in new office complexes and shopping centers as a number of big corporations moved their offices out of nearby center cities to less expensive and less crime-ridden surroundings. Cherry Grove's population exploded. Alongside older, 1940s- and 1950s-style residential neighborhoods of ranch homes, there are now rank upon rank of new developments with names like Cherry Pointe and Grey Fox Estates that are well-tended, carefully set into land-scaped grounds, and, in this land of two-earner families, also oddly de-serted during most of the day.

The Cherry Grove Mall is only the largest and most spectacular of several big shopping centers fed by wide and spacious boulevards that, throughout the day, are jammed and roaring with traffic. Cherry Grove, especially in these newer sections, is a city designed for driving, not for walking; it's rare to see anyone walking along the bigger boulevards that link the malls and the gleaming new glass-and-concrete office buildings that have dwarfed the older, fifties-style shopping areas—buildings that look as if they've been set down whole by a giant hand in the midst of what was until recently rural orchards and farmland. Though Cherry Grove is quite prosperous on the whole, the overall sense is that, as in Iron City, there has been no plan, that the city has been loosely assembled from disparate parts with no overarching sense of the whole.

Moreover, once you go a short distance away from the gleaming, newish city center and the malls, other parts of Cherry Grove seem to be peeling around the edges. Some of the neighborhoods have an aspect of slight dilapidation, of precariousness, of a struggle to keep things up. These are streets of small, often nearly identical working-class ranch houses, often with flaking paint and lined with aging campers, vans, and pickups. At the local 7-Eleven, kids in football jerseys and torn jeans hang around in the parking lot, or jostle inside the store over video games with names

like Bad Dudes Versus the Dragon Ninjas, or practice unnerving ma-
neuvers on skateboards richly decorated with fluorescent decals. There
are few black families in Cherry Grove, but there is a substantial and
growing Hispanic community—Mexican-American and, increasingly,
Central American—living mainly in the least attractive neighborhoods in
the city.

The River County Juvenile Hall squats obscurely in a working-class
residential neighborhood in Rivertown, a nondescript, concrete-block
structure that could pass for many others with very different functions if
it weren't for the barbed wire that tops the tall chain-link fences around
it. It is one of two medium-security detention centers operated by the
juvenile probation department; the other is a "farm" for boys some miles
away. On an average day, about three hundred children and youths are
confined here.

They are sent here for many reasons. Some have been convicted, in
juvenile court, of serious offenses—violence, repeated drug dealing, thefts
or burglaries. Some have been returned to the Hall for a second (or third
or fourth) time after having been released on probation because they have
violated the terms of their release laid down by the court. Many, for
example, have turned up "dirty" on a drug test, and returned to confinement. Some have been picked up off the street and are being held tem-
porarily, mainly because they have nowhere else to go. Others have been
taken from a dangerously abusive or drug-ridden family, and a few have
turned themselves in to the authorities in order to find temporary shelter.
(Both of the latter happened increasingly during the late 1980s, during
the time I talked with these young people, because there were not enough
resources in other youth-serving agencies to handle the growing needs of
adolescents in the county for protection and shelter.)

Many of the young people in the Hall are awaiting "placement," as
the county calls it, to some other part of the youth system. As in the rest
of the country, there are several options for placement in River County,
depending on the adolescent's specific problem and the state of their family
life, if any. Some are waiting to be sent to a live-in drug or alcohol-
rehabilitation program, either here in the county or elsewhere in the state;
long waiting lists for some programs, especially the more affordable ones,
can mean having to stay many weeks in the Hall. There are also often
long waits for placement in group homes—small residential facilities with

a live-in staff, often used to house teenagers who are no longer thought to need secure confinement but for one reason or another aren't considered ready to return to their families—if their families can be found. For younger kids, there is also the option of foster care with a private family.

The average stay in the Hall is about thirty days, but those convicted of serious or repeated offenses, or who must wait a long time for "place-ment," may stay for up to six months. The most serious cases, or those who cause real trouble during their stay in the Hall, can be sent to higher-security state youth prisons, which have a deserved reputation for being much tougher.

The Hall is divided into several separate sections, or "units," each holding from thirty to fifty kids. Inside, the walls are a drab institutional blue. The facilities are sparse and frayed; one dispiriting schoolroom with aging supplies and desks askew serves the entire population of the Hall. Concrete play areas with high, wire-topped walls resound with the shrieks of kids shooting baskets or playing brutal games of dodgeball.

At certain hours, the Hall bustles with activity. A stream of kids and parents, police and lawyers and probation officers flows in and out; youths are constantly being admitted to the Hall, being released to stony-faced parents or cheering knots of friends, or in transit to or from hospitals, emergency runaway shelters, or the county youth farm. But during much of the day the units themselves are quiet inside, the youths confined to their rooms or at school; the quiet is broken occasionally by a lone wail, a sudden, angry outburst, or the voices of kids shouting at each other from one unit to another.

Inside the units, where kids are usually bunked two to a room, the first thing you notice is rows of laceless, identical county-issue tennis shoes lined up in front of the rooms—the laces removed to prevent their use in suicide attempts. Periodically, a nurse appears with a tray of medica-tions, ranging from antibiotics for the endemic minor infections the kids bring to the Hall, to a battery of "antipsychotic" drugs and major tran-quilizers that are administered to some of the most disruptive or agitated wards.

The kids confined in the units are a diverse assortment of serious drug dealers, gang youths, frightened runaways, and depressed kids drying out from long bouts with drugs or alcohol, indicating again how much places like the Hall have become multipurpose catchalls for young people with a wide variety of problems in an era when other public agencies have been cut back or, at the very least, denied enough resources to keep up with the growing numbers of kids in trouble. River County is actually better off in this respect than many places; overall, despite considerable poverty, it is a relatively prosperous county in a relatively prosperous region of the country. Its public authorities, including those who run its juvenile justice system, have traditionally been more enlightened and progressive than the average in this state, or any state. Yet in River County, just as in worse-off parts of the United States, the juvenile detention facilities are now swollen with young people for whom there are so few accessible services that the detention system must take them in by default.

I chose the twenty young men and women in this book from more than sixty I spoke with in the Hall because each of them seemed to me to have something especially distinctive to say. My interviews with them ranged from single sessions of less than an hour to, in a few cases, several separate sessions of up to two hours each. They took place in a variety of settings inside the Hall: in dining areas, playgrounds, a laundry room, even a storage closet—whatever space was available that allowed a certain amount of quiet. You should picture a stark and utilitarian setting, with institutional-issue chairs and tables and identical T-shirt–and–dungaree outfits for the residents, often with chaotic and noisy activity going on just beyond the doors—kids arguing and shrieking, a weekly Bible class in the room next door, complete with hymns, providing fervent, if ragged, accompaniment to the interview; interruptions by staff whisking the interviewee off to dinner or school, or a nurse dispensing medication.

I went to the Hall with the permission of the county juvenile probation department, but I went as a writer working on my own, not as some sort of representative of official authority. I explained to the kids that I was writing a book about the problems that young people faced and I wanted them to be part of it. Almost without exception, they were eager to talk, open, and gracious, and very interested in the book itself. Most of them were sufficiently sure of themselves and confident in their views that they wanted me to use their real names in the book, but that wasn't possible; the law requires that their confidentiality be protected, and I would have insisted on doing so in any case. Most of them accordingly chose names for themselves, and if they didn't, I made one up for them. I've also changed some details and specifics about their lives—the names of relatives, friends, and streets, details of the layout of their towns and their parents' jobs, and so on. The names of the three main cities—Iron City, Cherry Grove, Rivertown—of course, are not their real ones, and none of them will be found on any map exactly where I've put them, or with exactly the same features. That's also true of the other nearby cities that figure in these accounts: "Hillview" is a medium-sized city in an adjacent county; "Valley City" is a sprawling agricultural center about two hours away.

I've arranged the twenty interviews into three sections, but the arrangement is necessarily somewhat arbitrary. The first section brings together the stories of kids who are drug dealers: many of those in other sections have dealt drugs too, but I put these together because I believe their stories, more than others, reveal something particularly important about the nature, meaning, and consequences of youthful drug dealing today. Likewise, the following section, "Child of the Air," focuses on the meaning and consequences of drug *use* among those kids in the Hall whose troubles with drugs were most crippling. Nearly *all* of the kids I interviewed used drugs, at least recreationally; but I felt that these seven illuminated the reality of youthful drug abuse in particularly compelling ways. And the final section brings together an assortment of the regular troops in the army of discarded kids in America: gang fighters, street kids, the ones who are behind bars for stealing cars or breaking into stores or vandalizing their schools. What they most have in common is that they illustrate, even more vividly than the others in this book, the consequences of our failure to provide a range of legitimate opportunities to match the energies and capacities of all of the American young.

Glossary

AA. Alcoholics Anonymous

Amped. High on methamphetamine

Base, basehead. A crack cocaine addict

Bloods, Cuzz. West Coast street gangs

Camouflage. A variety of LSD

Cisco. A potent fortified wine cooler

Crank. Methamphetamine

Crystal meth. Methamphetamine

Dime bag. Ten dollars' worth of marijuana

Dirty test. Urine test that turns up illegal drugs in the system

Dope track. A heavy drug-dealing area.

Droptop. Convertible

Eight-ball. Usually, an eighth-ounce of a drug, especially methamphetamine

Forty-O. A forty-ounce bottle of beer or ale

Four-way, four-way windowpane. An especially potent form of LSD

Freebasing. Chemical process by which cocaine powder is made into smokable form

Fry. LSD

Frying. Thoroughly stoned on LSD; as in "frying your brain"

Gremmie. Cocaine and marijuana mixed in a cigarette

Grinding: Dealing drugs.

Ho'. Whore

Homie, home boy, home girl. Comrades from the neighborhood.

Hop. Heroin

Hubba. Crack cocaine

IV. Intravenous: injecting a drug in the veins

KJ. PCP

NA. Narcotics Anonymous (similar to Alcoholics Anonymous, a self-help group for drug abusers)

Orange Sunshine. Another variety of LSD

PCP. Phencyclidine; once mainly used as an animal tranquilizer, often abused in the inner city

P.O. Probation officer

Rock. Rock cocaine; crack

Sheet. Sheet of paper spotted with droplets of LSD

Sherm. Cigarette laced with PCP

'Shrooms. Psychedelic mushrooms

Slam. To inject a drug, as opposed to smoking or snorting

Trails. Visual phenomenon sometimes experienced on LSD: a phantom hand, for example, appearing to "trail" hand movement

Tweaking. State of being stoned, especially on LSD

Twelve-step. The widespread alcohol and drug rehabilitation approach, originally associated with Alcoholics Anonymous, now common in many drug rehabilitation programs

Weed. Marijuana

Wire. Methamphetamine

Zig-Zag. Brand of cigarette papers

PART 1

DOWN FOR THE MONEY

I come from the town
called the City of Dope:
It couldn't be saved
by John the Pope.

—Too Short, "City of Dope"

During the 1980s, hard drugs spread into the communities of River County as they did across America, and so did the "war" on drugs. The arrests of juveniles charged with selling drugs skyrocketed; in the United States as a whole, the number sent to public juvenile institutions for drug and alcohol offenses leaped by almost 150 percent from 1985 to 1989 alone. By the end of the decade, when I first began talking with kids in the Hall, the county's youth institutions were jammed with drug dealers—some as young as twelve or thirteen, most of them small-fry in the hierarchy of the drug trade.

The younger kids in this book entered their adolescence as crack cocaine was first pouring into the black ghettos in Iron City and elsewhere in the region, and that accounts for the large number of low-level crack dealers in the Hall during the months I spent there. But though crack got most of the headlines, it was only one part of a much bigger and more diverse pattern of drug dealing throughout River County—a pattern which, as in the rest of the country, is sharply divided along lines of race and class.

Crack, and to a lesser extent PCP (phencyclidine), remain the most prominent drugs on the streets of Iron City. There is a distinct division by age between crack users and their suppliers: the serious users are typically adults, a big proportion of them women, while the dealers are mostly young and often in their teens. In this area, crack is usually sold in small chunks or "rocks," also called "hubbas."

The main drug trade among lower-income *whites* in River County, on the other hand, is in methamphetamine, what most people used to call "speed" in the sixties and seventies, and these days, in this area, is most often called "crank" or "crystal meth." Crank is endemic in many poor and working-class white neighborhoods in River County; in some places it's almost a family tradition. Middle-aged parents are at least as likely, in Rivertown or the poor-white neighborhoods in Iron City, to be "cranksters" as their teenaged children. Crank is manufactured widely in illegal laboratories, some close to home in River County.

The drug trade is so pervasive in the poorer communities of River County that the *majority* of kids I got to know in the Hall, whether black, white, or Latino, have sold some drugs at some point in their adolescence. For those I've assembled in this section, the drug business has been a big part of their lives; and what they have to say tells us a lot about the kinds of people we are now putting behind bars, in ever-escalating numbers, in the course of the war on drugs.

15

"We just like human kids"

I come from L.A. All the gangs, Bloods and Cuzz? Over there, only the strong survive.

I been livin' there all my life, and you know, you sort of get used to it. Same friends and stuff, then you come up here, you got to regroup again.

He's long, skinny, has a basketball player's frame, and says he'd like to "make it to the pros." During the entire conversation, he fidgets constantly, can't sit still; he turns his head up to look at the ceiling, bends down to look at the floor, scratches his arms and legs furiously. He's a small-time crack dealer, a private in the army of younger kids who swarm the streets of Iron City like foraging squirrels. The arrest that brought him into the Hall was for beating a man nearly to death with a board for making him "break his dope"—break up a large "rock" into smaller pieces— "for nothing."

They's a bunch of followers out here. Jealousy. They don't want to see nobody else *having* something. You have something what they want, they's envy and jealousy. That's one thing I don't like about Iron City, comparison to L.A. They don't want to see nobody else havin' nothing, they just think about they self! Like *you* driving a Benz, *they* want one. If they can't have one, you know, they'll try to tear yours up or something like that. Or kill you over it. (Scornfully:) L.A. ain't like that. They'll be *glad* to see a brother like us, you know, *doing* stuff and having things. There's jealousy, and everybody want to be followers. Instead of being the leader, they want to follow somebody: "Well, man, come on, let's go beat up somebody." "I'm going." And that'll be it.

You guys do that a lot? Beat people up?

That's all we *do* is jump people, man! You just go jump in! That's what I'm in here for right now, jumping a grown man! Wasn't worth it. Over ten dollars, we jumped him over ten dollars! (Soberly:) It wasn't worth it. Not trying to *rob* him or nothing, man, it was because of *our* ten dollars. Not even that, *eight* dollars. Eight dollars.

We used to jump a lot, pull guns on people, you know, throw rocks at the police cars. Used to do *anything* to have a good time. (A wide smile.) One time we used to kick in people' doors like we a Task Force! Having a *good* time. We just go kick in they house doors. One time we kicked this Chinaman's. They went off. And they was a little hole in the fence and around twenty people trying to go through the same hole, but I always go the opposite way. When I see them runnin' that way, I go the opposite way. I always get away.

We used to always shake cabs, get somewhere, we get stuck, "Come on man, let's get a cab!" "Oh, will you take us to this place, take us to our apartment?" and just run. Did that a lot, too. But then they start to get smart, they say, "You can pay the money first."

How come you jump on people like that?

Just to *do* something, man, you get a kick out of it! (Laughs.) But when it's *you*, you know, you don't think that way. What you think about sometimes . . . (Hesitates.) Doin' this stuff, beatin' em up, I think, "*Damn*, man! What if that was *me* be down there, you know? Around twenty niggers stompin' *my* head to the ground, brother? Shit ain't cool." You know? That's later. Then I say, "Motherfucker, now you don't let that get to you, man."

You don't let it get to you?

Sometimes it do, man, sympitty. 'Cause one time we beat a *lady* up! Most times we beat 'em up for a reason. (Indignantly:) Like these young niggers out there trying to sell dope, and they think 'cause they *little* they can take advantage of 'em. But it don't work like that! One lady try to get over, you know? She say [she wants to] taste it, gave him *another* one out of her mouth, but it wasn't real! (Laughs.) So we all just *beat* her up. "Don't you never come up here," you know. That's what we used to do. We'd just beat baseheads up cause they trying to get over on people. By havin' somebody break they dope for nothin'.

Happened to me a couple times. They get your money, too. They *try* to take your money. The real dope addicts, they'll just put a .38 to yo' head! They *crazy*. Those kind of people, you can't do nothing. Unless you see him one time, just take him *off*. (Casually:) Get him out of the game. You'll always see him again, and when you see him, be prepared, take him out.

I know when I first started, man, I first started like this. I grew up in a complex, one of the rowdiest places in L.A. And you know, my buddies, we grew up like *this*, man (fingers tightly crossed), like *this!* (Smiles.) All of us like a big *family*, you know? And the older ones was around three or four years older, and we saw *them* doing it. I started holding for 'em, say, "Here, you wanta make a couple dollars?" One time I made about forty dollars! I say, "Forty dollars, just for holding?" They say, "Want to make some more?" Said *fuck* it, come on, man! Got all my homies, say "Come on, man, we *all* gone make some money, look!" Forty dollars was a *lot* then, you know, I was around five and six years old, forty dollars was a lot to me. One little kid going to school with forty dollars! (Laughs.) You know? For a young *six*-year-old? Having around forty dollars. Then I started, you know, as I grew up, when I was ten years old I started *selling* 'em. That's when I first started.

That's pretty young.

(Scornfully:) That ain't *shit*, man, there's nine-year-olds out there, eight!

My manager got hip to the game, right, she was evicting everybody who was selling, so we got evicted and moved up here, 'cause I was getting into too much trouble. Moved up here, started doing the same thing.

I'm tellin' you, man; everybody want to *have* things. Fifteen-year-olds havin' *millions* out there right now. Kickin'! Most of 'em got mamas, you know, and you know how style is, how everybody want to go in *style*, and that's the only way they survive. By drivin' cars and everything like that, havin' money, that's how they survive.

You think there wouldn't be any other way to survive?

What would *you* do? In my category, if I see a fast buck I'ma go for it. I *tried* working, man. I just feel, I can work here for six hours, man, I make around twenty dollars a day! Well, if I can make twenty dollars in a *minute*, what I'm gonna go for? The twenty dollars in a minute! You know? Who have heart, have money.

Have heart?

Who have heart, have money.

What do you do with all that money when you're fifteen?

But you don't spend all of that. This what you do, you just stackin' and stackin'. *Save* it, buy you a car. Can't be buying *too* many cars. You can't just go in a car lot and just buy you a Benz or nothing like that, 'cause they get you for taxes. You gotta be smart about it! Have my sister or something, have her get me a car. Get a *used* car, you don't go buy no new car off a lot either, they get you for that. Don't flash, you know, like just drivin' around with Benzes, it's like the police know, they gone *hit* you, what's a young fifteen-year-old driving a *Benz*! (Laughs.) Having donkey rolls, having rings, you don't go like that, you know, you dress casual. You know, it's OK to have like a leather Troop* cost three hundred dollar, sweat suits, you know, Troop shoes, all that. You don't go like

---

* An expensive brand of jacket, very popular in Iron City.

that *every* time. I go casual, like when I go someplace I may throw on a sweatsuit or something like that.

(He's too young to have a driver's license, but cars are an important part of his life.)

I had so many of 'em. My first car we turned over. Went through the windshield.

How'd that happen?

Alright, man, we was in Hillview, right? What's the name of that kind of soup, it *hot*, a kind of soup, you be drinking the soup up? (Vaguely:) Think it's chicken noodle, something . . . and my homie have some, right? And the police is right on the side, you know, eating something, with his window down. I say, "Turn y'all head straight," you know, cause none of us have a license. I say "Turn yo' head! Turn your head!" And this stupid-ass nigger go flippin' the *police* off, man! The police say, "What are you doin', man?" I said, "Why you *do* that, punk?" (Laughs, shakes his head.) They some *stupid*-ass niggers, man.

So he get mad! Voom! We get on the freeway, we thought we shake 'em, we pull off for a minute, here they come. I said "Man, you drive, brother!" And we *strikin'* on the freeway, zzzzooom! (Laughs, excited.) Somehow he go to pull to the exit, I think he pulled it too fast, so we flip! "I'm OK, you OK?" Everybody was OK. And we got off the freeway, just ran! We made it.

And a second time we was striking, you know, screek! Bam! (He bounces around in his chair.) My head went like *this* through the windshield! I pulled it out, jumped out the window, the side window, and everybody got out and ran. We left the car there. We leave so many cars! (Laughs.) Wasn't too far from my house, so we ran home and my mama said, "Oh my God!" (Disgusted:) She called a *ambulance*, like a dummy. You know an ambulance come, the police gone come right behind him. They didn't do nothing! Gave him a ticket. I say I wasn't driving. He say, "Who car was it?" I say I don't know. 'Cause baseheads rent they cars out for rocks, then some of 'em call and say the car stolen.

Got one, a Poniac, what happened to it . . . ? Oh, I let my brother drive it, he around twelve? And the police got after him and he got out the car and run and leave the car there. Everytime we get pulled over, or like a siren or a ambulance, we pull over, just run out the car. Just leave it for 'em.

He's been arrested twice before for selling crack; both times he spent several months in juvenile institutions.

Were you in school all this time?

About school, alright. I get out. Soon's I got out, you know, I stay out, be good for a *week* and shit. (Laughs.) And my homie say, "Man, there's a spot in Hillview, man, you know, money be *rollin'!*" Said, "Fuck it, man, I've gotta go out there. Gonna go out there, have my dollars." I goes on Monday, my buddy get caught. I goes on Friday, *I* get caught.

So I'm in Woods County, you know, with a dope charge, and I'm the only Iron City nigger in there. Hillview don't like Iron City, so I've got to fight for my town in there! You know, I goes in there, "Man, where you from?" (Puts up his fists.) "Iron City, brother, wanta make something of it?"

I gets out. And I start going to school. My Mom went up to Roosevelt High and got me in there. Got in Roosevelt, did a good week going on and off. "Fuck it man, I'm droppin' out, man. I gotta have my dollars!" Man, I just got—you know, man, I just let that money go to my head! Some people can sell dope and go to school, but I can't, I just . . . (shakes his head, smiles) fuck it, I just let all of that money go to my head.

But she never knew I was doin' it. She had a *'spicion* I was doing it, on Christmas before I came here she had a 'spicion, 'cause I went and bought my nephews some bikes. I bought them two bikes, you know? She said, "You don't *work*—how can you buy them bikes?" "I found the money."

I went out, bought my sister one of them Tanky computers, you know? She working and she needed one, a big Tanky computer? Gave my brother around a hundred dollars, go do what he want to do, his little ass don't *know* what he want! (Laughs.) Bought him about five scooters, Elites, shit! That cost around eight hundred dollars for *one*, I bought him about *five* of 'em, they get towed in every month! Fuck it, I ain't buying him *shit*, he don't know how to take care of nothing. Then lettin' him try to drive, I won't do *that* again! (Laughs.) Man, all over the *curbs* and shit? I say, "I don't want yo' ass to drive this shit!"

He done been trying to go out there, too! Out there grindin', trying to have his money. (Thoughtfully:) Eleven years old, out there having his money.

How do you feel about him being out there?

I don't care. I care in a *way*. (Grins.) But if he down for his money, he down for his money!

It's pretty dangerous though, right?

I'm telling you, man, if you was out there, you wouldn't have no fear. You gotta—you know, what's the fear for? What's your fear; you go to jail, get caught? (Contemptuously:) Think! You gotta think. It's dangerous just walking the *streets* at night! It's dangerous for you to walk outside! It's dangerous everywhere you go! You gonna die *one* of these days! You know? (Agitated:) You gonna die young or you gonna die old, simple as that. You know, when you out there, you don't think about nothin' but "Man, I'm gonna get *all* the money out here. Police come, they gonna get everybody 'cept *me*." That's the way you think. You gotta think big-headed to survive. Can't just be paranoid on the track or you get caught, man. You *think* you gonna get caught, you gonna get caught! (He puts a finger to his head.) It's all up *here*, man, I'm telling you.

One week I was doing that! I got caught, right, in Hillview, and I started back soon's I got out. Grindin' again. You know this is the highest I ever got, but I was *shaking* . . . If I wouldn't know the person, I'd *run*, I'd say, "Damn, this ain't working!" I'd run somebody house or something like that? I was paranoid for a week. And I said, "Man, fuck this, brother, if I'm gonna sell, I'm gonna be a *good* one." And I just stopped being paranoid.

And one day my mind told me to go to school. (Softly:) Everybody was talking about dreams that morning. And I dream I was in *jail*, man! And *last* time I dreamed I was in jail, at night I dreamed I was in jail, the next morning I *went* to jail.

I goes out and a man come up, "Hey, man, can I get something for my eight dollars?" So my nephew broke him a eight-dollar piece and gave it to him. He said "Nah, man, this too small." "Brother, you better buy it, here you have me breakin' my dope . . ." I said, "Fuck this," man, I went like *this* (draws back his fist), but my friend grabbed me? I said "OK," went over there, got a stick: "Give it; whack!" "Give us eight dollars!" A boy hit him with a stick and a nail went in his knee! I said, "Fuck it, man, give it to *me*," just started slappin' him all in his *face* with it. Somehow he made it to a office and called police. I say "Damn, man, we beat his ass *that* bad?"

And my cousin say, "Man, the police is after us!" We shake 'em, pssh! (He's bouncing again, excited.) Somebody told us, "Man, yo' best bet is go into the park!" Man, I *knew* I shouldn't have listened to him, man! (Laughs.) This the first time I ever stay with the group. And got caught. But check *this* out. My two cousins get caught and three gets away. I gets away at first, and I'm hiding and shit. And my other two, one just go somewhere and the other one come *back*, like a fool (laughs), try to be *cool* and shit, I was laughin my ass off. Now *that's* stupid. You gets away already then you come *back*, that's a *stupid*-ass nigger!

Is there something you'd really like to do when you get older, a dream?

(Grins.) Make it to the pros! It's one way to go. But like LL* say, I gotta fight for it . . . (Pauses, scowls.) But I can tell you all *kind* of bullshit, man, brother. "I'm gonna go straight, man, I'm gonna be like a *angel*." But you know once I hit the gates I'm in a whole different story, man. I learned that for my own self. I tell the counselors, man, I'm gonna get my ass in gear? Soon's I get out, "Hey brother, what's up, man?" "Money roll into town!" "Oh, let me go get my dope, man!" Start the same routine again . . . (Laughs, shakes his head.) Here I go again.

I know some of my people, some of my cousins, died over this shit. You know people get too big they die.

Does that scare you?

Only thing I be scared of, man, police kicking in my door at night. And hurting my family. 'Cause they got a camera on my street now points

* LL Cool J, the rap artist.

directly at my house! This what *else* they doing. They get dope fiends—
like you a drug addict, they tell you to come buy dope from me and then
I have marked money and I get caught. I started selling out of my house,
and I said naw, man, I ain't gonna put *moms* in danger, shit . . .

What does she think about all this?

She can't do nothing, I do what I want to! I feel I'm grown. (Distracted:)
I *think* I'm grown. Just go away for a few days. I come back. Too *big* for
whuppin's, man, that shit played *out*, bro. (Laughs.) I wouldn't never hit
her back, though. If she *did* try. That's one thing I wouldn't do. And I
dare a motherfucker to *try* to hit her back. If she feel she have to whip
me, I think it's time for me to pack my bags and get out.
   Yelled at, that didn't do no good. Punishment, that didn't do no good.
I do what I want to do since I was twelve, since I was real little. She tell
me to go somewhere, "Go yourself." I cussed at her a lot when I was still
little.

You know that stuff messes people up, and you're selling it . . .
does that make you feel bad sometimes?

Alright, let me tell you, brother, this how I feel. I was thinking just
like you, man, I was saying, "Damn! *Look* at these motherfuckers, man!"
You know? I even try to *help* some of 'em, brother. Once said, "Brother,
that's too much for you, man. You better come off that shit," I tell 'im.
I says, I ain't gone sell to no *pregnant* people, no *old* old people, or no
young young people. But I found out this: if I don't sell it to 'em, somebody
else will. And I'd rather get the money than the next man get it. (Earnestly:)
So you can't have no favoritism about it, man! "Damn, I hurt her, or
hurt *him*" . . . I sold some shit to my own motherfuckin' *cousin!* You
know, you can't have it like that, man, if you don't sell it to them,
somebody else will, and you want the money, 'stead of them. You can't
think that way.

Say somebody was selling to your mother . . .

Aww . . . (Uneasily:) I wouldn't worry, though. I know she wouldn't
use it. Oh, if she *was* using, how would I feel if she *was*? Tell the truth

. . . I couldn't feel *nothin'*, man. Know why? 'Cause she a grown motherfuck—I mean grown lady, you know? If she want to fuck up her life like that, that's on her.

But I'd just tell 'em, "Hey cuz," you know, "you don't be selling my mom no dope," you know.

Or your little brother?

He wouldn't use drugs either. I teach him. (Laughs.) If I catch his ass, ssh!

Police get his little ass. He got caught a couple of times. I try to tell him you got to slow down, man, you end up in *here*. But he too young.

(Defiantly:) I sold dope to a couple people in *here* before. *And* they mamas!

What's your best quality?

I'm human? I'm human. I bet you if you ask anybody in this world you can't tell me nobody didn't do nothing illegal when they was a kid. (Earnestly:) Either they did it illegal when they was a kid or they doing it *now*. Like I know sure, when *you* was my age, you was probably doing something, probably not as *bad* as me, but old people was telling you, "Hey, you know that's wrong to do"—they said the same thing, and you wanted to learn the hard way! That's what it's gonna take me, the hard way, man. Cause I can be talking about all this—aw, man, I can tell you any motherfuckin' thing I *want* to, but when I get out there on the game, it's a whole different story. I'll do what I want.

Like people that be trying to help me, I say "Yeah, thank you for the help, but no thanks," you know? (Proudly:) If I'm gonna quit doing what I'm doing, I'm gonna quit on my *own* and for *myself*. Like they try to get me in NA and AA, I don't have no drug problem, I don't need no NA, AA. I'm gonna help my *own* self by quittin', I ain't gonna need nobody else to do it. I'm gonna control my own brain. If I feel I'm gonna stop something, I'ma stop on my own. You know? I got that much manpower on myself to quit. If I want to quit, I know rights and wrongs for myself. And what I need and what I don't need.

I'm tellin' you, man, I never took nothin' from nobody and that's one thing I don't do, take nothing from nobody. Steal. And that's the worsest.

I think that's worser than anything, taking something that don't belong to you? That's one thing I don't do. I don't take nothing from nobody.

*If you could change something in the world, make things differ-
ent . . . ?*

(He smiles ruefully.) Cocaine. Man, I'm telling you, some people think—like selling cocaine, some of these people, "Oh man, I sell *dope*" . . . They *dream* of it. I say, Man, dream of sellin' dope, that don't make you a big man by sellin' dope! (Contemptuously:) A little *baby* can go out, "You want hubbas?" A little *baby* can do that! So that don't make you a big man to be doin' that! You know? Some people just want to be, you know, one of the fellas. But some people sell it 'cause they have to.

You were saying it would be good to get rid of cocaine.

But they *cain't!* It'll always be here. Just like weed. Look how long weed been around! They can't catch *every*body. I'm telling you. Half of the police is involved in it theyself. I'mo tell you that much, I'mo tell you that's the truth! (Laughs.) *Half* of the police. I know so many police—judges, too! You know. They'll do anything for *money*, man! Like somebody said money don't make a difference? Money make a *lot* of difference, man.

I wish it could be like this, man. Wasn't no bums on the street. . . . This what I dream of, everybody be peaceful, man! Nobody would have to sell dope! You know? Just think if cocaine wasn't here how many kids would be alive, how many homies would be alive right now. Over that. I bet you more kids'd be having money, dressing more neat, and decent, than they are. I see little kids running around . . . (Trails off.) 'Cause one lady spent her whole check and her kid say, "Mommy, I'm hungry!" and she was running, bring three little kids and a baby, "Can I buy a rock?" I had a little sympitty, I bought the kids something to eat, but I wasn't gonna buy *her* nothin' to eat. A lot of dope dealers'll do that, they'll buy the little kids something to eat? Like one Christmas he bought all the little kids bikes, *all* of 'em. So you can't say they ain't trying to help 'em. They didn't buy the mama nothin'. (Laughs.) They say, "I dare you to try to pawn this for a rock." So you can't say . . . And some of 'em, you know, be takin' the little kids in, buying 'em clothes and everything, you know? You can't say all dope dealers bad.

How come so many people are like that—ready to let their kids go hungry just to buy a rock?

I don't know, I never tried it. And I'd never *try* it! (Scornfully:) See, y'all don't understand. Why'd I want to try something like that if I seen what it's doing to people? People going around *broke*, starving to death, lookin' . . . Ladies, it's easy for ladies to get it. You know, "Want to make a deal? Come on, let's go to a hotel or something." You know. And mens be *robbin'* you for it. But why'd I want to do something like that when I know what it's doin' to people?

He's also been dealing long enough to know that what you get on the street isn't the same as what you're looking for, at least in Iron City. "You know speed? Speed is cut with epherin and rat poison. You know Sherm? PCP? Call it Sherm? How they make that, dip that in bleach, Raid . . . I don't smoke it, man. That's one thing, I don't do nothing, I don't even drink, man! I very seldom, I don't even smoke cigarettes! One time we may just drink a wine cooler, like a Cisco or a California, just to kick it, man, or a forty-ounce Old English, maybe a joint or something, but I don't fuck with that. Don't have none of that shit. Nobody smoke gremmies or nothin' like that, primos, that's like cocaine crumbled up?

But you know what? (He's incredulous.) Big dope dealers— this what I don't understand—out here, big dope dealers smoke powder cocaine! In my category, they ain't no bigger than a person on the pipe! It's all cocaine! I guess they feel they having they money still. They snort out here, they don't do that in L.A. either! That's a damn shame. I feel once you using, man, you using, don't matter what you doin', smoking gremmies, you still using cocaine. So they don't get no respect from me. How can you call somebody a basehead when you doing it yourself?"

I just seen how some people who was doing good? And how they just went down so *quick.* (Quietly:) You know who suffer the most? The kids, man. The kids. I know a lady who stay right up the street from me. Kids go *dirty*, man. Everybody know they mama a base 'cause everybody go to their house if they don't have noplace to go. Just give them a little piece. I used to sell up at they house. But I stopped, man, 'cause that smoke'll get to me, man (laughs), that stuff fuck me, shit have me all *sick* and shit? And you know, when you on probation, take pee tests, and shit, man, I know I'm coming up dirty, *smelling* that shit!

So the mother was basing . . .

And the father. They had around five kids and they was going dirty, man.

They suck penis for the rocks. Have sex with little, *little* kids! One time, man, it was so funny, my brother and a couple of his friends, around *five* of 'em, was all having sex with a grown lady. Two had they penis in her mouth, one's fuckin' her, another was . . . (Shakes his head.) That's a shame. With a grown lady. I said, "Man, I should take a picture of this and show everybody." I say, "How you *feel*, doin' that shit?" "It don't bother me." For one twenty-dollar rock. Five people.

A lot of 'em'll ask me, "You wanta work something out?" Shit, I got better things to do. You want something, you can just *ask* me for it.

And you know, you never give credit, you gotta kill somebody over your money. But one thing I tried out one time, was the fifteenth, no the *first*, I went to a house, I left school early and everything: "Let me get credit." I say, "I'll make a deal. I give you twenty, you give me back *forty*." And they showed me they checks* and everything. So I made around four hundred dollars off that one house. Other five I go to, made about four hundred dollars off each house. I turned in early *that* night. (Laughs.) Just put it back in the safe, just waited till morning, went to school the whole day: "Why you didn't come to school?" "My stomach was hurting," you know, give 'em any excuse, have my girlfriend write a note.

She don't like me selling dope, though. But she can't tell me what to do.

She gets mad, though?

---

* He means welfare or disability checks, which come regularly on the first or fifteenth of the month.

Fuck her, man. It's just like a bus. You know? You miss this one, another one'll come along. That's the way I look at it. She ain't putting money in *my* pocket, I'm putting money in *her* pocket. She ain't doin' nothing for me. I don't need her. She need *me* more than I need her. She be right here, I still go right in front of her face and talk to another one.

So you're not thinking about getting married . . .

Aww . . . (Laughs.) Be a bachelor, man. Can't be tied down, man. I'd rather tell her, "Well, I ain't gonna marry you, rather be a bachelor," better than cheating on her.

I had a letter from this girl today. Her boyfriend just got killed. So she say she don't want to talk to nobody else. So I tell her you gotta *relate* to them things, shit. Something bound to happen. You can't let that hold you forever. It's just like I know people said just because they husband died, they ain't gone never marry again. Can't hold that.

What do you like to do when you're not selling dope?

Aw . . . man, we *do* be playing basketball! We play *foot*ball! We like *human* kids! (Laughs.) We act just like human, man, you know? We like to have a good time and stuff like that. We play football, like go play like ten houses against another part of Iron City. We play football and have a good time, still. We go bowling a lot. Sometimes even, adult dealers be taking a lot of us bowling. We have a good time. We used to go to a carnival, they just take the whole group! You know, we'll go to parties. (Softly:) We still . . . like . . . human.

Some people think I guess 'cause we sell dope . . . we gotta be some . . . I know selling drugs is wrong, (indignantly:) but it's just as wrong as robbing! Stealing! Adultery, that's wrong! So they can't whup on selling dope, 'cause a lot of these . . . they do wrong things too, they ain't no angels! *Every*body do things wrong! So I don't sweat it, man!

Some people have different ways of coming up. Like *you*. You say you maybe makin' money by this *book*. Some people want to make money by prostitution, some make money by robbin', some people *hit* mens, you know? Some people sell *drugs!* You know?

Like Ronald Reagan. You know, I bet you he do a lot of things illegal, too, man, so he can't say . . . (Trails off.) There ain't no person on this world that don't . . . I bet you now, out of this whole week, shit! I bet you can't *nobody* say they didn't do nothing illegal. Parking in a red spot, that's illegal. Running a red light, that's illegal! So selling drugs is just as illegal as that! (Earnestly:) But the society look at it like selling drugs is *harm* people. What if you ran a light, and an accident was started? But they don't think that way! Society just full of shit, that's what it is.

They should get around seven or eight billion dollars, you know, get peoples tested for drugs, and alcohol, *all* the government, not just some. Like I bet you if you test some of these counselors in here in Juvenile Hall who's worse than the *kids*—some of the counselors come to the job high, man! (Laughs.) I ain't gone say no names, but one day we was outside, we come back and the unit smelling like *grass!* And *I* can smell weed, you know? And the counselors trying to tell us what's right and wrong, and they doing the same damn thing theyself! So I feel this way: How can you tell *me* something if you doing the same damn thing I'm doing?

So the first thing you'd do is have more drug testing, drug treatment.

Yeah, but then we'd be out of jobs! (Laughs.) How many people you think is in the United States?

Two hundred million.

Two hundred million? I say *half* of them use drugs. Or even a little *more* than a half use drugs. I'd say a hundred million of 'em use drugs. Could be *more* than a hundred million. You know drugs gonna be a problem wherever you go. It ain't just in the United States. I read a little about Russia, how Russia was having a drug problem? But it ain't as bad as America.

But America, I'm telling you, this a pussy-ass country, man. You need somebody up there who know what they doing. A younger person, man, who understand, who *relate*, man! Ronald Reagan can't relate to *nothin'*, man! And we even wrote him a letter! We wrote him a letter and he wrote us back talking some bullshit. We did it at school, gonna help Niggeragua or something, you know, he was spending money on Niggeragua, you know, buy nuclear bombs, and shit . . . How 'bout if you gave every kid that graduated a couple thousand dollars, I bet you more kids'd graduate. Help our *own* country, man! We goin' down the drain! Goin' straight down the drain! Watch, wait till we have a war, all our army men's gonna think about is hittin' that pipe! (Laughs.) They gone be all based out while Russia just *killing* us, bam! (Jumps out of his chair.) Just gonna overpower our country, man. Need somebody up there who know what they *doin'!* He *senile,* man! Then he *lie* about the shit, that's what I hate. He do things then he lie about it. And Congress just back him up like he's some hero, man. He ain't nothing but another human being.

If you could be the president, instead of Ronald Reagan . . .

I wouldn't want to be no president, man, I couldn't stand the pressure. I'd end up blowing *all* of our asses up! (Laughs.) I'd send a bomb straight to Gorbachev! Man, I mean it's just . . . the point is . . . This what I'd relate to as my president, man, a person who would *rule* the country, make *good* decisions to help his people . . . But *his* ass selling nuclear bombs, you know, they'll overpower us, it be funny if they just sent one back to us, you know? He helping them blow *us* up.

We're talking about whether there's anyone else he'd like to see as president.

How about Jesse Jackson?

I wouldn't want him to be president. I think he'd probably last around a *day* or so. (Laughs.) Me and my friend bet it, though. Bet C's on how long he'd last if he was elected. I said a day. He said a *hour.* Somebody'd get him. Like Martin Luther King, man! I ain't saying *all* white people like that, but some white mens don't want to see no black mens, you know, get nowhere. They think they *better.*

And that's another stupid thing we got, is prejudice. Like in this juvenile hall I lost twenty-three days cause of prejudice. A white boy called me a nigger, man: "My granddaddy *owned* yours!" I just couldn't take it, man, just went off on him. Lost twenty-two days. Security risk. Then I think, "Man, it wasn't worth it," but in a way it *was.* I don't let no white boy call me nigger, man. You know. I don't disrespect *you* like that.

Then they start singing the Iron Man song,* man . . . That's one thing I can't stand is a prejudiced motherfucker. I look at everybody the same, man, color don't mean nothin'! It's just I'm darker than you, you lighter than me, man, we all *human*, we all got a brain! But some people moms didn't teach 'em different.

Most of 'em just wannabes, man. They start slidin' notes under my door, say "Come on y'all, y'all want to start a riot, man?" I say, "Fuck you, man, let's do something about this shit, man, I hate this shit, man." (Thoughtfully:) But you know, let me tell you something. After I hit him, no one else called me a nigger, man. That's all it took is *one*, man. They learned they lesson. It was still "nigger" talk, but it wasn't like that, most of 'em were singing, that's what was trippin' me out. But then I said, "Come on, man, we gone get 'em in a way" . . . *I* was like saying "nigger," man, I was playing against my own color, like. "Come on y'all, let's sing 'Iron Man,' make the white boys look like fools!" Let 'em know this ain't hurtin' us by singing "Iron Man"! They call me stupid, I say "No, *I* ain't stupid, *you* stupid, I'm just letting you know, man, by singing 'Iron Man' and calling me nigger, that shit don't *hurt* me, 'cause *you* can be a nigger as well as *I* can be a nigger!" We got 'em back, they was mad! Then they shut up and the halls was quiet. All the blacks are singing "We are iron men, killing niggers in the night!" (Laughs.) Some shit.

How it go? Something like:

I am Iron Man
leader of the Ku Klux Klan
wearing sheets so white
killing niggers in the night

And we start singing it, and the white boys is gettin' mad! Say, "Y'all stupid, why you singing that prejudiced . . ." Cause! It don't hurt us! (Laughs.) And they was gettin' mad. Then they stopped singing it.

What would you say to someone your age who was reading this?

---

* A racist song. Blaster attributes it to the Ku Klux Klan.

(Quickly:) Don't be a fuck-up, man. Drug, drugs, drugs ain't gone get you *nowhere*.

But they got you somewhere.

But look how many of the hundreds that have tried, though. Around ten succeed. When I get out of here, I think I'm gonna go with this side of my brain, man. Get me a honest job, man. Police, every time something come up first thing they do, come to your house. Once you get the jacket, man.

Thinking about working at Taco Bell 'cause they hirin' now. But you know how, one half of your mind telling you to do it, go for it, other mind say, "Man, you could be a *millionaire*, keep selling dope." I don't know which one to go to yet. I worked before for the summer, it was all right. (Laughs.) Then the motherfuckin' *government* take all yo' motherfuckin money, though. I don't like that. I feel they ain't earned it. *They* ain't working for it.

I think one time, probably around *five* more time, maybe I'll get it through my mind. I got to go to school first, that's the biggest problem. It's up to you to decide. Like I came up to Roosevelt [High School] supposed to get a good start, right. I get kicked out of school and I just there two *weeks!* Started getting suspended for five days every other week!

How come?

Just didn't like it. I used to be a fuck-up, you know? One of the kids that just like to clown and shit, want to be a hero, one of the guys, just walk up to somebody, "What's up, man?" and *bam!* Just hit 'em for no reason! You know, "Why you hitting me?" *Bam!* This what I used to be: I used to be one of the kind of guys, if they had a enemy or something, I'd be the first one, "Hey, man, you mess with my cousin?" I'd just light 'em up, *bang!* Sometimes I'd just knock on they shoulder, bam! Then one time we just both hit him at the same time! (Grins.) *Bam!* Just like jumping people, man!

What'd you do that for?

Just *do* it! Just to have a good time! That's fun! Just do it for the hell of it . . . (He's quiet for a minute.)

That's the first thing to do, man, get your education. Drugs ain't gonna be here forever. I mean, it may be here forever, but it ain't gonna be as popular. You know, I'm gone tell you, this the only three things you get out of drugs, you either get to the top and get off the game—when I say get off the game, I mean quit—get hooked up, or you die. That's your only three alternatives. So far that's the only ones I seen. I'd say out of around fifty million who sell it, five get out, five thousand. The rest get hooked or die.

Die?

Get *killed*, man, jealously. See—if *I* seen you with a million dollars, I wouldn't sweat you personal, but somebody else would. Like, you know, "Man, brother, he gettin' too rich for me!" Like Mafia? Man, like you know, they want a part of everything. If some money in *this* game, they want to be in it. If the money in *that* game, they want to be in *it*, want to be the top of it. But some people, "Fuck Mafia, man, they don't mean nothing to me, man," but you say that . . . (Cocks his finger, shoots.) *Bam!* (Laughs.)

And the Cubans, too, man, they's a lot of Cubans in Iron City now. Cubans, Colombians, that's where everybody get they dope from, Colombians. I bet you, now this would help too, if the Colombians stop *making* this shit, I bet you, give it a year, man, it'd be gone. Nobody else, you know, they don't grow this shit in America. Can't be grown, I don't know why. 'Cause of the climate.

Anything else you'd tell a kid?

(Muses.) I'd tell a twelve-year-old, or a ten-year-old, this ain't no place to be if you don't want to get turned to no bitch. Come in a man but leave out a girl. I know a couple of my friends used to do that shit in Juvenile Hall. That shit, that ain't cool. I feel—fuck it, man, they ain't been in here *that* long. (Laughs.) Long as nobody try *me*, I don't sweat it. I tell him I *kill* his ass. That's one thing I'm scared about going to prison.

Won't be scared till it happen, though.

I'm telling you man, this the last time I'm gone come to this motherfucker. Next time they gone *kill* my ass to get me in here. I'mo give 'em a run for they money. Usually, I'm just, "Fuck it, man, I give up, brother," ain't no use in going through this, you know? Next time I'm gone give 'em a run for they money. *Telling* you, man. They gonna want to *quit* police when I get through.

I stayed seven months in this motherfucker and I didn't learn *nothin'*, man. Only thing I learned, tell you the truth, I'm telling you, you come in to this motherfucker you learn *more*, 'cause you be with so many kind of *thieves!* Only thing I learned, how to break into *houses* more, how to hot-wire, how to use red and green wire, to hot-wire a car? Or *steal* better, how to *kill* somebody and get away with it, that's the only thing you learn, you don't learn nothin'! I bet out of around fifty people around *two* of 'em probably'll learn something, you know? I been in every institution there was. This ain't nothin'. Jail, this Juvenile Hall ain't nothin.' This don't mean nothin'.

I been coming here around, how many years now, for . . . around two years now. Just seem like every time you come, the same things. Nothing change! Telling you, like I bet you if I go around a month, I come back I see the same faces, from the last time I was here, the *third* time I was here. See the *same* faces, see the same routine, you know? Day after day, nothing change.

You can't be a loner in jail, man, you have to be one of the guys, and survive. Can't just be by yourself. Everybody think you a punk! Only the strong survive, man, can't be no pussy. Some of this shit these niggers pull up here, man, go down to L.A., it won't work. But in L.A., man, its hard to come in jail! Counties like this they put you jail for any little thing. In L.A., you gotta *kill* somebody (laughs)—not kill somebody, but like beat somebody down or bust they head or something like that to come in jail. Jail's overcrowded there, man, people sleepin' on the floor! And like here, man, this a hazard! Four people to a room, man, one time we have four people to a *room?* And when juvenile crowded, judge don't know what to do with you.

Just too many kids, man. You know, institutions ain't workin'! They should come up with something *else*, man. This is too old! I tell you, this Juvenile Hall ain't nothin', man. (Angrily:) This *county* ain't nothin'. It ain't nothin'. This don't *mean* nothin' to me, man. To a fifteen-year-old, jail ain't nothin'. Jail ain't no place to be. You lose your freedom, your respect . . . You know, 'cause when you come out, people be *looking* at you all crazy? Like this what I hate, my cousin look at me crazy 'cause I was in jail. And that hurted, your own *cousins*, man?

Sometimes, I'm gonna tell you the truth, it's fun here! (Smiles broadly.) You may think I'm crazy but sometimes it's fun . . . You know, like for Christmas I was in this motherfucker here, I had a *great* time. You know, you wasn't with your *family* and everything, but since you in here you make the best of it, you know? It take the place of your family, everybody was singing, you know, kicking it together. We had fun stealing people's presents and stuff? We had a *good* time, man! One of the best Christmases I ever had, even if I was free, even though there ain't no place like home, but I'm telling you man, we had a good time. Doing things, you know, playing with each other, kicking together, you know . . . and everything? I had a *good* time, man.

(Suddenly:) Man, it don't *mean* nothin', man! It's just like this ain't shit! You know, I be gettin' *out* in seven more weeks. I ain't set no goals for myself! I'ma do the same fucking thing!

"Spooky"

"There's nothing out there but dope and trouble"

I love animals. My dream for my future is I'd like to be a veterinarian.

Tall and wiry, with tousled blond hair and a turned-up nose, she looks like what used to be called a tomboy. She's shy, softspoken: she blushes easily and giggles a lot when she's nervous. She's from a rough, mostly white neighborhood of small stucco houses and wood-frame bungalows, not far from the oil refineries and the bleak, shut-down industrial wasteland on the outskirts of Iron City. She is a very successful methamphetamine dealer.

What else is part of your dream?

Well . . . I wouldn't have the dog pound the way it is. I don't think that's right. It's like; if *kids* ran away from their homes, and people picked 'em up and put 'em to sleep? No way! When they put animals to sleep, I hate that. It's not fair. And I'd make them be able to get their dogs fixed free. I would! Because it's the population that's doing it. And they punish us because a lot of people don't have the money to get their dogs fixed. Because it costs a *lot* to get your dog fixed.

I've got a rabbit. I've got so many animals. Four pit bulls. One Doberman. My horse, but it's really mine and my brother's. And I have goldfish and two cats.

I raised birds for a while. Like if a baby bird falls out of a tree, I'll take care of it. It's fun, because they grow up and you let 'em go, and they stick around the house. Not *all* of them, but like some of them will come back, and I can tell they're mine because I banded them. I hate to keep animals locked up in a cage. My *rat* runs free! Around my room.

She lives with her mom and thirteen-year-old brother. Her parents divorced years ago.

I used to deal. Before I came in here. It was . . . uh . . . rich-man's aspirin* and crank. Right now somebody's working for me while I'm in here. *Several* people. Making money. I make a lot of money.

How much?

Sometimes two thousand dollars a day. Cop dope with about half of it. Spend the rest. I have a Camaro T-top, it's brand new . . . but I'll say it wasn't from dope money, because then if I ever get busted, it won't be—how do you say that word?

Confiscated?

Yeah, confiscated. But I'm not going to do it anymore. I'm gonna get a job. I'm gonna go to school and get a job. 'Cause I don't like it. I mean I *like* it, but I don't like getting *dirty* money. I like getting money that I *earned*.

But don't you have to work pretty hard at this?

No! (Scornfully:) I just walk down the street and somebody'll come up to me. And they'll give me money. And I never got busted, because I

* Powder cocaine.

know how to play my cards. You just don't be stupid. You don't make a deal right on the streets. You don't make a deal with a stranger. You keep a runner—(She looks hard at me, suddenly suspicious.) How come you wanta know this, just because you wanta know?

Yeah.

You keep a runner, that sells your dope for you. *You* don't sell your dope. You have someone else do it, so if they get busted, the rap goes on *them*, it don't get on *you*. And you *never* carry your dope with you. And the person that's running your dope, selling it for you, is willing to take that risk because you pay them good.

How much?

Maybe a third of it. But like, if he brings me in two hundred dollars, that's not good, I'll give him like fifty. But if he brings six hundred dollars, he gets maybe three hundred.

Sort of an incentive?

It's so they'll want to sell more so they'll get more.
But I'm going to quit.

Could you make enough money, if you quit dealing?

Yes, I can make enough money. Like my mom; she makes more than I make—well, no. (Laughs.) But if she makes thirty thousand dollars a year, that's good. And if she can do it, I can. I can make more in two days than she can make in about two years—I'm serious! (Laughs: she knows she's exaggerating.) But I don't like it that way. I like to *work*. Like my mom comes home all happy because she got to *finish* something that she was looking forward to. And I could just go out there and make what she makes—like that she tried all *week* to do—and I'd get it; and I don't like that. I like to be happy in what I do.

So you don't really feel good when you're selling?

At the time, I do. But to me, selling dope—well, you're making your money but you're also hurting other people out there. I've seen people get messed up on bad dope. It wasn't *mine!* But, like, people put real, *real* acid, car acid, and stuff like that? And it—like—melted his *tongue* all away, because he tasted it first, to see if it was fake, and it *was* fake! Well, not his *whole* tongue, but melted a hole in it.

It's not worth it, giving somebody dope that's all cut and everything, giving it to someone and getting money. It's not worth it because they're not gonna come back to you, so you just lost a deal, lost a customer. That's why when I deal I make my dope *good*, and I have people coming to me every day, fiendin' for it, because my stuff is pure.

Fiending?

Fiend; you know what that is? A dope fiend. A fiender. That means they'll do anything for it. They have to have it every day. Every single day. When they get up. Before they go to sleep. They *never* go to sleep.

What about eating?

No. Never.

People do crank to make 'em *go*, to make 'em hyper. I'm hyper automatically, so I don't care a thing about it! (Laughs again.) To make 'em up and moving. Some people need to do it to get up in the morning, they're so addicted. It's like people smoking cigarettes, you know how they have nicotine fits? Some people have *crank* fits. They're fiendin'; they're fiendin' bad. Like they'll do anything to get it. That's how you get good customers, good buyers. Cause like . . . you let 'em try your stuff and you make sure it's the best. So they'll fiend for it and they'll do anything for your stuff—always come back to you. That's how you get customers.

Does that make you feel . . .

Bigger? Yep. Kind of like you're an important person. But not really. But in a way, yeah, you are. You're not important cause you're *yourself*, you're important cause you have their dope that they want.

Who buys your dope, mostly?

It's mostly my friends that buy—(quickly:) well, not really—yes, I guess my friends. And some people I don't know who they are.

But how'd you feel about getting people, your friends, to fiend for your dope?

I don't know . . . (She's nervous, looks at her shoes.) At the time, I felt *good*, because I was making money. But now I think about it and I think it's stupid, it was dumb.

The people who buy dope from me aren't really my *real* friends. They're just people I'm making money from. That's why I don't get my real good friends hooked on my dope. Or if I do, I let 'em have it free. I don't charge my friends.

Did any of your real *friends get addicted?*

No, not to *my* stuff—well, I guess yeah. (Earnestly:) But I supported their habits, so they wouldn't go off and do anything just to get someone else's 'cause I wouldn't give it to 'em.

One time I even had a girl who was gonna sell her body to someone else to get money for my dope. And I was gonna be her pimp.

Did you go through with it?

No! That's *sick!* (Indignantly:) I don't like doing that. I just *gave* it to her. She was fiendin' bad.

See, I was a close friend of hers, and she needed the money, and she was already *doing* that, you know? And she was telling me that she was gonna live with me and in order to support her dope habit she was gonna go out and do that, and give me half of whatever she got so I could give her my dope. And I told her I'd just give it for free. No way! I would *never* do that to a friend.

But really, most of my friends all *sell* dope. They're not buyers at all. Most dope dealers aren't fiends. They're not much users, or else they'll go downhill. Because they'll do their dope. Like one of my friends had an eight-ball and was supposed to sell it for about three-hundred-some dollars? And just *done* it all. Not at one time, but like day in and day *out,* just done it. And he lost a *lot* of money. An eight-ball? It's crank, it's like . . . you ever see a dime bag of weed? It's one of those full.

But most of my friends don't.

Why not?

Because they're *strong*; they know what they're doing, they don't do dope, so they're not fiendin' for it, and they can just make their money. I mean, sure, *some* of them use it, but they're not *fiendin'* for it, and if they are, they *have* it, so it's not like they're going downhill.

Sounds like some of your friends are pretty hard characters . . .

Thugs! *I'm* not a thug, but some of them are, because they're out there selling dope when they should be making something of themselves. Instead of hurting other people.

If you think they're hurting other people, how come they're your friends?

(Quickly:) Because that's none of my *business* what they do. Cause if I was doing that I wouldn't want anybody putting *me* down. Because that's my business. People out in Iron City mind their own business.

If drugs hurt people, should we try to stop the drug business?

No! I mean, *I'm* not addicted to drugs, I don't do drugs, but almost all my friends are—pushers. It's like they'd be—like . . . (She's searching for words.)

Out of a job?

Yeah! And I don't like that; I don't like to see all my friends out of a job. But, like, if somebody *helped* them get a job and get their lives together, I wouldn't care, because I don't do drugs, drugs don't make no difference to me. I can get it any time I want, as *much* as I want, but I don't.

You mean if they had a different job, they'd quit selling?

Yeah. Because these days, you go and apply a job or—however you say it?

Apply for a job?

Yeah. And they don't accept you for who you are, they expect you to *know* a lot and get a high school diploma, and you know, some of these people out here can't do that. And they should at least give them a fair chance, to try and do something else. They have to make a living somehow.

If I could be president, I'd give people a fair chance. And I'd change the way things are built. I'd build 'em better. Like houses, and jails.

A lot of the friends she deals to are older: "Most of my friends are adults. 'Cause I'm immature and I don't like being around other people who're immature. They're stupid, and I act stupid when I'm around them. If I was dealing with kids, I'd get so busted it isn't even funny. Some of the kids at Roosevelt High deal their dope in school and leave it in their lockers? No way! They're stupid. They don't know how to do nothin'. There's always narcs there. There's narcs that walk around that place."

If my mom knew what I was doing, she'd beat my butt. I used to get spanked by a belt. The last time was when I was about thirteen, fourteen. We were just messing around in my room. And every time my mom'd spank me, she'd go over and spank my little brother. And I'd start laughing, and she'd come spank *me* and he'd start laughing. (Laughs.) It was funny, 'cause my mom never wanted to hurt us, she felt bad after she did it, and she'd come in and say "Sorry," so we just made it funny so she wouldn't have to say "Sorry." The one thing I hate is when I tell my mom I'll be good and I'll do this? And then I put her down and I don't. I *hate* that.

She's the world to me. I'd do anything—I'd kill myself for my mom. I would.

My mom *made* something of herself. Like she used to deal dope and stuff when *she* was younger. And her dad didn't like it, my grandpa? And he wasn't—I don't know how to say that—he wasn't *impressed* with her.

And before he died, she made something of herself and made him proud.

I get scared talking about these things.

I never used to run away, but I used to stay out all night with my friends for like three nights and stuff, which is *bad*. Like when my mom used to run away from her mom when *she* was sixteen? She ran away one time? And when she came back one time her mom killed herself. Cause she ran away. And I don't want that to happen to my mom. So I don't do it no more. And my mom never got to say she loved her again.

What did you do when you stayed out all night?

Just out with my friends and making money, all night. Once you're on a mission of making money, you don't want to stop. Cause it's like: *Man!* all this *money!* I had, one time, money—this much (she gestures, her hand about a foot above the table)—and I mean it was no *ones* in it. Not one! Tens, twenties . . . I had about four hundred-dollar bills, the rest were fifties and stuff. Making money . . . (Suddenly:) Do you have a kid?

Yes.

How old's your kid?

Fifteen.

Oh, man, *you're* in trouble! (Much laughter.)

You think anybody with a fifteen-year-old is in trouble?

Yes. (Soberly:) If they live in Iron City . . . yes. Because there's nothing out there but dope and trouble. Seriously. There's Twelfth Street, and I live right up the street? And it's where people drive up and down the street, and I mean it's just, it's *all* dope people. I'd never, never, *never* want to raise my kid in Iron City, ever. Never, never, ever. Oh, I love Iron City. I don't want to ever move. But if I ever decided to get a decent job and be able to raise my kids right, I'd move from Iron City. 'Cause I wouldn't want my kid going through what I did.

I want my kid to *earn* what she, or he, is going to work for. 'Cause when you're a dealer, you have to worry about a lot of things. Like who's gonna buy next, and if a cop is gonna be undercover. You don't know. You *never* know. I worry about my runners, that they aren't gonna be honest, that they're gonna—like—take my stuff home and take it in their house and cut it, you know; make their stuff less pure so they could have some of it? Take out half, put the other half baking soda or something. But they never done it.

Do you ever get worried about anything else?

Yes. My parents. And sometimes, that something'll happen to my little brother.

My dad got shot in the head, but he's still alive. My real dad. The story I heard was two guys were gunfighting and my dad put his head up to see who it was and they shot him. I don't believe that. It was about—it was when I was six years old. I was *crying!* And my friend Duane. They thought that he was a person who owed some dope money, but it wasn't him. *He* got shot. I'd known him for four years. All I know is he supposedly owed some money and the guy shot him because he couldn't pay.

Down where I live, if you owed a person a *quarter*—just like a dime or a quarter?—they'll shoot you for it if you don't pay 'em. *I* won't do that, but . . . (She's quiet for a long minute, hesitant.) I packs, too. A little .25-caliber. I packed ever since I was thirteen. My dad gave it to me.

You carry it because you're afraid?

Mostly, I'm not afraid. I'm not afraid of *anything.* But in *that* job I am. *Heck*, yeah. 'Cause you don't know who . . . someone *crazy* might come up on you. I don't really use it. I mean, I don't even put *bullets* in it. I never told anyone that except my best friend, but . . . It's like I have one bullet in the safety, in the chamber. But the clip I have in it? If a cop was to pull me over, I could take that out real quick and I would get only concealed weapon, but it wouldn't be *deadly*.

Would you ever use it?

No, I never want to use that. I just carry it because, like, if you pull *that* out . . . (Grins.) Plus, it's attempted murder, no way! No way. Even for packin' they'd put me away for a long time, if it was loaded. Minor with a concealed weapon? No *way*. And I don't want to ever have to shoot no one, uh-uh. 'Cause if someone shot *my* family, they wouldn't see the end of it. No way. I'd have a task force after 'em.

I've got a beeper, too. It's not working now, but as soon as I get out, I've got to get it started. But not for me, 'cause I'm not gonna do it no more. My brother wants it, just to have his *friends* calling him. He's *dorky!* It's like—he's square, but then again he's not. He can act like he's so *innocent*, though. Sometimes I wonder. But he likes to ride skateboards; so I know he's not out doing drugs.

I'm gonna get my brother out of this place, too. Yes I am. He don't do nothing, but I know—with the schools he's going to? He's gonna go to *Curtis* [Junior High] and then he's going to *Roosevelt High?* I mean he already knows *everything* about dope because of me, and I feel bad about that, but I'm glad he knows; that way he knows what's wrong and what's right. And I tell him that he shouldn't do it, and that if he does, I'll disrespect him, and I won't have nothing to do with him. And he says, like, "Well, *you* do it, why can't I?" (Laughs.) It's like I'm a *parent* to him! Because kids'll say that to their parents: "Well, *you* do it, why can't I?" And I'm like, maaan, what is this?

But I'm gonna get him out of here. I'm gonna go to school, get a job, and then I'm gonna help my parents. Even though they don't need my help. I don't know, I'm just gonna help them. I'm gonna make something of myself, and I'm gonna help my brother.

One time he got caught stealing in a store. A little water gun, squirt gun. I took the rap for him. 'Cause he was *so* scared! They knew someone took it, and like right when you walked out of the store, they got you. And they said, "Come with me," and we were walking, and I took it out of his pack and I took the rap for it. They took us upstairs at this place, and searched us . . . My little brother was so scared it made me cry. And I was *hecka* shakin', cause I could've gotten in *big* trouble for that. But I didn't want to see my brother get in trouble. Over a squirt gun. My mom just came and picked me up and I told her what happened, and my brother got punished. I wasn't gonna take the rap at *home*, no way!

I love my brother. I want to see him have a whole bunch of girlfriends. I don't know why; I don't want him to have just one girlfriend.

My experience, all the young kids are really getting into a bad environment, however you say that. And some kids will do things because their *friends* are doing it, just to get into the crowd. And that's what most of *my* friends do; just to get into crowds. And it's like—if one person does it, they'll call you names to make you do it and then you *will* do it, just so you can be one of the crowd.

I don't like listening to other people. That's my bad habit. I mean I love listening to my mom, because she's my mom. But I don't like people who don't know me telling me what to do. You know how they think they're *bad*, and they can tell you what to do, and you'll just listen? (Scornfully:) *Forget* that. All my life I was never told what to do, besides from my parents; no one on the streets told me what to do. At home I'm perfect, I listen to my parents, because I try to do things to make them happy.

That's my habit, though. I like to be the leader, I don't like people telling me what to do. But I need to get out of that, because I'm going to be told what to do all my life, at my jobs and stuff. Even President Reagan has somebody telling him what to do! I guess that's part of the reason I'm dealing, though, to be my own boss. But that's not why I want to be a veterinarian. It's because I love animals and I want to help 'em.

We're talking again about her fears. Does she worry about the possibility of war?

I don't worry about it, because if it's gonna happen it's gonna happen, and it was meant to be. To me. 'Cause I believe in God a lot, and if he wants me to go to heaven, then he'll make a bomb come . . . (Laughs.) No, but seriously, if I die, then it was *meant* to be, that's my opinion. I'm not really scared. Like if I get shot or something, then I think it was meant to be. Because to me, God won't make you die if he don't want to.

I talk to Him all the time. But I do it when no one sees me, in my room. He helps me. And it comes true! When I pray and ask for something, it comes true. All the time. You never pray to God and ask Him for stuff? And don't it come true most of the time? Not if it's really *bizarre* stuff. But like I'd pray sometimes that people will like . . . help themselves instead of trying to help other people. Like quit selling dope. And I prayed for myself, and that me and my boyfriend stay together, and that he gets out of jail. And it *happens*. It really happens. And I pray that, like other people . . . Like I have some friends who are real, real old? And I go over to their house and I cook for them and I pray that they have good health and stuff like that, and they *do!* I have a ninety-year-old friend, and she's still alive! Yep, I pray for her all the time. Her daughter died; her daughter was like fifty and she died. And now she's all by herself. Something was clogged in her throat, I think.

My wish? That everyone would live. Really. And I wish that people wouldn't, like, destroy animals; that's what mine would be.

I won't even kill a ant. I will not do it, I hate it. Like if there's one on the wall? There was a cockroach in this bathroom and they were gonna kill it. I said, "Don't kill it, don't kill it!" And I picked it up on a paper and took it outside. I'd go in the swimming pool and I'd take the bees out, just to make them go free. Sometimes I'd go swimming just so I could do that. Take 'em out. And like I can't see a fly in a spider's web and him wrapping it up. I'll take the fly out and let him go. I will.

Shaniqa Brown

"You for your own and your self only"

My mother she had whupped me bad once and they called Child Protective Service and had took me to the shelter over there. I was about fifteen. And so we called my house, and my stepfather he said, "Keep her there till she *good*." And he hung up the phone. And I was there about two weeks, and my mother said she didn't want me. They said some of my relatives could come get me, but wouldn't anybody come get me. So I came here. So they was calling all over the place and stuff, to see who'd come get me. Wouldn't nobody come get me. So I stayed here, and I went to placement.

She is athletic, quick in her movements, vibrant, and expressive. As we talk, she's alternately lively and animated, and deeply depressed. Born in Iron City, she moved back and forth between there and Rivertown, as she was passed from one parent or guardian to another: "And then to group homes, back and forth." She dropped out of school at fifteen, was pregnant twice and miscarried both times, and has just been arrested for selling cocaine, working as a low-level dealer for her twenty-nine-year-old boyfriend.

"My mother said, 'Well you shouldnt've been out there,' or whatever, and I haven't been really with her for like two years. And my father didn't say nothing. I haven't even lived with him. I lived with him on and off but not really lived with him. I was with my stepmother's brother, my uncle. And he was mad, 'cause he told me not to be in his house with that stuff. So it's like now I can't get released to him, but my aunt, one of my other aunts, is gonna come get me. They don't really care. I mean . . . that's just how they are."

When you were selling cocaine—were there a lot of people in your neighborhood doing that?

Uh-huh. It was like our whole street was, and it was like—people like *little* did it? And I have one of my cousins, he sells it. And then my boyfriend sells it—or he *sold* it.

Sold it—he doesn't anymore?

Oh, he, uh (she chokes, starts to cry, holds it back), he got killed about . . . it'll be about two months on the twenty-fifth of this month.

I was in *here*. And I was wondering why he didn't write me. And so then my cousin wrote me a letter, and she told me. And I wasn't supposed to know until I got out.

It wasn't an accident . . .

Uh-uh. Oh, they *got* him.

Why do you think so many people were out selling drugs?

Money. Money, and then there's always—when you sell it, then people *respect* you out there, 'cause you're taking the penitentiary chance out there selling it. You know. It's like an adventure, because you're playing tag with the police. I mean it's like a risk—you want to see how far you can go without getting caught. But it's like, you get caught in the end. I mean, it could take three years for you to get caught, but you're *gonna* get caught in the end.

*But people still do it even though they're pretty sure they're going
to get caught . . .*

Uh-huh. Some people are still out there selling now, that I know,
that's been back and *forth* to jail. And they *still* sell it. But like me, I
figured, well, that was my first time selling it, and that was like my first
serious charge. So I doubt very seriously . . . (pauses) not *doubt*, I *know*
that I won't go out there and do it anymore.

I don't really—I don't know, I didn't want to become no *big* dope
dealer. I just wanted to be having money in my pocket, you know, like
if I wanted to go *eat* or if I wanted to go get a coat or a pair of shoes, or
something like that. I mean, it wasn't something I was gonna make a
career out of. It was just something into the time being.

Cause it was like—during that time I was pregnant and stuff, and I
really did need the money. Or what*ever*. And I couldn't get my checks,
from Social Security, 'cause my mother wouldn't sign them over to me
and she still was getting 'em. And I wasn't at home. And then, too, this
dude, this guy that I used to go with, he was in trouble or whatever, so
I was helping *him* out, too. So it was like I was helping him out *and*
myself out at the same time. And I got caught, and so he left and went
somewhere, Florida, and I came back out, and that's when I got involved
with somebody else.

I don't think it was respect I was in it for, I think it was just money.

I've never had a job. 'Cause I was always too young. I mean it was
like—fifteen or sixteen, it's hard to get a job. So now when I get out, I'll
be seventeen and a half and so it'll be easier.

But a lot of people do it for the respect, because of the risk . . .

Respect. Yeah, and then, too, it's money, and then with money you
get *cars*, and with cars you get girlfriends and boyfriends, and stuff like
that—'cause I know a lot of females out there who sold it, too. Some are
in it for money, some are in it because they want to be noticed, or they
want people to have respect for them, what*ever*. I mean 'cause sometimes,
money . . . (She pauses.) You know, it's just *throwaway* money, whatever.
Some people, they be stackin' G's after G's, I mean *thousands*, and don't
care! It's just the simple fact that "Oh, you know such and such? Oh
yeah, he's a big kingpin," you know, stuff like that, or "Yeah, such and

such is my *cousin*, you know him? Yeah, *I* used to sell dope for him," you know, stuff like that. That's what it was all about. Say I sell dope in Iron City for somebody, and somebody in Hillview sell dope, but they come from Hillview to Iron City to sell what they have, see, and then they come mess with *me*, the person I'm selling dope for can go after that person from Hillview, you know, and then there'll be a whole bunch of confusion against such and such: "How are you gonna come from Hillview to Iron City to sell this?" or "How you gone come to *my* territory?" stuff like that. (Laughs.) They don't want nobody to be bigger than them or what*ever!* That's all it is, you know, who's bigger than who.

But when you boil down to it, there's really nobody bigger than *nobody*, 'cause they *all* stupid for being out there! (Laughs.)

See, they stupid, and *you* is, if you out there and don't know what you doing? You gone get *hurt*, I'm telling you, somebody gone come out there and *rob* you, or something, that's what I say.

Did you ever get hurt dealing drugs?

You mean physically? Uh-uh. Not me. I guess it was because I was a girl. And it was like it was guys out there that I knew, like my cousins, and friends that I grew up with and stuff, they were out there, and they would like watch me and stuff, make sure wasn't nothing happen.

Is there something you would do so that people didn't have to be selling drugs in order to make money? I mean, should it be that way?

No. But then, too, there's not really nothing I *can* do. Because if somebody's illiterate, like say we have some illiterate drug dealer, and they make so much money, but yet, I can't give them a job, because they're illiterate. And what if it's like—in some *science* factory or whatever (laughs), you know, and they mess up the *potion* or what*ever!* (Laughs.) You know, what would we have?

And I mean it's fun, it's fun, but then . . . (Pauses.) You know, 'cause you get the cars, you know, and people say like "Oh, yeah, did you see that car such and such, it had *this* on it, *that* on it," or, you know, you come out with some type of Troop sweat suit, leather sweat suit, what*ever*, they'll be like "Oh, yeah!" Like this guy I know, he got a big ring, and

it say "Buddy," it's about *this* big, and it got "Buddy" on it, or whatever
. . . You know, they'll be wearing it, flash it . . . And stuff like that, I
don't like. You know, it looks *cute*, but you know me, I can't imagine
myself walking around with some type of ring like that or some big *me-
dallion* . . . I'm not into that.

And like I got a brother, my stepbrother? and my father just told me
that *he* out in Valley City sellin'. And I mean, I didn't expect *him* to be
out there selling drugs. But it's gettin' *everybody*, and I mean, like I keep
telling my sister, don't do it, don't do it, because you don't want to be
locked up. I mean, right now I done wasted half a year. Cause of that.
It ain't worth it.

I don't even associate with Iron City no more. 'Cause it's a bad area.
I mean even the *dope* dealers that was *selling* dope smoked out now, you
know, smokin' dope and sellin' they *cars* to get this hit, and that hit, and
stuff like that.

I know this guy, the one I was telling you about with the ring? I got
out and I said, "Where Buddy at?" And they say he's smoked out now,
off of gremmies—you know what gremmies are? Has somebody told you
that? That's cocaine and weed put together, rolled up together like? OK,
that's what gremmies are. Everybody told me he smoked out on gremmies.
I said, "You lying." So I went to Iron City, right, to see my mother, and
I seen his car, and (sadly:) it was like the *hubcap* was missing, had a *dent*
on the side, and stuff like that, and I asked this dude Leon, I said, you
know, "Ain't that Buddy car?" And he said he rent his car, in other words,
you know, like when you rent your car out to somebody for twenty dollars
or whatever, two rocks, stuff like that? And I was like, that's *sad* . . . that
is really sad. (She shakes her head again.) And when he came to the
Valley, he was in this car, I mean it was just like this little *small* car?
And he *had* such a pretty car, he had this like Cutlass Supreme, it was
like a gold color, and he gone come in his little *small* car . . . And his
shoes, he used to wear like Troop tennis shoes, stuff like that, he had on
something like ten-dollar tennis shoes. I was like, that's sad, how . . . it
could take you over.

Drugs, I'm telling you, it could ruin you. I know a lot of people who
smoked it, so therefore . . . pssh . . . (Uneasily:) I mean . . . I've got
aunts on this stuff, cousins . . . *everybody* on it.

And my mother, she stay at these condos, right, and it's a lot of people
who sell dope where she live at. And sometimes I'll be like, "God, I hope

don't nobody get my mother mixed up in it," you know? Like say somebody gets shooting guns and my mother *walkin'* or whatever, the bullet can hit her, whatever the case may be, you know, or she get involved in a raid 'cause the apartments got mixed up? Cause a house can easily get raided because the apartment numbers got mixed up. And it's like when you selling drugs or whatever, it don't . . . they . . . pssh . . . (She laughs uneasily, shakes her head.) Honestly, they'll go to your *baby brother* or who*ever*—your daughter—whoever, to get to you. They don't care, it's like I said. It's like the picture *Colors?* Did you see that picture? They don't care *who* they get.

Like my godsister was telling me, somebody was looking for her friend, this guy, and they couldn't find him. So they took his runner, in other words the person who sold dope for him? Kidnapped *him* and shot him eleven times. To get at the guy. And I told my godsister, I said, you shouldn't be out there, because see, if they taking his *runners* to get at him, imagine what they'd do to his *women*, you know what I'm saying? Because she used to mess with the dude. I mean that's how they—that's how it is now. And like this one guy that my friend in Hillview knows, he got shot 'cause he came up, you know, he was having a lot of money and stuff, like that . . . I mean it is *dangerous* out there, pshh . . .

And I told my godsister she better be careful 'cause some of the people be mistaking me for *her*, and I swear to God if somebody try to kidnap *me* and shoot *me* (laughs) . . . I mean I would be so *mad* at that girl I wouldn't know what to do. I'm serious. She was like "Well 'Niqa I don't think they after me now, that was just *then*," and I'm like yeah, alright, um-hm. Let somebody come after *me*. And I've never had the experience of nobody having no contract out on me or nothing.

That's another thing, when you play with people' dope like that, or money, that's another thing you can get hurt over. So I mean you can get hurt over the littlest things. Even if it was five dollars or what*ever*. It's just the point of, don't nobody want to look *stupid*, you know, as far as, "Oh, well, um, yeah, such and such took this much dope from you, and that much," you know, they don't want that, they want this *image*. And so that's why they don't allow stuff like that.

I used to stay on a dope track. The house I *lived* in was a dope track, it wasn't nothin' *but* dope dealers out there, or either people coming to buy dope. I went there three weeks ago, the street is—pssh, so quiet. It's like you got to go *find* the dope, and I mean the place where you got to go find it is way in the Ridge, that's another part of Iron City. And it's like if you go to Eastville you might see somebody out there with something, but it's like, either they in jail, they smoked out, or a task force came, you know, or whatever. 'Cause I was out and it was like "Where is everybody at?" you know, and my godsister's telling me "Well it's been like this since you left." I mean it was *nobody* out there. I even went to my uncle's house and *he* was in the house. I was like, man, this place done *changed*. And I mean that's just like within six months.

So there's not as many people selling . . .

It is, but they're like doing it on the *under*. And you know, the worst way a person get caught is by a beeper. Because some people sell dope by a beeper, you could *easily* tap, I mean not tap but you know, give the beeper number to a police, police gone check it out . . . 'Cause I mean this guy had got killed, I mean somebody shot him, through his car. What it was was, they set him up through his beeper, beeped him on his beeper, called him from somewhere—I think his name was Arizona— and said they wanted to pick up a package. I think they wanted like a half ounce of dope or whatever. So he came, and they *shot* him, I mean, they *killed* him (laughs), they took his money, and the boy—they killed him and they killed the passenger, person who was in the car. But that's why beepers—it can be either from a dope dealer or police, either way you can get set up from a beeper.

And you gone have money for a minute, but now you *gone* get caught *sometime*. And it's lucky for me I got caught and I wasn't selling it too long. And most people, that's they *living*. They don't know how to do nothing else *but* sell dope. And some people start off by selling weed, and they graduate, you know, to the cocaine. Or either it's the heroin, the hop, whatever you want to call it. And I mean . . . (hesitates) it's just a trip. And it go way, way back. All of it do.

And I mean I don't do cocaine, but I smoke weed and I drink, but it's not like I *have* to have it. And as far as that, I wouldn't—OK, I've seen what it does to too many people to even *try* to indulge in it myself. Even people like my next-door neighbor, and I just *give* it to her, you know, and it's like she'll be normal one minute and talk to me like I'm talking to you, and the next minute be like, it's like a Dr. Jekyll–Mr. Hyde thing. I wouldn't want to mess *my* life up like that.

'Cause you know what, that one hit could be your *last* hit. It could either be that hit to get you hooked, or it could either be that hit to put you six feet under. 'Cause I know this guy, he said he had smoked it one night, he said his *heart* stopped. And he said he was so scared that he put it down. Now it's, wouldn't you know, this brother smoking it again! (Incredulous:) I'm like—wait a minute, you know, *my* heart stop, I'm gone put it *down*, you know I ain't gone *touch* it no more, or whatever the case may be.

But see . . . you know what? I figure like this. Black people the most stupidest people, though, you know what I'm saying? 'Cause they don't realize, if you—if something wrong with your *body*, physically *and* mentally, then you *know* you gone stop what you doin'! But they get so strung out on—like this girl I know, she got so strung out on it her *face* broke out in a rash, her *lips* was cracked in a rash, and her hands was like old *lady* hands, and stuff? And you know, it was like, they was just—skinny, period, and it was like—they *chest*, they didn't *have* none, you know, you could see they *ribs* sticking out and stuff, and they be wearing pants, you know, that you got to roll 'em to keep 'em up, and stuff? (Laughs.) And that's why I was like uh-uh, ain't no way in the world, I mean . . . (She points to her own chest.) I don't have *much*, but trust me, I cherish whatever I got too much (laughs) to indulge in all that, 'cause, um, it's *crazy*.

Like my uncle, *he* on it; my aunt, *she* on it, and she stole—she went to my mother house, and my mother had like four holes in her ear, she had like three diamonds for the last three holes on each ear that was different sizes. And my aunt went and stole my mother's diamonds. My aunt Letitia? She went to my mother's house in Iron City. But it was like my mother had these diamonds for years, she got one pair for her birthday, and she bought another pair, and I don't know who she had the other pair from but it was like, you know, she had *memories* of those. And now it's like they *gone* and stuff . . . (trails off:) you know, just little stuff like that, then they go to my grandmother's house and steal *her* stuff . . . and so it'll be like . . . be a trip. You know, that's why my mother don't let relatives go to her house. I mean it don't pay!

And I was reading this book called *Carmen*, have you heard of that book? It's about this drug addict, and she ran away from home and stuff like that, and so then she came back home, it was like years later, and her mother said that she had read somewhere that drug addicts come to their house and steal their jewelry, so the mother put her jewelry all *on* her at *once* and stuff (laughs) so the daughter couldn't steal 'em! And her daughter was wondering why her mother has it on . . . then she finally realized. You know, that goes to show you how far they'll go. To get it.

And then, like boys still be locked up in here and they do like, "Well, I'm gone do the same thing, but this time I'm gonna be *legit* about mine, I'm gonna be stackin' my dollars," stuff like that. And like my cousin Sidney, he started here and he in County [Jail] now. They say once you been here four, five times you go to prison. And he got a year to serve now. And you know . . . it's sad. And he just turned eighteen in February. And right there, you know you can get your record sealed six months after you eighteen, he can get his Juvenile Hall record sealed but he can't get his adult record sealed, he got a record, straight off the top. I mean *he* was even strung out on drugs! I was like, God! I said, not *Sidney*, he used to be so bright in school and stuff, I said, not him . . . When my mother told me, I didn't believe her.

And somebody tried to pressure *me*, too, long time ago, about two years ago. It was like, you know, "Here, here! Just this one time, just this one time!" I said "Uh-uh, I'm all right, I'm all right," you know. And so they was still doing it and finally I just left, 'cause I'm not the one (frowns), like I say, I'm not the one to be, pssh! into that. If *they* want to go down, fine. That's them.

When you were selling—knowing what you know about how drugs mess people up—did that make you feel kind of weird, knowing they were buying stuff that messed them up?

I don't know . . . (She looks at her hands.) I mean, like if it'd be like *older* men coming out there, I mean like my grandfather's age, now . . . *that* I would feel guilty about. And like this little ten-year-old boy who'd come out there, *that* I'd feel guilty about, and I wouldn't sell to him. But I look at it like this: an adult is an adult. And . . . they are responsible for them own selves and if they know . . . I mean it's just like a sixteen-year-old, you know what you getting yourself into, when you start it, so why do it? You know what I'm sayin'? And if you get hooked on it, then . . . there's nothing *I* can do, I mean, you know, it wasn't like I was being cruel or anything, but it's like—I need the money, you needed the dope, OK, you, I mean . . . (Starts over.) You're responsible for your own self, so it's like, OK, I'm gone sell it to *you, you* gone have your habit, *I* get the money in my pocket.

There was a ten-year-old boy out there looking to buy dope?

Uh-huh. He stay somewhere around there, I didn't know him.

But you wouldn't sell to him . . .

Uh-uh. I mean . . . 'cause I couldn't see my little sister, or, you know, my little half sisters, stepsisters or whatever you want to call it, coming out there, you know, somebody else selling it to her. So I wouldn't want to do that.

Her boyfriend hasn't been caught yet, and she hasn't told anyone they were together for fear they'll find out he was supplying her and arrest him too. "And Ray, as much animosity as I have towards him, I don't think I could go out there and say me and him had, you know, some type of relationship going, 'cause I wouldn't want to see that man go to jail because of me. I'm not so immature to be going, 'Well, uh, he's twenty-something and I'm only sixteen,' I couldn't do that. I really couldn't. I figure if I'm trying to be old enough to go with somebody older than me, then I figure when the heartbreakin' comes, I'm old enough to handle that."

What are guys like out there these days—guys your age . . .

(Much laughter.) Oh, God! That question is . . . I don't know. I don't know. If they're not sellin' dope, they in *jail.* You gone very seldom find somebody graduating—I mean they don't graduate but barely. Then most of the guys out there that's doing something with themselves, they're *older.* Like my boyfriend—not the one that just passed but the other one, that I was going with before I went in here? He just turned twenty-nine in March, and *he* was even selling dope! And so it's like . . . I don't know about those guys out there.

If all these guys are all either selling dope, or doing dope, or in jail, how does that make you feel about getting married?

OK. I'll put it this way—for the last couple years, five or six years, I've always said I'm not *never* getting married. As far as relationships are concerned (laughs), tell you the truth, they come and go. 'Cause I mean, it's after this person, after we done broke up? Alright, I go to the *next* person. You know, it don't be like I'll be . . . what you want to call it . . . OK, it's called a *toss-up*, where a girl goes from one guy to the other guy to the other guy? I'm talking as far as having sex with 'em. It's like . . . the guys that I go with are like people I don't know, just met 'em or whatever.

Like Ray, he used to come around and I used to say, "God, he look so *good!*" Like that. And then this one night, next thing you know, I was driving around with him, and then he dropped me off, and then he came back and got me, next day, and we went to the motel room, he had me (laughs)—I was kept a prisoner, you might as well say . . . I mean, God, this brother wouldn't even let me out of the room to go get no *cigarettes!* And like one time he got me so scared I locked myself in the *bathroom* (laughs), you know, and I mean, it be a *trip!*

And when Ray had asked me how old I was, I never did tell him. It was like he was drunk or whatever, not drunk but he was under the *influence*, 'cause he used to do gremmies, and smoke the pipe too. And he still sold drugs. He would ask me how old I am, he'd be like "Baby girl, how old are you?" and I'd be like "How old are *you?*" You know, trying to avoid the question. Then by time he get through all that he done forgot that he asked! (Laughs.)

God, it be a trip, though—the relationships I have is not even funny. I tried going with somebody my age. See, I was messing with two guys, one's this guy in Hillview, and then I was messing with a guy in Iron City. And that guy in Hillview just turned eighteen in February. So at the time he was seventeen. He did not work out for nothing. He got a little girl—I can't understand how these boys be gettin', so young—to be having children, I don't understand it. I mean, like me, I would have had two kids by now. But it was just a matter of you got to be able to take care of yourself first, before you try to take care of somebody else. And this boy staying with his *mama* (laughs) and stuff like that, and I'm like . . . I don't know what to tell you. And so that didn't work out, so I just stopped calling him, off the top. And that's when I started messing with Ray.

And he was nice, though, he really was, he would take me to the hospital—my mother was in the hospital, and he would go take me to the hospital to see my mother, and you know, if I needed something, he'd get it, stuff like that.

I'm so mad at him, though. 'Cause when I got busted, he asked my godsister, all he asked about was his dope! (Indignantly:) "So where is my dope?" or what*ever*. I told her, I said, I was so mad, I said, "I'm in jail"—I mean I was *cussin'*—I said, "I'm in jail and he up here asking about his *dope*." And when I got my pass, my godsister was saying, "Well, 'Niqa, Ray was asking about you." And my exact words was, "Fuck that punk!" like that. So I got to thinking. And I said he got nerve, asking about me, and when I got busted, all he asked about was his dope. I was like, "He probably out there messin' with the *next* bitch," like I was so mad, God!

Then I got to thinking. And Ray married, too, right? I was just committing sin after sin, and this brother up here *married*. And I got to thinking. I say, "OK, I'll get back with him, but I'm gone *charge* him this time." I say, " 'Cause I been locked up for half a year 'cause of that brother." So I was like, OK, when I get out I'm gone make him buy me all *type* of stuff. And I mean Ray, he got rings all over his fingers? Take some of them off, you know, I would go give some to my mother. Whatever the case may be, you *paying* for my being locked up. It was my fault, but still, when I get locked up 'cause of you, 'cause I'm trying to help you out, you don't ask about your *dope*, you know? You ask about *me, then* you ask about your dope.

Yeah, he was married. You know what, I didn't know, but then he start saying something about a *wife*. And I wasn't really trippin', 'cause he was having problems with her anyway. Oh, he has a son, too, about five years old, old enough to be my little brother, and he took his son away from her. He have a sweet little boy. And you know, we'd take him to McDonald's, stuff like that.

But one night he *really* got bogus. One night he brought the broad to our motel room! And he gone tell her that I was his *friend's* girlfriend! I was so mad I flew out that door, I mean, I was literally pissed, I mean I was so pissed off. I told him, too. I said, you know, I said, "You are *no* good." 'Cause he get on the phone, and call her, talking about all types of stuff? I said, "Now if I call Richard, and talk to him, while the next nigger in the *room* with me, I mean, I couldn't do that, I really couldn't." He was like "Yeah, you right, you right, you right," stuff like that. (Laughs.) It's bad enough I'm accepting the fact that you got a son, and you married, and whatever the case may be, and you bringing the broad to where I'm *at* . . . I mean, I can take a lot, I'm serious, 'cause that right there took the cake off, took the icing off the cake, put it that way.

I'm gone tell him, too, this time: "I'll get back with you, but um, pssh . . . yeah! You try to be married this time and, I'm telling you, we just be friends. 'Cause I'm not into that no more. I'm not into sharing, put it that way. So you go mess with that girl, come mess with *me*, give me some type of *disease* or whatever . . ." (Laughs.)

You said you decided a while ago not to get married . . . how come?

Cause, my mama married twice, and all the people I know, I been seeing too many bad marriages. And then, too, I'm the type of person, I don't like to be tied down to nobody. I really don't. 'Cause you know, I mean, just think—I wasn't even *married* to Ray and he trying to tell me where to go! I couldn't go here, and I couldn't go there—I mean just imagine if I'm married! That means I'm living with this man, and he can (laughs), you know, he can put the *bar* on the door and I can't go no . . . I'm serious! I'm not into that. And you know, then somebody'll try to *hit* me, and I'd be *lost* then, it'd be all over. I don't know, I might get married about when I'm forty. (Laughs.) I'm serious, I really couldn't see myself being married at twenty- . . . three, thirty, thirty-five, stuff like that, I couldn't.

Even if somebody came along that you really cared about?

I just cannot see . . . (Muses.) That's why I guess . . . You know what? The longest I ever had a relationship was like a couple of months, I'm so serious. I have never went to like a year, eleven months, stuff like that. 'Cause I get tired of a person. And when I get tired of you, *trust* me, I'm gonna stop calling you and all that. I'm not . . . (shakes her head vigorously) uh-uh . . . I'm not into it. I'll have *kids*, but I'm not getting married.

Won't that be hard, though?

(Laughs.) No, it wouldn't, I'm serious! It wouldn't . . .

You'd be there with these kids, and it's just you having to deal with them . . .

Yeah, but I'd rather have two kids than be *married*. (Laughs.) That's *bad!* I'm serious, that is bad, but I really would, truly. God . . . I don't know, I can't be married. And my brother, I guess he gone get married, or whatever, but I'm not *getting* married!

But you want kids . . .

Yeah. I want one. Two. Not ten! (Laughs.) And by the time my first child would be fourteen, or ten, or whatever, by then, that'd be time for me to get pregnant again, if I was to have two kids. 'Cause as far as having kids a year apart and things like that, oh, get out of here! I don't know . . . And I just think about it a lot, too. I rather be a single parent.

Do other people you know feel that way, too?

My *mom* does. She is, now! She just got a divorce February before last.

And she's happier now?

Uh-huh, she *is!* And you can tell. She looks better, she acts better, now that she's not married. I mean we actually *conversate*.
(She's quiet for a moment. Suddenly:) I hate it, I despise it. I hate women, I hate marriage . . . I hate it *all*. I don't know.
And that's another thing, I'm afraid of getting old. Seem like just a few days ago I was fourteen. Now I'm seventeen, next thing you know I'll be eighteen in about March. I mean when you get old . . . it's all over! I mean you can't . . . go dancin', you know what I'm saying? And you see your son, your daughter growing up, and things . . .

But that can be good.

Naw . . . Next I'll be envying my kids, I'll bet you. There's a lot of things you miss out on. You know, I ask my teacher, she's forty-four years old, this lady work here? I ask her if she still have sex! (Laughs.) See, that's another thing I'm afraid of getting too old for, I'm serious, 'cause all these guys . . . Who gone support me when I get *fifty* and . . . stuff like that? I don't want to be on Social Security when I'm fifty, and things . . .

That's one of the things about being married—you support each other . . .

No. What if I was married and all of a sudden my husband became an alco*holic?* Or what*ever?* And then I'd get a divorce, and this brother don't want to move out of my *house,* and things like that . . .

Guess it depends on who you marry—if you married the right dude, he'd be taking care of you.

True. But . . . since they're all *gone* . . .

Gone?

There is no more *around.* (Laughs again.) They're all gone. The good ones. Or either they're like fifty, forty, stuff like that. They *gone.* I'm talking about the *good* guys are gone, that're *my* age, twenty-nine and stuff like that . . . And you know, there's this girl, she was here, she just turned eighteen, I asked her how old was her boyfriend, and she said something like thirty-two, and I said, "Oh my God!" and she said that her boyfriend's *son* was her age! I said uh-uh, uh-uh, no, I say, "I would never go with no man whose *son* was my age, never" . . . It'd be like, who is that, you mother, your stepmother? (Laughs.) Oh, no, uh-uh.
I was pregnant twice. I had a miscarriage. Both times.

Did you want them?

Uh-huh. And my aunt, she was—she wasn't like my mother. She gave me support, like, 'cause she had got pregnant at sixteen. And she was like sometimes: "Maybe that'll be best for you." I mean, 'cause the daughter that she had when she was sixteen, my cousin, is now—she'll be eighteen this summer and she's getting ready to go to the Olympics! So it's not like her daughter turned out bad or anything. I mean she didn't down me because I was pregnant. And she was more or less like, you know—she was letting me know about that was a big responsibility to take on, but then, too, she also let me know that there's also, you know, if there's only a little good in it, there's *some* good. Or there *can* be some good, but it depends on what point of view you look at it, of having a baby.

So you weren't upset . . .

No.

What about the father?

The first one was this guy in Iron City. And it was like it happened when I was on the run from a group home, and I barely had contact with him, and when I finally had contact with him, it was like after I had a miscarriage. And then the second one was this guy in Hillview. And we had broke up and I had went with somebody else and he said, "Oh, well how do I know it's mine?"

I saw this commercial about this lady, she had a baby in her stomach, she smoked cigarettes, and they showed the little baby inside her stomach smoking a cigarette! (Laughs.) I said, "Oh, God!" I said, they done cut it *low*, they done made they *point* right there. I think that's one of the reasons why I had my first miscarriage was I smoked weed, and smoked cigarettes, and I was drinking. (Matter-of-factly:) And then I got run over by a car, too. This guy I used to go with ran me over.

Uh—you mean he ran you over on purpose?

Yeah, he ran me over on purpose. I flew up in the air, and I came back down, and he took off. And a lady said, "I'll take you to the hospital, I'll take you to the hospital," and I said, "I'm fine!" I was *bleeding*, but I was fine, my feet got scarred up . . .

And then one time he saw me talking to this guy. On the street. He stops me, tells me to get in the car, and he *hits* me! I said, "I'm out of here," you know? I'm *serious*, I was like uh-uh, this brother done went *crazy*. And so then he came—he stay in Hillview—he came to Iron City, and he was like "I really wanted to hurt you, 'cause you try to talk to a lot of dudes," you know. I mean, that's me: somebody ask me my name, I'm gonna give 'em my name and a phone number, too, you know, if they want it. And so, right to this day, we friends and stuff like that.

Still friends even though he ran you over with the car?

Yeah. That was *then*. I just feel sorry for the girls he going with now, 'cause he be knocking 'em upside the *head*. (Laughs.) God! I be like, uh-uh, how could you guys *take* that? And I can't stand pain, so if I see a situation where somebody gonna try to hit me, I'm *out*.

Is that one reason why you're not too excited about getting married?

Uh-huh. That's another reason. My father used to beat my mother a lot. And I'm not for no guy puttin' his hands on me, I'm serious. Playfully, yeah, but you know as far as *seriously*, to whereas my *teeth* get knocked out, or black *eye*, what*ever*, concussion, stuff like that, I'm not—un-uh, I'd of just shot 'em, I'm serious, I would be in *jail* for murder. I don't know, I'm not—like I say, I just don't like pain.

It's sad, too. I'll tell you the truth, I think the guys that beat on females, they *weak*. In other words, you *know* they sissies 'cause, you know, they got to beat on somebody lower than them. You know what I'm sayin'?

See like . . . this how dudes is now: if you call them, and you tell them to come get you, that automatically means that you want to go to the *hotel* with 'em or what*ever*. To they house or wher*ever*. And do this and do that, that's what they think *that* mean. And that's what they gone expect of me or what*ever*. 'Cause you know they gone be like "Oh, she just got out of, you know, Juvenile Hall, jail, whatever you want to call it, so she gone be willing to do this, willing to do that," stuff like that. And I ain't into all that. They expect somebody to be a toss-up or whatever. That's how they expect the girls nowadays, 'cause I know girls they still with dudes that's *beating* them and stuff like that. And that's how they expect me to be, but I always let them know that I'm not the one nor the other for them to think that they got some type of control over.

Like this guy that I used to mess with, the one that tried to run me over, he in Iron City now. And this dude, I mean, he one of these people like to *beat* people. And when he first came to Iron City, my godsister said, "*Look* at that dude right there," you know, he had waves in his hair and he had a little drop-top Firebird, and I said, "Don't even talk to him 'cause I know him." I didn't tell her how, but I told her I knew him. So now to this day he out in Iron City with some girl, she ain't nothing but like *sixteen*, maybe fifteen, and this dude, his name Chris, he about twenty-something. And he out there *beating* the girl! You know? And she's still with him! And like he was messing with this other girl, and he slapped her in front of all his friends and stuff. Un-uh. Putting her on show and tell. And I say they *stupid* for trying to stay with this dude.

And like I say, that's all today is about anyway—this new generation, *us*, kids, that's what it's about anyway. 'Cause even little fourteen-year-old dudes'll be trying to hit on their little girlfriends, and stuff. 'Cause they think that 'cause they got *money*, and all this, that that give 'em the right to hit on somebody.

Whole world is that way, I think . . .

It *is!* That's true. Because my daddy used to beat my *mother.* And I remember it, but I *don't* remember it. I mean God, he used to have us wait outside, nights, with no *shoes* on, and chasin' after my mother and stuff . . . I mean like one time she had a car accident, she hurt her back—it was a Vega, them cars is not good. The whole top came in, the front squished, all stuff like that, and I was in her room and he gone tell me to get out, you know. And like he'll be hitting her and stuff and she still got a *neck* brace on her neck . . .

My father used to *slam* some dope. I don't know if he smoke cocaine or what, but I know he used to be a straight drug addict, and I guess that's what brought on his seizures—to this day he have epileptic seizures. But like when I was little and stuff, after him and Mama had got separated, he would come and try to talk to her. One time he busted our window out. And so it was like nighttime, we was goin' somewhere, he was like "I want to see my daughter, I want to see my daughter," we all up in the car, I'm crying, my mother tellin' me to be quiet. And she almost run him over, and stuff, I was like "God, how I get into *this* one!" (Laughs.) I won't never understand it.

And like when me and my brother and sister had got in trouble, for that little shoplifting thing when he was little? After he came to pick me up, he went outside, he got all types of switches, tied 'em together, and I got all *beat* and stuff, and it's like right down to this day I've got a cut on my back, like it's a scar, and I don't even know how I got it there. I mean it could've been from when he tried to nearly kill me with them switches or whatever.

And like when we got in trouble, my mother called my grandmother, her mother, and it was like "Mama, come get these kids before I kill 'em," you know. And that's why I guess they decided my grandmother was gone take my sister and I was gone go with my aunt.

It was like I'd get in trouble if I didn't clean the *toilet* stool right! We'd get whuppin's, you know. And to this day—I went back to Iron City and this dude name Leon, he was like "Yeah, Shaniqa, I remember when your mama used to *beat* y'all like that!" He said, "Boy, your mama used to tear you *up!*" It was like (uncomfortably:) all these people *know* all types of stuff . . .

And it was like one time I was in kindergarten and I cut my hair, like one big plug from my hair? My mama came and got me, and she took me home, I mean she tried to beat the living daylights out of me. And so then they had to cut all my hair off, to even it up with the plug that I cut out.

Child Protective Service had to come into it. And that's when I first went to the shelter. It was like my mother had whipped me badly. And I had told my counselor that my mother had took my purse and my lunch card and I needed my lunch card to eat. And she ax why did your mother take it, and stuff like that, so I just told her. First I didn't want to, but I told her. And my mother got all upset, said, "You called them peoples on me," and stuff like that.

Why did *she take your lunch card?*

You know, I don't even remember. I think it was something so stupid—I don't know if it was 'cause I had makeup in my purse or what, but she took my purse, and she kept it in her closet. I mean, gettin' whuppin's was something I was *used* to, though. Like when I was in Iron City, and me and my brother and sister we cut school, 'cause my sister got suspended. And she wanted us to cut with her. And so we went, you know, and picked up—we shoplifted little pencils and stuff—I was like six, seven years old. And my father—we got busted so they called my father, and he came and got us, so my father whupped me badly. And it was like he didn't whip my sisters and them. And we all got sent off. And it was like, I went to my aunt, the same thing happened *over* again! And like when she'd hot-comb my hair, she'd burn my scalp and *laugh*, you know, just stuff like that.

"Then I went to my father's house. And he was trippin', and he gone tell me—I had met this guy and he came to my daddy, my father house, he was older than me though, so my father got to trippin' like 'Man, my daughter can't come out,' stuff like that, like I was a little kid. And so he got to talking 'bout 'I don't want no ho's up in my house,' stuff like that. So then me and him got into a fight, he was choking me, it was in his shop, his wife was there, she gone try to say I provoked him to choke me, and so he let me go, and he grabbed me again, he was choking me again, I mean I was crying, I called him all types of names . . . And he spose to, be, so-called, a church man, and all this, and he up here chokin' me, I'm laying on the ground, he up here chokin' me. And I was like God, for a minute there I thought I was gone die. I'm serious!

"And then I went to Hillview. And I was staying with my stepmother's brother. And my father done come up and told 'em I can't stay there, it wasn't even his house, but he gone say I can't stay there, I got to get out of this house, stuff like that. And so we driving, we going to Iron City to my mama's house, they spose to drop me off. And so he talking about as much trouble as I cause, he should drop me off right there. I said drop me off, I said, 'cause I can find my own way back. And it was like my little sister was there, my little half sister, and she was hearing all this type of stuff, and I felt bad. But wasn't nothing I could do. So he just dropped me, straight dropped me off at my mama's house. Mom's talking about I can't stay there, then she's talking about spending the night, I was like what I'm gone spend the night at my own mama's house for? And then got to leave the next day. So I was telling her I leave my clothes, then I come back and get 'em. So she was like 'Well, um, if you don't be back such and such a day,

*get your clothes, you ain't gone have no clothes.' It was like I had
to drive from Hillview to Iron City, this was like right after I got
finished selling my dope, it was like five-something in the morning,
to go get my clothes."*

In between that time I was just like jumping from school to school. I
never stayed at a school long enough to get too many credits. I had been
to ten or eleven different schools already. It was like either I'd move from
relative to relative, or from group home to group home, or whatever.
Confused life! (Laughs.) It was like I was going from Hillview to Iron
City, Iron City to Hillview, back and forth. And I was like, this is *crazy*.

For some reason I ain't never missed a year of school. I mean I done
been to about eleven different schools. I mean I went to so many schools
it ain't even funny. I mean I'd go to one school for like preschool to
kindergarten. Then I'd go to another school for second grade, and I'd go
to a *different* school for third and fourth, and then another one for fifth
and sixth . . .

(Softly:) I think I *liked* school. It was just—I don't know, I got to the
place where I was just fed up with people trying to tell me what to do. It
was like—I don't know—I just got fed up with people trying to push me
over and stuff, like I said, using their authority, abusing it, rather. I got
tired of it.

My brother was illiterate. And my sister was too, and it was like I was
the only smart one. And it was like all three of us had came from the
same background. Same homes, or whatever.

What do you think made the difference?

I don't even know. (Quietly:) I was always the type of person that I
liked books. And I liked to read. And that got me in trouble, too, with
my mother. 'Cause one day I brought this *Foster Child* book home, it
was—that was the *name* of the book—it was about some little girl who
went to a foster family, or whatever. She gets on my case, "Oh, so you
want to go to a foster home?" and blah-blah-blah this, and she took my
library book and she kept it . . . I was like, God, I don't know what's
wrong with her . . .

I've always liked to read. I mean I guess that was the only freedom at
least that I had, was reading. (Laughs.) And I would get a book, or whatever

. . . It was like one day when I was in third grade I cut school and I went to the library and I checked out all these books! And I snuck 'em home. And she found out I cut school.

She didn't encourage you to read?

Un-uh. And now it's to where "Oh, Shaniqa *was* so smart . . . and she *was* an honor student, and I don't know what happened now . . ." And she's like "Well, if anybody would've told me you'd turn out the way you did, I would've told 'em that they were lying . . ." You know, it's stuff like that that irks me. But it's like there's nothing I can do about it.

My mother's the type of person that after I leave for school, soon as I turn that corner, she would go in my room. And I always said one day she's gonna—I mean I never had nothing in my room for her *to* find, but it was like I always said, well one day if I have something in my room, she's gonna find it, and she's gonna find something she don't want to find.

And it's like even when I was a virgin, like when I was fourteen? My mother—I got sick, 'cause I went out lying in the backyard and it was all hot and stuff, and I didn't eat, and so I got dizzy. And I ran in the house and I thought I had to throw up and she's like "What's wrong with you?" And I said, "I'm sick," you know, and she's like "I know what's wrong with you." So she called her friend on the phone and she told 'em that I was pregnant. So it was like nothing I could say would change her mind.

Did she apologize when she found out you weren't?

Nope. My mother only apologized to me like once, and that was like one time the store had cheated me out of five dollars. I don't know how it was, but I got a whuppin', 'cause I couldn't find the five dollars. And so like a couple days after that we came to church and they said, "Well, did your daughter tell you that the man cheated her out of the money," or something like that, so like she said, "Sorry," but she didn't want to say it. And it was like after that, "sorry" was too late 'cause I had got the punishment for something I didn't do. I mean it was like I was in the third grade, it's a grown man, and I'm gonna go with what he says, I'm not interested in counting her money.

I mean one day my mother saw me in Hillview, it was like three o'clock in the morning, this was when I didn't have a place to stay. And I just got off the bus and I was walking and she stopped and I was trying to figure out who it was and she's like "Where you goin'?" So I told her and she dropped me off. And so then I read my report and it says my mother said that my daughter has been prostituting and selling drugs . . . OK, I was hurt at that. I mean the part about selling drugs was true, but the part about prostituting was not true.

I don't even talk to my mother 'cause its always I'm *wrong*. And it was like I asked her could I come home for like three hours one day, then six hours the next day, twelve hours: "No." She told me, "No"! (Laughs bitterly.) I said, "OK." And so I didn't know who was gone come and get me after I did my program here. So I was crying, it was like she wouldn't take me, so I finally contacted my aunt and she said yeah.

How come your mother didn't want you back?

You know, I really don't know. I can understand that I wasn't the *perfect* child, or whatever. But I couldn't tell you right to this day . . . (Bewildered:) Everybody ax me, "Why don't your mother want you home, what'd you do?" I don't know! It's like one day after I ran away from home I came back home, was there two or three days, I came back from somewhere, she left a note on my bed that said "You have to leave my house." I call her on the job, she says, "You know why," I *didn't* know why, but yet she insisted I knew why, she wasn't gone tell me. I was like "OK."

I don't know. I got to the point to where I didn't care anymore. So I just started being rebellious and running away from home. 'Cause I'm the type of person whereas I refuse to stay somewhere where I'm unhappy. I mean what is that gonna do for me but make me more depressed and more rebellious, and stuff like that? 'Cause I can't get out.

It was to where I had got to be like an independent minor. I got tired of adults taking over, abusing their authority that they had. So I just left. I mean . . . (Pauses.) I'd rather live on the streets, and live from here to here with a friend, than have to sit at home and get abused by my parent. Or a relative.

And my aunt, and my grandmother, we were talking about a year and a half ago, and they told me, "Well, your mother used to *beat* you and put you in closets," and stuff like that? And it was like . . . I guess it got to the point to whereas I didn't remember, or whatever, 'cause I didn't *want* to remember, and I blocked it out, or whatever.

Why do you think they'd beat on you all the time, over these little things?

I don't know. Pshh. I figured it this way. My father beat my mother so she takes it out on us. What*ever*.

My mother have all type of restraining orders out to keep him from coming. But I don't know, somehow he'd come.

When I was younger, he was like my *father*, so *therefore* we got along. But then as I grew up, I could not *stand* him, it was like my stepfather, I hated him. And everybody would ask me why, and I'd be like, you know, 'cause of the way he treated my mother. And to this day I can not stand him 'cause of that. And now it's like he try to play Mr. Holy Roly.

And to this day—this what I don't understand about adults. You know, I figure it this way, in order to *get* respect you got to give respect. And no matter how old you are. I mean if I have a little seven-year-old daughter, or little cousin, whatever, I've got to give him respect in order for him to give it *to* me. And if I'm not giving him no respect, he don't give me no respect. So therefore I don't see how they can say, "Well, I'm older than you," and stuff like that, 'cause really, I say age have nothing to do with it. It's like my father, I don't give him no respect—why? Because he don't give *me* no respect. So therefore it's all over, I don't see no sense in . . . you know. And then it'll always be like my grandmother and all them, "Well, 'Niqa, you're *fast,* and you can't mind," and stuff? If I don't agree with something, I might listen, or whatever, but I'm not gone go buy it.

It's like . . . (A long pause.) I've come to a place, you know, where I'll ax my mother for stuff and she'll say "No," and it's like I'll either ax my friend to give it to me or I'd ax somebody for money. It was like I got to the place to whereas I didn't depend on nobody for nothing. 'Cause it was like—if you *ax* somebody for something, that means you *owe* them something, and I got tired of it. And so I just said, "Look, Shaniqa, you for your own, and, you know, your self only." Right now to this day, if they was to release me? I would find some way to get from here to Iron City, you know what I'm saying? And then, if I didn't have a place to stay in Iron City, I would still *find* someplace to stay, food in my mouth, clothes on my back, stuff like that, you know . . . proper rest . . . Like my uncle, I axed my uncle for a place to stay, he gave it to me, that's all I axed for, that was it. I didn't ax him for nothing else. I didn't ax him to buy *clothes* for me, nothing, because that was my *own* responsibility. And that's how I figure it to be. I mean I'm old enough, it's like I can read, I can write, you know, so if I can do *that* (laughs), I figure I can do just about anything. I mean I'm not dumb or nothing, so . . . I see no point in depending on somebody.

Oh, I'd call Iron City first, and I'd call my aunt and say, "Well, you know, Delores, they released me, can I get—can you come get me?" She says no, I could call my godsister, I mean—I could call many people in Iron City, but if that didn't work out, then I would go by my own measurements. I mean not as far as *prostituting* or anything like that, that's out of the question; I mean as far as, you know, asking somebody for do they have a dollar, or whatever? Now, *that* I would do. That's just me, I don't know.

(Quietly:) Just think, next week on this day I'll be gone. I'm serious, this gone be like a *dream*, that's what it's gone be, a nightmare, trust me. And I'm gone just wake up.

Does it scare you, going back out there?

You know what? Somebody else asked me that, and I said no. 'Cause I'm not like most of these girls in here use drugs and they're scared of going out and using again. And it's not like I'll be scared that I might go back out there selling drugs, 'cause I know I won't, 'cause look where it got me *this* time, not very far.

What scares me, though, is growing up. Getting older. I don't know. It's just like . . . (Softly:) I'll be eighteen next year, and then it's like . . . I'll be nineteen, and then there's no turning back. And then after that . . . after so many, twenty, thirty years from now, whatever, I'll *die* . . . I just think of that every day. I mean I could just look back a couple of years ago and I was saying, "Boy, I can't wait till I turn sixteen." Or "I can't wait till I turn fifteen." And it's like now I'll be seventeen and it's like what have I done, I mean what have I accomplished? I know! I worry a lot . . . I don't know what it is, but it's like I think about it every day.

Soon as I hit my teens, it's been a bad year. And I'm telling you, I have not enjoyed not *one* teen part of my life, whatever, I'm having. And next year is my last year. Or no it's not, the year after. So . . . something better happen. Like *God*. I guess I just grew up too fast. Or what*ever*.

Tell you, when I get out I'm gone be a different Shaniqa. I say they ain't gone know who I am, I mean they gone *know*, but you know as far as attitudewise and my personality, stuff like that, I'm gone be different. It's gone be all over, I'm serious. I'll just speak for myself, when I'm in my room I'll be thinking. If somebody ask me what I'm gonna do soon as I get out of here, as far as my plans is concerned, I can tell 'em right off the top, 'cause I done thought about it so many times before. It ain't like I'm just like these people right out the pen and stuff like that and they go do what they was doin', 'cause I know these girls, or these ladies rather, they just got out of jail, you know, and they still going back to doing drugs, something like that? See, me, I'm not gone be into that. And I just ain't gone be as dumb as I was before. 'Cause I'm not the one to be gettin' hurt over nobody, or nothing, or what*ever*.

Postscript

Next week. She's all ready to leave, but no one has said they'll come to get her. She's been placed under observation because she's been badly depressed.

You know, I already packed my stuff, too. My stuff's been packed about two nights ago. I can't believe I'm finally getting out of here. I am *tired* of this place. *Trust* me, I am.

Neither parent has made contact with her: she hopes her aunt will come, but she hasn't heard from her either.

The thing that's depressed me the most is like I said I wasn't sure she was gonna come get me. Like she only visit me once. Now it's the problem that I've been callin' since last week and I have not got in contact with her yet. So . . . I don't know. She doesn't have a phone, so it's like I have to call my godsister's house, then I have to call my *grand*mother . . . Then my grandmother gets to trippin' 'cause she don't like long-distance phone calls on her bill? I mean Iron City is really not that far away from Rivertown . . . so therefore I don't see why she won't let her use the phone.

And that's why I'm telling you, when I get out, I don't have to—pshh, like right now, I feel that I have to *beg* somebody, you know what I'm saying, 'cause I'm stuck. But when I get out, I don't have to depend on nobody to come and get me from nowhere. I don't have to beg nobody or what*ever*, and my actions can't move around them. God, I'm just . . . (Exasperated:) I don't know. Soon's I get out that gate, I'll be fine.

And I'm gonna tell her about it, too. When I get out the gate. (Laughs.) I'mo wait until we get home. Then I'm gonna tell her that was not cool, what you did. I'm serious.

Sean O'Farrell

"After a while, I just couldn't do it, without the drugs"

He's slender, anxious, moody: "It's my Irish background." He's doing serious time for having stolen several thousand dollars from the fast-food restaurant where he'd been working as a cook. Before that, he was dealing small amounts of methamphetamine and LSD, and had been kicked out of Rivertown High for cutting classes. He lives with his mom, a waitress and hairdresser, in a small apartment in Rivertown. He speaks softly; he says he's depressed a lot of the time.

The reason I got myself into this situation is my mother was having problems with bills, keeping up with all the phone bills, and mainly our rent, and we were about to be evicted. We had the eviction notice and nowhere to go but to the nearest curb. And the manager there, nobody cared, it was just kick them out.

So I was working for Chicken City at the time, and I was giving my checks to my mom to help out with the bills. But it wasn't enough, it's like we just still couldn't do it. Three dollars and thirty-five cents an hour minimum wage just wasn't cutting it! (Laughs.) So I decided to steal some money from my work. And at first they put the case down as extortion, which would have put me away for a long time. But then after the circumstances came out, the reasons and all, they brought it down to burglary, felony burglary.

Were they hassling you at work?

They weren't that bad. I felt they rode me pretty hard, but it was necessary because some of the workers there would screw off. In other words, they were stealing money from them by lounging around and not doing the work and yet being paid for it. I was never really like that. I always got there, did my work, punched out, that was it. They rode me hard, and it was frustrating at the time, but I was OK with it because my boss was pretty understanding. He'd ride me hard on something and then if he noticed that something wasn't quite right, he would stop me and ask, "Is there something wrong?" And I'd say, "Well, you've been riding me pretty hard and I've been trying." We'd talk about it, we'd get through it. But the work was hard.

They felt that they gave me a lot of trust. (Softly:) And I screwed them. I felt *extremely* bad. I ended up writing a large letter apologizing and explaining the reasons why. I don't know if it helped them as much as it helped me. It kind of made me feel a little bit better, but it's still a big burden on my chest right now. Like how could I be so stupid to do something like that?

But at the time, it seemed appropriate. It was the way out. She worked two jobs, seven days a week. My father doesn't pay any child support, so it's real difficult for her to support me and her. She was waitressing, cocktail waitress, bartending, and stuff like that. And the time she had off she was housecleaning. The only real time that she took off was when me and her went to church.

It wasn't like I wasn't *getting* enough from my Mom. I felt bad because she was doing so much to *give* me what I was getting. Instead of being happy about what I was getting, I'd get upset at her for doing it. Because she would go without a lot of things to do for me, and it wasn't—I didn't feel right about it. So I decided to try and help *her*. It just didn't work. (Laughs.) Bad decision.

I was going to Rivertown High. I'd been dyslexic all through grade school and junior high. And in high school, they felt that I had achieved above being special ed anymore. I ended up having a hard time, so I stopped going to school. I'd get up every morning, dress nice for school, take a shower, and I'd head straight for school, and where I'd end up was sitting on the newspaper bins in front of Safeway. Because that's where most of the traffic between school was. That's the place where everybody went to, Safeway, to meet, because it was a place where some people got lunch. It was between the continuation school and Rivertown High, so it's a general meeting place. Sitting right out in front, I'd talk to everybody that's going by.

Didn't the school try to find out where you were?

No, they didn't try. (Puzzled:) They let me go and go on, didn't even call my mother. Until I got too many absences and they kicked me out of school. Yeah, they acted like they didn't notice I wasn't there, which surprised me, because in junior high, the second I was even *tardy* they used to call my parents, call me in for a meeting, and find out why I wasn't making it on time. And in high school, it was like they were just too busy to notice that my name was even down on the list. I felt that they should have noticed, but I was kind of happy they didn't because I was getting away with what I wanted to get away with.

That was towards the third quarter of school. I'd been going the first quarter, and then I started skipping in the second quarter, and then I stopped going to school completely about the middle of the second quarter, and by the third quarter, they eighty-sixed me. (Laughs.)

Besides being dyslexic, it was hard in class, and I was teased about that. And I developed migraine headaches from it because there was just so much pressure. So the easy way out was to go sit in front of Safeway, you know, and just not even *deal* with the school. If I'm not there, I can't get upset, right? Well, by sitting there I ended up getting bored, I started into drugs. Drugs were a pastime, a tremendous pastime. The day *existed* around the drug use. Like I planned to see certain people so that we could do these certain things . . .

I got to the point where I was selling methamphetamine. I never got busted for it, I was never a big dealer or anything, it was just like school friends, which now I feel extremely bad about because all I did was help kill them and I would never do it again. That's one way it helped screw up my life, mainly school, it was a way out of school, of not having to deal with the pressure.

My mom thought I was going to school every day, so she had no idea of my problem. She had thought—she suspected drug use, but never really had any substantial proof, because I never really came home messed up. She never saw any of it, so she wasn't sure. So she took the benefit of the doubt, saying I didn't, because I told her I didn't. I lied to her. Of course. (Laughs.)

One reason I was selling methamphetamine was that when I worked I also used it, because it helped me in my work, made me faster, kept me awake, put me in a good mood. Then it got to the point that I ended up using as much as I was making profit off it. And then it got to the point that I wasn't even making enough profit to pay for how much I was using. And that's when it got so bad that I started using a little bit of the money I was giving my mom for it. Maybe twenty bucks out of my paycheck, and that would go to a gram I would buy, and I would sell three-quarters, and get enough for *another* gram, and then it got to the point that I wasn't even—I couldn't hold it long enough to sell it, and then right after that was when I got into trouble.

And yet I wasn't really addicted physically, but I *wanted* it. I mean it wasn't like, if I didn't have it, I'd go into convulsions or spaz out or something. But it was a mental addiction. I just *thought* I wanted it.

You didn't even have two minutes to use the bathroom. It's a continuous line. (He's making cooking motions with his hands.) We would get the chicken frozen, it was fresh. We'd bring it in, tear the fat off it, put it in the marinater, marinate it, take it out, flour it, season it, put it in a rack, deep-fry it, take it out, put it on racks, bring it up front, and then it would start over again. We had to do this in a certain amount of time. One, because of the salmonella? Before it was deep-fried? We had to do it fast. And plus, it came to the point where people were coming in so fast they had to wait for us to make the chicken. And we were cooking four chickens at a time, six chickens at a time! So we were running just constantly and didn't have time. Then afterwards the cook, which I was, had to clean up the back, so I was there till eleven o'clock every night.

When did you start?

About four-thirty. And then yet have to go to school. (He stares at the floor.) After a while, I just couldn't do it, without the drugs. And that's when marijuana use came in, too. Then I couldn't go to sleep, and used marijuana to go to sleep.

What scares me? Mainly, going back to my old routine. Getting back in the drugs again. That's my major scare, but I'm pretty much—with my religion, it's pretty much out. From being in here, I've become very religious. I've found where I stand now.

I've never been a really big-time drug dealer but I have tried it, alcohol and marijuana and methamphetamine, which is crank. LSD. And now that I've gone through this situation and have become closer to the Lord, I know that I don't need to even deal with that. It's not even on my list, not even a *thought*. It's just something I know was killing me, not doing me any good. It basically was one of the reasons that screwed up my life. (Nervously:) But I don't know if I'm going to get into some problem that would be pressing me and I'll go back to it. I definitely don't want to, now. I *say* that, but I can't be absolutely sure when I get out.

A lot of it's peer pressure. It's not exactly the type of peer pressure that says "Come on, do this, do this," it's more like "Look, *I* can do this too, I'm doing just as much or more as you right now. I've got more than you." That puts you up with the crowd. That puts you in there. That's one of the reasons I was selling, is because in school I was nothing. Just a little freshman. Nobody noticed me. When I was selling, even the *seniors* in high school would come to *me* and ask me for fronts and stuff like that. It made me feel a little more important in school. I made a lot of friends through drugs. (Pauses.) I don't know if they were really friends, but *so-called* friends.

A lot of other kids have more time to put into school, their jobs are just for spending money. All their money, they went and blew it on drugs, stuff like that, buying stuff that they wanted. And I never really had that, except for when I was selling. At first, I was making big money. I was carrying around six, seven hundred dollars at a time, and anything I wanted I'd buy. And then (softly:) it got to the point I didn't have a cent in my pocket. Because of my own use.

I'm going to go back to Rivertown High School. A guy that comes in and talks with me is also a contractor, and he's offering me a job, so that when I get out I'm going to be working for him. I'm going to help my

mom with some bills. We feel that we can make it this time, really do it
this time, get my life together.

Do you ever think about what you'd like to be doing, say, ten
years from now?

I've got a problem with that. There's so much that goes on *now* that
I don't have *time* to think about what's going to happen. And it's so fast-
paced, it seems to come before you know it. (Nervously, wringing his
hands:) You don't even have time to *think* about it. It might be, some of
it, that I just haven't been thinking about it. But a lot of it's because it's
fast-paced. If I thought about it I wouldn't know even what to say, what
I want to be as a so-called grown-up.

You worry about the future . . .

I *am* worried about my future, because I feel that I have some responsibilities of supporting my mother when she gets—she's right now at
fifty-six years old, and I feel by the time I'm old enough to start working
a full-time job, that I should be able to support her and help her out.
(Earnestly:) I feel obligated to do that. For one, I just love her a lot, and
two, it's just all the stuff she's *done* for me, I feel that I need to repay.
    I'd say that I'm lower than middle-class. My sisters are, um, what I'd
say, real middle-class. They've got hundred-fifty-thousand-dollar homes,
hot tub, and all that stuff. But my mom has a hard time accepting money
from them. She feels that if she borrows money from them, she will pay
it back, and she has. And it's just difficult for her to do that. My sisters
help out as much as possible, as much as my mom will allow. The reason
I can help out more is because—she doesn't like taking money from me
at all. At all. She actually disagrees to it completely. But I've got the edge
on her, telling her I'm giving this to her because it's for *me*. I'm paying
for myself. And she feels that she should be supporting *me*, but we've
kind of made the agreement that I'm going to help out. Right now my
mother's living with my older sister, who's thirty-two, and with my
nephew, who's twelve now, in a small apartment, a two-bedroom apartment here. And she's getting her life together. (Laughs.) Kind of like a
break.
    This experience has been real tragic in a way and yet it's been a miracle

in another, because I've become a lot closer to the Lord, what *I* call the Lord. (Earnestly:) I've learned to accept responsibilities and I've got a goal, a so-called goal. I never really had a goal to reach before, and now I've got a goal. To achieve in school and help out my mother, and have a good family.

I was always what I'd call a part-time Christian. I believed in Him, I went to church. I very rarely prayed, and I very rarely obeyed his rules. Now I've come to know the Lord a lot more. It's helped me out tremendously. Accepting his rules and just following them has made my life easier.

Postscript

Sean attempted suicide three months after we talked.

"I just started loving money"

My mother long time ago she left us in the house by ourself and my brother was trying to change my diaper, he didn't know nothing about it. I was like only a baby three weeks old and he poured *cornstarch* and stuff all over me, he thought it was baby oil! And he put *flour* all over me, I had flour all in my face and on my everywhere, and Cheerios and stuff, and he tried to put peanut butter on me, and then he tried to cook his peanut butter, right, and he had me still laying on the stove and he tried to put some peanut butter on the bread, a whole big half a jar of peanut butter on one little piece of bread, and put it on the stove and turned the oil on it. He set the bread on fire, my diaper caught on, too, and I'm *burning*, the whole house was really blazing, he was so short he couldn't reach the knob . . . He threw water on me and took the fire out of my diaper, my brother did, but he couldn't get out because the house was so smoky and he couldn't reach the top lock because he was so short. So he just jumped through the window and his neck got caught on the window when he jumped through it, so he got this big cut on his neck, right here on his little neck. So they took us away from our mother.

She's a strong, stocky kid with a warm smile and an infectious laugh; this is her third arrest for drug sales. She lives with her mother and four brothers and sisters in a small apartment in Iron City's Eastville, the busiest "dope track" and one of the poorest neighborhoods in the city. "I don't like it, really. Too much drugs and too much things to get into. A lot of trouble. That's the reason why I'm in here, for being around drugs. And everywhere I go there's people who sell drugs on the street. It's a lot of blacks that's bringing out the drugs." She remembers a time when the drug scene in Iron City wasn't nearly as bad: "But I was much more smaller then. It started getting like this in, like, the eighties really." Why did it change so fast? "People these days are really in desperate needs of money so I guess that's probably why."

I think it's got worse, it's real worse now. When I first started it wasn't that worse, but now it's so worse that . . . (laughs, shakes her finger at me.) Don't ever drive out there, 'cause if you drive out there in my neighborhood, someone'll jump on top of your car, and "You want some drugs, you want this?" (Laughs.) No, seriously, that's the way they are. They'll get in your window and you'll be sitting there driving and oh, God . . . (Laughs.) And I mean it's like there's not that many, um, *Caucasian* people in our neighborhood, and like when they come through, it's like they think you some type of *narc* and they'll start shooting at you! (Laughs.) And you think I'm talking, *they* wouldn't talk to you, they'd be trying to get your money, they be all up in your car . . . I wasn't like that, but I was *almost* like that. I was getting to the point where I'd come up on your car and say, "Is you gone buy his or is you gone buy mine? I tell you mine the best." I was the type of person that'd steal people's business, you know, "Look at this, look at this."

Did you ever get into trouble trying to take other people's business?

No, 'cause we was all like brothers and sisters and everybody, we all stuck together. If one of them lost some money, say if somebody came in a car, (matter-of-factly:) and they said, "I want to buy some drugs," and they snatch your money *and* your dope, we would shoot 'em?
One time this man came, he had a BMW, it was a brand-new drop-

top, or it was like one of them *sunroof* tops, it wasn't a drop-top? It was pretty, it was like white and gold? And he said, "I wanta buy an eight-ball," right? An eight-ball is like a two-hundred-dollar rock, it's like two-sixteenths of dope. So I was like "OK, OK, I got it, I got it, I got it," so I held a eight-ball out, it was about this big and it's all rocked up—really *that* big (her fingers are a couple of inches apart) it's all rocked up. I said, "Here you go, here you go," I said, "Look, it's pure," right, and I said, "Now give me the money," right? And he was just *staring*, right, and I say (laughs) "Is you gone give me the fuckin' money or is you just gone *stare*," right? And so he snatch the dope and he try to pull out. And one man just came by and shot the tires, and he can't go too far, so then we got him and was just (laughs) *beatin'* him, tore down the *sun*roof, whap! One lady, she was a drug fiend, she threw her *TV* down on his car! We was *mad* that night! (Much laughter.) She threw the TV out the window!

It's really wild over there where we live, ladies come out with mops after they boyfriends and stuff, it's crazy. (Suddenly serious:) I mean, if you lived in that neighborhood, you'd try to get all this drug stuff shut down out of the community, because it's so terrible. I mean you could be just sitting there in the park and stuff, just *smiling*, and they'd think you some type of narc and come over there and kick your *ass!* (Laughs.)

Why do you think it got so much worse lately?

Because drugs started tasting good to the little dope fiends and they start turning they friends on, and they friends turn *they* friends on, so then it got wild and we just started making money, too much money. It's like when I first started out selling drugs, I had like five hundred dollars' worth of dope. I cut it down so low that I came out with a *thousand* dollars worth of dope. See, that's what you can do when you start getting used to it, you can cut it down, you can cheat people and you can give 'em less than what they supposed to do. If you really want to make some money, you could *really* cheat them, and if they fiending bad enough, they gone buy with you.

I remember one time when I didn't have no more dope and I was selling *baking soda* and they was *buying* it! (Laughs, amazed.) I was selling fake dope and nobody never knew, they was just buying it. And when they put it on that little screen on they pipe and they started smokin' it, the smoke wasn't coming through the pipe! It started flaming! (Much laughter.) And they didn't like that!

Did they come after you?

No . . . One time this lady did, 'cause I sold her a piece of *soap!* It was this lady, she was like *hella* big, and I was like "Ma'am, uh-uh, you couldn't have bought that from me!" (Grins.) I say, "'Cause everything I got right here, really, you couldn't have bought that from me." She said, "I remember you, you had on that same leather jacket, I remember you—give me my motherfuckin' money or give me my dope!" I said, "Lady, I gave you this?" (laughs) right, and I was laughing in her face. She was so loaded she didn't know what to do, she was just "I want my motherfuckin' dope or I want my money. You sold me that soap—when I set the fire to it, it started *smokin'!*" So I said, "If you think I'm the one, I'm just gone *give* you some dope, OK, but don't come back and buy no more dope from me," right.

But now today that's probably one of my best sales I ever got, 'cause she come *every* day.

(In a singsong voice:) Dope fiends go for every line—if you got the dope, they got the time.

It all started when I was like twelve. My first time out, my mother made me mad and I ran away from home. I went over to a friend of mine that I knew? But I never knew she was into bad things. I thought she was good because we went to school together. She told me to go to her house. I stayed with her for like a day, and she introduced me to all these *drug* dealers and things, but I didn't *know* they were drug dealers. I just seen a whole bunch of guys just standing out in this one complex, apartment building, and they're all just standing there and I was just like new to them all, and so she was introducing me to them. Then I seen one guy pull out some dope and I thought he was smoking it or something, and he sold it to this man, so then I knew I was in the drug traffic.

So then I went back home. And then I ran away again and I went to the same friend, and this time I stayed with one of the drug dealers. We talked for a long time, and he said, "Well how about you working for me?" I thought he was meaning prostitution or something, right (laughs), but he said, "Naw, selling drugs!" He said, "Whatever you make, I'll give you half of it." I was still too young to get a job, I didn't know nothin' about that. And I wanted to live the *big* life like everybody else, so I didn't want to do like my mother say. She told me to stay away from them apartments, but I'd just sneak off. I didn't care what she said, really.

And then I just started being like all the rest of the people. I was sellin' drugs—oh (she's breathless), I was doing *everything*. I mean I just started making a *whole* bunch of money. You know people get checks for disability, and all those type of checks? I'd be out there on those days that they'd get their money, and I'd just get so much money I just started loving money.

So I just kept on and kept on and kept on doing it. And one time I started trying to teach my friend how to sell drugs. At this time, I had stopped selling *for* anybody, I was just selling drugs for *me*, I had that much money. So me and my friend, I was trying to show *her*, and she had this stolen car, right? But I didn't know it was stolen and I was in the car with her. So then I just had a whole bunch of narcotics with me and she ran into something (laughs)—I don't know *what* was wrong with her, I was just in the car asleep, right, and I felt—*crash!* Right? And the police was behind us, and they made me get out and I was like, oh, *God!* I was ready to run, but I just couldn't. I just thought maybe this can help me, this can put a stop to what I'm doing.

So they arrested me and brought me here for my first time. I went to court. My mom wouldn't get me out, because she was happy because she couldn't stop it from *nothing*. It was like I'd come home, change clothes, *go* back out, *go* home, take a bath, go out. She never stopped me. I never paid attention to her that much. She'd say something, I'd go, "Awww . . ." Just go on about my way. So then finally when I came in here, it made her a little happy, but in a way she was sad. So mainly that's what happened, how it started.

I'm one of those people that have a hard head. I do have a hard head. Somebody can tell me something and I'll say "OK, I won't do it no more," and before you can say abracadabra I'm in it again. (Smiles.) So it was like, here I am again, back to drug sellin'. This time I wasn't selling cocaine, I was selling like weed, you know, hash . . .

You never get scared selling drugs?

At nighttime, but not in the daytime, 'cause I can watch. Like this last time it was me and my friend and a whole bunch of boys was out there. And I seen this task force, you know, police force, for the people with drugs? I seen them and somebody started saying "Task force coming!" and I started running, right, and my friend was behind me and I jumped over in this backyard, and there's a whole bunch of dogs. And I was scared, and my friend she was in a *dog* pen and the dog was trying to bite her? and we was on top of the house and the task force people was standing right under the house and she was standing right by them. And she didn't have no drugs, no nothing, and she was calling my name, she said, "Tasha, come on, Tasha," and they knew me all the time.

That's mostly the time that everybody's out, at night. In the daytime, like if I see something happening wrong, I could go home. And my mother don't know nothing about it, 'cause she be at *work*, she don't know *what* happening! She don't even know when I get suspended from school. That's how long she be gone. It's like—it's *weird* for my mother, she pay the bills, go to work, come home, sleep, go to work, pay the bills . . . It's like mainly she's paying the bills and paying for us to go to school and stuff. So it's really hard on her.

My mother had five children. She worked three jobs and she made pretty good money. But it was like I was the spoiled one in the family. I was the oldest out of the girls, I was right in the middle of everybody, out of all the kids. And I'm used to getting everything I wanted, and she just stopped doing that 'cause she had four other children to take care of. So I just started getting mad! I just wanted everything, I was just a little brat. If I seen my friend having something very expensive, I wanted it too: "I want that, I want that, I want that." (Laughs.) If she couldn't get it, I'd say, "Well, forget it, I know a way to get me some." So I'd sell drugs. So it's like I never listened to my mother. That's mainly the reason why I'm in here too, 'cause I never listened to her.

Three jobs?

Now she's working two because it was too much for her. My mother's a medical technician. She works for, I forgot . . . (vaguely:) some hospital. She's like a surgeon, you know . . . She's got her B.A., A.A., she got all her degrees and stuff. She can like work anyplace in the hospital, she can do everything she want of medical things. She done went through the whole medical course.

(She's silent for a while.) She used to leave . . . I mean like the only time I seen my mother was like seven o'clock in the morning when she be gettin' ready to go to her other job. It was like I never seen her. Like when she comes home, I'd be in school, it was like that. I could never see her until like seven o'clock—she'll wake us up and say, "I'm gonna go to work, I'm on my way to work." At three o'clock when we come home from school, "I'm on my way to work." It was like she really never had time for us. And that's mainly why we had to take care of ourselves a lot, we didn't have our mother that much. She wasn't really there all the time to help keep us through everything. In a way, some ways I fault her, some ways I fault myself for everything that's happened to me. But it's like I didn't have too much discipline behind me. So therefore I was really free to do anything I wanted to do.

Right now I'm about to go to the tenth grade. (Casually:) I'm very smart. I am. I like school, but sometimes I tend (laughs)—when people tend to put their hands on me, I tend to *hurt* them. For instance, I won't call nobody bitches, and I don't want them to call *me* one either. So if somebody call me a bitch or something, it's like I've got this temper that, um . . . (Smiles.) It takes a lot to get me angry. It's like you build up a whole bunch of bricks, then when you get to the top they just all fall.

And it's like I got suspended like five times before. Fighting. I don't fight unless somebody . . . (Shakes her head.) I got bad kids in my neighborhood, we have *bad* kids. And I don't like living over there. So all the time I have to be on guard, I have to defend myself. And I'm the type of person if somebody just say something to me that I don't like, I'll confront them about it, but if they just keep on and keep on I just *goes!* (Laughs.) That's what happened at school. I used to be just a quiet type, I didn't bother nobody. And one day, it was like these girls used to always pick on me 'cause I was quiet and I was very thin, I was real bony, I looked like a little *nerd* or something. (Laughs.) I was the quiet type. And one day I was walking home from school, I remembered I cussed this girl out in the hallway. They was saying, "After school I'm gonna beat you up." And I forgot about it. So I'm walking home and there's a lot of kids that walk the same way. And I heard somebody say, "There's gone be a fight, there's gone be a fight." And some girl just ran up behind me and hit me in the back with a rock! And I don't know, something just turned over in me, and I don't know, when I got up, I had my foot on her neck and she was . . . (laughs) very unhappy! And ever since then, girls didn't mess with me. Ever since I hurt her. There wasn't too many people botherin' me. Mostly, they was just trying to be my friend.

But mainly, I had a little rough school year. But I made it through it. I don't let nothing get involved with my schoolwork. If I got into a fight, it'd be like after school, it'd be like on Friday. We always fight on Fridays.

You could say I'm on a higher level than I'm supposed to be. I know a little more than I'm supposed to. I'm learning all type of stuff. I'm learning algebra. I'm learning how to—like—you know, like squares? and they got numbers on the side? Yeah, geometry. I'm learning a lot of stuff that I didn't know. I'm learning more about history. I like reading a lot, so like math is like second. (Brightly:) I'm pretty good at everything, mainly! I try to be the best. I try to be the best.

I'm really basically on a higher level. I can read from twelfth-grade books, you know, *college* books. I can read from my mother's medical books. (Proudly:) Yeah, I be reading *big* old words . . . I teach my mother how to study sometimes, she had these big old hard tests, and I like, you know, helped her study.

I love school. That's one thing keeps me out of trouble, school. But when school's out, all that time is so *vacant*, there's nothing else to do! (Laughs.) I mean I could be a *normal* kid, maybe go home and read a book, but that was like in the *sixties*, you'd go home and read *books!* (Laughs.) But now these days it's like, going home and reading a *book*, you must be some type of nerd!

I have to *go* somewhere. I'm just . . . (Pauses.) We the type of kids these days, we don't like staying in the house. That's mainly what made me run away, 'cause my mother she kept me in the house a lot. So it's like I wanted to just break away. I don't know, she was afraid. She wanted me to be a square, you know, a square? . . . (She searches for the right meaning.) Somebody who didn't know nothing about the outside world. She just wanted me to be the type of girl that *go* to school, *come* home, *go* to school, *come* home, cook, clean, cook, clean, go to school, come home. (Laughs.) And as long as I did this, my age kept gettin'—I kept aging, then when I started getting up to my friends' age, like fourteen, thirteen, the big girls, I just didn't want to be by myself anymore, I wanted to be like *them!* 'Cause it's like they were getting more attention. It's like I didn't get too much attention when I was younger. Sometimes I feel that I don't get enough attention. Somedays I feel like that and I'll run amok!

What did your Mom do when you got suspended from school?

When she found out, she whupped my *ass!* Mainly, when she found out, it was like she wasn't gonna spare the rod. She was just gonna . . . *whap!* It was just "Bring your ass to me!" That's the way she'd say it, "Bring your ass to me!" (Laughs.) So therefore it wasn't too much discussion going on. I knew what was going to happen. (Grins) That's why I used to beat her to the mailbox. When they'd come in the mail (her report cards), I'd run to the garage. And I'd just tear them up and flush them down the toilet and then go wander around for a whole day until it's time to come home from school, and I'd walk home with all the rest of the school kids. And she'd never know. Until she'd like go to school while I'm at school, she'll go up there and check on me and stuff: "How my daughter been doin'?" "Well, she's been suspended such and such and such a day." And she said, "Really, um, *I* didn't know that!" (Laughs.) And then it all piled up at me, and I'd just get me a whuppin' for it. But I'd rather take *one* whuppin' than take like six of 'em for each *one* of them like that! (Laughs.) I'd rather take one *big* whuppin'!

But it's very seldom she whupped me at all. She whupped me I'd say about seven times in my whole life, but she ain't never just went AWOL on me like some mothers do some children. But I had brothers and sisters who really, *really* harmed me (laughs)—they abused me real bad. I always got slammed around by my big brother, so mainly my mother didn't have to really discipline me, I had a big brother who just . . . (Laughs, shakes her head.)

It was like I was making, say . . . I think it's a lot of money to be so young. I was making like a thousand dollars every two *days*. Because I didn't sell like *little* rocks, I sold like *big* rocks. I'm talking about *this* much of a rock was like five hundred dollars. And I'd sell this to the big dope dealer so he could break it down into a lot to make *his* money, to make a whole bunch of money. He'd break it, cut it down, cut his dope down, cut it into little ones, little rocks, and he sold it for like twenty and thirty and ten and five, he was selling it for the little money. (Proudly:) But the rocks *I* sold was for the big money. I was making so much money that when I put it into the bag—I put it in this big bag, all my money?

and I used to just sit there and take *pictures.* I got all kinds of pictures of me holding all this money! Like I got a whole bunch of money in my hand, just *sitting* on money, (incredulous:) I had so much it was like, God! It felt like I won the lottery. It was like that.

I had a car, I rented motel rooms, I ate fast foods every day, it's like I went out to clubs, Great America, I just started having all the fun that I wished . . . (a long pause) that my mother couldn't have *with* me. I just started going to Disneyland and stuff with my friends.

I had *two* cars. And I just wrecked this person—I ain't supposed to be driving, I didn't have no license. I had somebody buy the car for me so that they gave it back to me, and I paid them for buying the car. (Sagely:) See, money buy a lot of things, people just don't know. But the only thing money won't buy is a good relationship. I found that out.

So you were just doing stuff that was mostly what you would have wanted to do anyway . . .

. . . with my mother, but she wasn't around, she didn't have the money to take me, she didn't even have a car at the time. She couldn't take me out of town and everywhere I wanted to go. I'm telling you I done went some *places* ever since I started selling drugs. (Wide-eyed:) I done been to almost six different places. I done been to Hillview, I done been to L.A., I went to Disneyland, I done been to Spruce Lake, I done been to Valley City, I done been, (breathless:) ooh! I done been to *places* . . .

And like when I bought the car from my friend bought it for me? He didn't show me how to drive, but I didn't *know* how to drive, so I had to learn how to drive on my own. (Casually:) So I learned how to drive. The first day it was fun, because it was like *whoo!* (She's grinning, pretending to drive fast.) And I hit this lady' car, it's like I hit her *soft,* hit her bumper, right, I didn't hit her like *boom!* I didn't put no little *scar* or nothing on her car. So I just started *crying.* I said, "Please don't call the police, I just learned how to drive!" I was only thirteen! So she said, "OK, just learn how to drive!" She said, "If you don't know how to drive, get your ass out of the *car* and don't drive no more," right? So I was scared and I just drove the car home. So then I just started driving by myself, in hills and mountains and stuff. And I learned around a whole bunch of dirt, when nobody would be around. So now I know how to drive and stuff. So that's one thing I learned.

So mainly I was just going a lot of places. I done been to places, I mean . . . (Hesitates.) I wasn't trying to be like the other dope dealers, I wasn't just trying to sell dope for the money, I was just trying to sell it for just the *fun*, really. But the fun finally ran out. So now we see how much fun it really was. But in a way, it was. At that time, it was. But now this time, it's like it wasn't even worth it to me.

Well . . . it wasn't really *fun*, to tell the truth. It was just like I was . . . (she searches for words:) just *used* to it, you know how you get used to something? Like say *you* used to talking to people a lot, and you know mainly how to come *at* a person? *I* was just used to making money! That was just the easy way out. I didn't go to school some days, other days I'd be making so much money I'd never get to sleep and I'd be sleeping in class. And they'd call my mother, and that's the only thing I didn't want them to do, so I had to stop staying up late. But I'd come out at night and just . . . (She holds up calloused and cracked hands.) My hands . . . they're rough now 'cause I had my hands on too much money. To be so young. (Shakes her head.) If you threw me a bag of money right now, I think I would give it back to you because money gets me in trouble. It really does.

You made that *much money?*

Oh, it was plenty people. It was *full*, I mean it was so many dope fiends . . . it'd make you never want to touch the pipe. (Laughs.) It was like, *God!* All times of night people come through, they eyes all like *this* (crazed, staring) and they be *looking* and pull out they money: (whispers) "This what I want" . . . I'd say "OK, here you go, come on . . ." But see, I understand something that this chaplain just said on Sunday—he said you are stupid for selling drugs, he wasn't saying *me*, but I could just put my feet in those shoes. 'Cause it's like I was taking the drugs, saying "Here, here's something that'll *kill* yourself, you want to buy it? Here, give me your money." And I was taking they money and I was giving them something that'd kill them. And people that I done sold drugs to, they like *this* skinny now, they like . . . (stumbles) all, you know . . . so mainly I . . . like I don't know, I was just . . . liking money.

But I'm a good kid after all that. (Laughs.) That's all I know I got in trouble for.

When I grow up, I want to go in the army, really, but first I want to start off with Job Corps. And maybe when I'm like twenty-three, I'd be ready to have children. Raise *one* child. And maybe be married. I'm sure I'll be married. I'm sure I will be. 'Cause I get engaged too young, so when I get up to the age, I'm sure I will be married.

One kid . . . is that because you had so many in your own family?

Hell, no! (Laughs.) That ain't why! It's because I don't want none of *my* kids to be like *these* kids! So that's why. Mainly, I just want one kid 'cause I want to just see . . . (Quietly:) Maybe I could give my child some of the love that I didn't get when I was that age. Maybe I can bring it up better. That's mainly gonna be my goal, to be married, have a job, and have one child. When I'm ready, when I have enough money to support my child. Not selling dope. *Legal* money. I just want to live a good life, 'cause I've already lived my *bad* life. (Smiles.) I just want to take this life and black it out so like it never happened. I'd never tell my kid that I used to sell drugs when I was his age. I'd never tell my kid.

How would you keep your kid from doing the same thing you did?

To keep my kid from doing the same thing? (Softly:) I think I'd give it a little *freedom*. 'Cause I didn't get freedom and that drove me to that. I think I'd try to tell my kid the good things in life and I'd try to explain to him the bad things in life. Mainly, I'd try to explain to him what's out there on the streets before it's time for him to go out by himself. I'd try to teach him what's out there. I'd take him around so he could see all the different kind of things that go wrong and all the things that could happen to him. Or her. I'd *show* them. "Look at this, don't ever put yourself in that position." I'd go show him one of my old friends, say, "Here's one of my old friends, she used to be real nice till she started messing with drugs and if you want to look like her, you keep . . ." (Nods.) I'd try to influence my kids, tell 'em it's not worth it to be out there doing nothing like that. That's mainly what I'd do.

What about stopping the drugs—what do you think we could do?

Well, really, the only thing that I think that can stop all this drugs is
. . . (Pauses.) Well to tell you the truth . . . if the world come to an end.
Because you got to get the dealers. And there's too many damn dealers
to be trying to get some dealers. (Laughs.) I mean it's *too* many dealers.
It's like so many dealers that it ain't gone stop. It *can't* stop until people
stop using the drugs.

DeWayne Thatcher

"She's my mom, you know"

*He's big, lumbering, and muscular, but gentle and painfully shy.
He recently moved to Iron City, and now lives with his mother in
a small house in a working-class black neighborhood. Never in
serious trouble until this year, he's been sent to the Hall twice
in six months, both times for selling cocaine.*

My dad stay in Valley City and my mom stay in Iron City. So I
wanted to come stay with her for a while.

Just a little town, nothin' to *do*. I was going to Roosevelt High. I didn't
learn nothin' there. Teachers let you do what you want, you know. Plus,
I hardly went to school anyway. I was just going out with the guys, you
know, messing around. I didn't like school. (Smiles.) Hate sitting in class.

In the city, I never got into trouble, *or* my friends; none of them
breaking into houses or anything. Move to Iron City, everybody *around*
is breaking into houses and stuff! There was a lot of things to do, that's
why I didn't get into trouble out there. In Iron City, there's *nothing* to
do, so you know, you get bored: "Let's break into this house or something."
Just feel like doing *something*.

Lot of pressure from my friends. Might try to make me want to do something. It's hard to say no to your friends, you know, all your friends? Like sell drugs; it's like "Oh, come on." Break into a house, all type of stuff like that. Steal a car. You know. *Money*. Get the money. Sometimes they have a drug problem, buy drugs for whatever they get.

Lot of drugs everywhere. Wherever you go, people on the corner selling drugs. *Every*where. Mostly *all* the kids sell drugs. Everywhere you go, there's drugs in Iron City. Kids, like teenagers, you know? They want to have money, just want to have a *lot* of money. *Fast* money. That's the only way to get it, you know, fast money, real quick. I know guys have thousands and thousands, have all type of Mercedes-Benz, all type of gold diamond rings, big gold chains, and all that; cars, and all that? Man, *women* . . . (Laughs.) They'll say, "Why go to school when I could be out here all *day?*" Instead of like say go to school, get out at three, nine o'clock to three? Be out all *morning*, selling this stuff. That's how they do it. And stay out all night. They be up all *night*. All night, people just come driving by all night. People come from all over, Iron City, River-town, Cherry Grove, people from Hillview, just everywhere.

I don't like it myself, 'cause people will do a lot of things to you, people will even kill you over drugs. *Lot* of people get killed over drugs. Say a little five-dollar piece of rock, get killed over it, get shot over it.

I've seen guys, say somebody comes by in a car they want to buy some drugs? And the guy in the car try to take the guy's stuff, and the guy drive off, and the guy just *shot* him all through! Lady and her boyfriend one time tried to take a guy's drugs, and he just shot up the car, he didn't care. Shot 'em. Yeah, they died. All type of stuff.

I've seen a lot of things. I've seen guys get dragged all up the street. 'Cause somebody's trying to take their stuff and they hold on to the window, you know; dragging him all up the *street!* Seen a lot of people get shot. I was up in this house, you know, these Cubans that sell drugs? This Cuban let this guy sell some drugs, and the guy didn't bring the Cuban back his money, and the Cuban shot him in the arm.

I've seen a lot of stuff. I've seen guys get shot with a Uzi before, shot the whole car up. Uzis, MAC-10s . . . Guy was selling kilos, guy did something to him, I don't know what. Seen the guy drive around the corner, the dude's parking his car, they just psssht! Shot up the whole car. They're dead, man; they're dead! (Laughs.) The police came, about twenty police cars. Started jacking everybody up. And that was it, I left.

I've been around violence a lot in my life. I'm just used to it now, you know.

I've seen guys like eleven years old selling drugs. 'Cause if they see their brother selling it, they want to be like their brother. *Little* kids . . . I seen a little kid get run over before. Some guy was chasing some guy in a car. It was in the newspaper and everything. Little kid was out there on his bike. Guy come flying into this court and just blam! hit the kid. Didn't even stop. It's like a court? and the guy's chasing him, so he's got to turn around. So he "eeeerk!" just run *over* the kid and just kept going. I seen the *police* run over a kid before! Police was driving and just *hit* the little kid, blam!

I was selling drugs for this one guy, right, and I messed up. I didn't give him all his money back. He was talking about he was gone kill me. He put a gun all up to my head and stuff. Then he had a few of his guys, you know, beat me up. That was it. And I gave him his money back. And I don't mess with him anymore. He hit me with the gun on my head, I got my *head* all busted! (Laughs.) Few busted lips, that was it.

Yeah, it's scary, it is. Specially now, guys in the street all carrying guns now, you know. *Big* guns. Guys carrying sawed-off twelve-gauge under their coat, now, walking around with Uzis and stuff.

It's a trip. You don't know *what's* gonna happen. Might get to shooting, might hit *you*. Some guys from Hillview came up, they were just *messin'* with the guys, and they were shooting at some guy, accidentally shot my friend in the arm. So then his brother started shooting back at the guy from Hillview. Shot him in the leg, then after they shot him, beat him up. Then shot him *again!* It's like a feud, you know? People from like Hillview, Eastville, come out here and mess with 'em, shooting people and everything, just for *fun*, just for kicks! Or say some guys from Hillview come up, try to sell some drugs out there, the guys from Iron City don't like it, taking their business away, so they just get into it, you know. Just start shooting and fighting.

Once out there, some guys were just shooting back and forth from car to car, pssht! pssht! (He ducks.) Man! I was *mighty* scared, right there. That was down around Trident Street, you know, by Rockwell. Right around there. I was *left*, man; I ran. I just left. I didn't want to get shot. My cousin got hit in the shoulder, that was it.

How could they stop it? I don't know. You know, I don't think they can. Maybe . . . (Hesitates.) I think they could solve the problem if they get the higher guys, the big dope guys, dope men. If they get all them, I think it'd stop, because they're the ones supplying everybody.

Or if they'd get something—like say, a big rec center, with basketball courts and stuff? Just for something to *do*, 'cause there's not anything to do in Iron City! People just kind of *stealing* everything. Usually, some people do that because their parents, you know, their parents are kind of like . . . poor, you know? They don't get what they want, can't get a lot of stuff, so they go sell drugs . . . (He's quiet for a long time, staring at the floor.)

Now, like my mom, she's just *all* messed up with the drugs. That's why I don't hardly see her anymore, 'cause she's just messed up on that cocaine. She's just selling all her stuff. Lost her house, cars, and stuff. She had a nice house, five bedrooms, and she just didn't pay something—not the rent, she bought it already—but something? Yeah, the mortgage. And then they took the house from her. And she didn't pay off the stuff for her car, so they took her car. Took her car and everything, selling all her stuff, stereo and stuff.

She can't stop, man. You know, everybody try to help her, my uncles and everything. She just won't listen.

I try to tell her, you know. I talk to her on the phone sometimes. She say, "I'm *trying* to stop." You know. I don't believe it. If she want to, she can. But she don't want to. We can't help her, she's got to help herself.

She lost her job, too. She was a nurse at Veterans' Hospital in Iron City. She was working there, she never came to work, you know, so they fired her. (Softly:) Don't know *what* she'll do now.

(He shakes his head, frowning.) Trip, you know? When we was in Valley City, she had a job and everything was going good, nobody messed with the drugs. Then once we moved to Iron City, everything just started messing up. All of a sudden, I see she's just always smoking that stuff. She met some lady, and I think that lady got her into it. She was doing it, I didn't think nothing was wrong with it. And all of a sudden, she just started selling her stuff, jewelry and stuff. I *knew* she had a problem then.

I'd tell her about it. She'd say, "No, I don't have no problem." I'd say, "Where the VCR at?" Then she'd try to say "Somebody took it or something, I don't *know* what happened to it!"

Then some of *my* stuff would come up missing. My jewelry. Clothes and stuff. But you know, it was my mom. (He wipes his eyes with the back of his fist.) I'd tell her about it, but then I didn't really care. 'Cause she's my mom.

Then she'd just start selling all type of TV's and stuff. I said, "Man, you gotta *stop* that!" My uncles and aunts come up there, try to talk to her. She just don't listen to 'em. Try to tell her she's losing her job and all that. She won't listen.

When she came to see me last time? She came about a month ago. I looked, she didn't even look like my mom! You know, she's real skinny, she's got all kind of *wrinkles* and everything? You know, she don't look healthy. She gettin' *old*, like. She used to look young, she's only thirty-seven! But she just look *old* now. She's just real thin.

I just have to keep telling myself she's my mom, you know.

PART 2

CHILD OF THE AIR

Forgive me father for I have sinned
I'm a child of the air, a witch of the wind
Fingers gripped around my brain
No control my mind is lame
I'm in the astral plane, and I'll never be the same
Never, never, never, never, never, never
Never, never, never

—Megadeth, "Mary Jane"

In a year and a half of interviewing young people in the Hall, I talked with exactly *two* who said they had never either sold drugs or faced a substantial drug problem of their own. For many kids in the Hall, drugs provide much more than momentary euphoria or stimulation: They are a central focus of life. Acquiring and using drugs provides a degree of structure, purpose, and challenge that most do not find in the rest of their lives, and it is often the foundation on which they construct a working identity, a sense of who they are. But for some of those I talked with, the drugs had, at some point, come to rule their lives. Here, some of that group talk about the effects of drugs on their bodies and their minds, the pleasures and terrors of being high, the difficulties of quitting, and the fear that they may never escape the pull of drug use.

What is most striking when you talk with young people in the Hall is how ubiquitous and diverse the youth drug problem has become in places like River County. Most of the seriously drug-dependent kids in the Hall are what are called, in modern jargon, "polydrug" abusers; they typically abuse two or more hard drugs and, frequently, marijuana and alcohol as well. But in River County, the specific mix of drugs of choice, like the drug trade, is strongly shaped by race and class, and by proximity to particular sources of supply.

The problem of crack cocaine—"rock," "hubba"—in the inner cities gets the most attention. But the communities from which most of the kids in the Hall come—white, Hispanic, and black—are awash in an illicit pharmacopeia. PCP remains common in Iron City and among many Latino kids throughout River County. There is little crack or PCP use among white kids in the Hall, although powder cocaine is common. Crank, on the other hand, is rampant among working-class white youth in River County: it's snorted, inhaled off of heated aluminum foil, and sometimes injected intravenously. Cranksters tend to go on "runs" or binges that last up to several days; the really badly strung-out ("amped-

out") often lose so much weight that they look like refugees from a con-
centration camp. Indeed, methamphetamine is sometimes deliberately
used, especially by young women, to lose weight.

Crank vies with acid—LSD—as the primary drug of choice for lower-
income white kids: there is a broad subculture of white youth in the
county for whom crank and/or acid and heavy-metal music are the central
diversions in life. Acid, along with cocaine and alcohol, is also abundant
in suburbs like Cherry Grove. Heroin, too, is also very much alive in
River County, and not just in the inner-city ghettos: there is a long-
standing and thriving white-working-class heroin culture in Rivertown,
and the drug is readily available in the less affluent parts of Cherry Grove
as well.

"I just got this crazy idea: shoot the principal"

I'm from Rivertown. It's a pretty nice town, though it's small. There's not much to do there. But it's fine. A lot of rock bands came from there. It's a pretty neat little town. Go fishing, down by the riverfront.

My dad's a craneman at [the steel mill]. Now it's called Korean-American Steel. The Koreans are coming in. But he still has his job. He got cut back, they took wages from him and stuff. But he's still working there. Couple of his friends got laid off. But they had other jobs to fall back on. My dad doesn't have no other job to fall back on.

Drugs. That's the main reason I *don't* like Rivertown. Lots of drug deals going down there. I mean that's where people go to get their main drugs. It's real bad, in the schools and stuff like that. There's a *lot* of drugs in Rivertown, I can guarantee that.

Why I think it exists is too much authority. Teachers, you know, get on your case. That was *my* worst pressure, teachers. Like in fourth grade, you know, I was laughing at a kid for flipping off a teacher. She *slammed* me, you know; I had a mark from here to here.

So I had a rough time in school.

At one time or another, I was like suicidal. Real deep depression. It was pretty much about school, peers, parents. I went off for three days, didn't go home for three days. Then I used to party a lot, didn't come home. I didn't know how else to handle it. My mom and dad, they misled me, I think; keep things inside of you, and don't cry, you don't want to go off or nothing. Till I exploded and I went to school with a BB gun and, well, shot the principal.

He's big, athletic, with broad shoulders and wide blue eyes. He'd probably be playing high school football, or wrestling, if he were still in high school. He greets you with a warm sunny grin that fades to a puzzled frown when, as often happens, he remembers something that makes him angry. He's been in the Hall for several months, but he still has recurrent flashbacks and hallucinations from his heavy use of LSD over the past year. He speaks softly and rapidly, the words tumbling over each other.

I was hallucinating a little bit, you know, thinking there was people behind me, following me. I was doing a little bit of leaving trails.* Playing with my trails. Like with your hand moving through the air, it leaves a trail? Then I thought I heard voices, you know, calling me, and . . . I just got this crazy idea: shoot the principal. He came after me, I thought he was a monster or something. Can't remember that well; I just shot, you know. He went down to the ground. Then I pointed the gun at *my* head and that was it.

It's like I wanted attention. I was just fed up, didn't know how to ask for help or nothing, so I just went to school with a BB gun cause I didn't know how to control myself.

The night before, I got arrested for drinking. They said it was intoxication? Dancing on cars. (Laughs.) And I blacked out and I don't remember nothing. Also, I took LSD. And that didn't help me none (laughs), so I was pissed off at myself. I guess I was really trying to kill myself. Everybody'd see it then, at school, you know, that I'm fed up with them, so . . . (Trails off, frowns.)

I didn't have a *real* gun. If I'd had a real gun, I would've . . . it wasn't

* He was on LSD.

really a BB gun, it was a CO_2 [pellet gun]. (Grins.) My dad killed *animals* with that thing, so I thought it was powerful.

Lost my self-control. And I was blaming it on them. You know, they kept on saying it was my home life, and everything else. But it was that they were really messing me around. And I just got sick of it. So I just remembered that, when I was on LSD.

It really started in kindergarten. First *day* I was in kindergarten, I got kicked out of school! The teachers thought I was retarded. 'Cause I acted silly, you know, and stuff; and they didn't know why. And they had permission to hit me, and stuff, from my parents; to spank me, and stuff like that. (Frowns.) They thought it would help me straighten up in school.

Schoolwork was kind of hard for me, 'cause I couldn't—I was slow; I was always in special day classes, or something. I was in *all* special classes in sixth grade. And I got kicked out of a lot of schools; I wasn't getting along with teachers. I used to climb around in class, on the desk and stuff, just to get the teacher mad and riled up, you know.

When I was in second grade, they wanted to know why I didn't get along in school. (Laughs.) I tried to tell 'em that I thought it was a bunch of baloney.

They weren't responsible enough. It was like they were trying to weed me out of school; that's what it felt like. It's like I was rejected? It's just what teachers are like, I guess. Never trust teachers again, that's all I can say.

I think I get my temper from, like, generations. I'm like the sixth generation out of control in my family. Abuse, or something like that. Hitting on things, hitting myself. Broke my hands. Ripped a toilet out of the wall, threw it up against a metal screen, left a big dent in the screen. I did a lot of that. I don't do it anymore, but at the time I thought it was necessary. 'Cause I'd always see my dad, when I was little, you know, breaking doors down and stuff. He was alcoholic.

Taking it out on myself, that's pretty much what I was doing. I was mad at everybody else, but if I took it out on everybody else, I'd get in trouble. So if I just took it out on *myself*, how could I get in trouble? Banging my head on the walls, stuff like that. Thought maybe if I did it hard enough, I'd die. One time I tried to hang myself with a shoelace. (Smiles.) Almost succeeded. It was kind of scary. Even tried to hyperventilate a couple of times, but all that did is trip me out, woke me up. I was hoping that my heart would stop. I was hoping that would be a

painless way to die or something. Pretty hard. I still have thoughts about
it sometimes, but I don't do it. I just figure life has to go on, that's just
the way.

Once in a while, I still see a little bit of trails, you know—a flashback
or something, like when I sweat or something? I didn't take that much
LSD—the stuff was *potent*. I guess it wasn't bunk! (Laughs.) At the time,
when I was with the BB gun, it didn't seem like it was working. I could
feel like I had a little more energy than I did when I was really down,
that's all.

You did a lot of drugs . . .

(Quickly:) But I can still *think* and everything, though. There's a kid
here named Wilson. He's kinda wasted out on acid. He can't think straight.
He's eighteen years old, acting like an eight-year-old! He doesn't really
have his senses there. You talk to him, it takes him five minutes to answer
"Yes." (Laughs.) Real wasted person. I want to help him out, though.
He's gonna be eighteen and he's got no place to go. It's like the only thing
he knows how to do is sell drugs, and take it. I don't think he really
wanted to take drugs, but if you're gonna be a good dealer, you've got to
try 'em out to see if they're bunk. Otherwise, you'll get shot. (Laughs.)

It was mainly LSD, crank—my parents never knew—they still don't,
like, believe it. (Shakes his head.) Some parents are *weird*, you know?
Because they're suspicious, but then again, they're ignorant. You try to
tell them, they think you're playing around or something. Or they think
you're just doing it just to get attention or something. You know: "You
don't look like the type" . . . Or that I was trying to make excuses for
what I did. I don't think they *wanted* to believe it. I don't know if it was
a shock to them or what. So I said OK, you know, I'm going to get help
for *myself*.

I did 'shrooms, too. I used to go pick 'em, go up to the hills. There's
a fortune up there. Just go there and take some. But all that does is make
you have trails, doesn't make you hallucinate. And it can make you have
a bad trip. You can *die* from that. So don't mess with that. You don't
know which one to pick. (Pauses.)

I've been to occult things before, too. I thought I was satanic at a
certain period, seventh grade. Really started getting into it eighth grade,
ninth grade. I went to a Satan church.

You had to eat a raw goat's heart. I said, "No, you eat it! I ain't eatin' it!" (Laughs.) I've seen people eat it. It's very tough, you know, I tried it.

I played around with it. I told the reverend here, "I believe in Satan, but I don't believe in God." I know it sounds kind of funny. I just did it because everybody else was doing it. It's funny. They're thinking, if they worship Satan, they think they're gonna get *powers* or something. Me and my friend are just sitting there cracking up, you know; "Uh-huh!" (Laughs.)

It's funny, man; it's hilarious. (Grins.) Started going, I said this is better than *regular* church. You can get a laugh out of *this!* They took a dead cat, you know; took out its skull. We said like, "What are you doing *that* for, what's that supposed to do?"

The only reason we went there is to get free acid. Just to have fun, I guess, just playing around with their heads. You had to pay thirty bucks for a pentagram that had a goat's head, ruby eyes, something like that. You had to pay thirty bucks to get it. I said, "No, that's okay."

Pretty weird. Went there a couple times with this guy, this kid. It's a trip. Decided to take off. Like an adventure. It's like Dungeons and Dragons but like in 3-D, you know? It's the best place to trip out, because it's like stained-glass windows? And what's so funny is, it used to be a so-called godded house, and they just painted the walls black. It's a trip.

I've seen people, you know, move things, and I thought they *did* have powers. I don't know if it's fake or not, but I *did* see 'em move things. (Uneasily:) And I wasn't tripping at the time, either. I think it's mind over matter. I believe in that. You know, since I've seen it. I'm pretty sure I wasn't tripping. It wasn't like I was having trails or nothing that day. It's so weird.

It's fun, till you really get into it, you know. Then it gets kinda weird. It is. I'd go back, just for a laugh. But, I don't know. You could be . . . (Hesitates.) I don't know if it's really *true* or not. You could be playing around with something you don't want to play around with. I mean I don't take it too seriously, but then again I *do*, because you don't know if this stuff's really true. There's no proof that it's true or it's *not* true. You might sell your soul to the devil or something, and you might go *down*. If there *is* a life after death.

If you could change things, make the world different . . .

Well, first off, stop all the wars, and all the prejudice. God's not prejudiced. The devil's not prejudiced, and he's supposed to be evil! And if *he* can do it, why can't we get along, you know? How I'd change things, we wouldn't need government or nothing. Just, I guess, police officers. Then take the A-bombs and stuff and throw 'em all in the ocean. Get rid of 'em. Then you wouldn't have to worry about destruction.

Do you worry about that?

Not really. Just if it's gonna happen, I wish it'd happen *quick*. I'd kill myself if I got exposed to radiation. Or at least, I'd try to find a mainframe computer somewhere, and try to stop 'em. (Smiles.) I've got a computer at home; that's what I do when I get bored. Play with my computer. An Atari XL. But I'm gonna get the new Atari 520, it's got one megabyte. I'd like to get my bachelor's degree. Maybe go to State. I hear they have a pretty good computer course there.

I'd like to go back in time and kill the person who invented the A-bomb, you know; then we wouldn't have any of this. Go back in time, tell 'em not to do it or something, you know. But I guess life has its own destiny. I guess all of our destiny is to die.

I'll tell you straight off, I'm not really afraid of dying. Just *painful* dying. Like with the gun. Why I thought it was going to be easy with the gun was I thought it was only gonna hurt for a couple of seconds and then I'd be dead. Then something just stopped me from shooting myself. I think I just wanted attention or something. It was pretty weird. It's like I wanted to kill myself, but then again, something wouldn't *let* me kill myself. It's pretty hard. I don't really care about living or dying. I'll just hang around awhile, see what goes, y'know. That's the way I feel about it.

(He pauses, frowns.) It feels like my life's just like a dream, you know? It's like anything can happen. It's too fast. This world nowadays is too fast. When I was a little kid, it was like I didn't know what was going on, so it didn't really matter.

That's what's so hard about life in the eighties.

Postscript

Eight months later. He's back in the Hall. He'd gone back home, but it didn't work out.

Got out, moved in with my mom and dad, and then my mom she went into the hospital and stuff. And me and my dad weren't getting along too well. So I had to come back. (Embarrassed:) 'Cause I got drunk, you know, took some LSD, started getting in trouble. Stayed in here for about six months, then went back to my dad again. See if it was alright. And then me and my dad still didn't get along, so they put me back in here.

My mom doesn't like my dad at all. 'Cause he's the same way with her! So my mom said she needed her freedom, so she left. She had to go into the hospital, 'cause of mental illness or something. Guess my dad caused it 'cause he was hitting my mom all the time and stuff. She has mental illness because of it. I don't hold it against my dad, I just hold it against what he does now. He had problems with *his* father so I guess he's taking it out on me.

My Dad doesn't drink no more. He quit that. I thought things were gonna be different. Made it worse! (Laughs.) I said, "I can't handle this." So I told him I was gonna live with my friend. He didn't like that idea, so he called the cops on me, saying I did all this stuff.

I didn't really do nothing, 'cept for this time I took my mom's car. I was gonna go and live with my grandma, grandparents, go to school there, try to finish school, try to work my booty off! (Laughs.)

Didn't have the bus fare, nothing like that. Never drove a car before. Pretty nice, though. Cops seen me, so I turned, went over curbs, left the car there. Ran for about two or three miles. Had a good run though. (Grins widely.) I was *sprintin'!* Ruined the transmission when I went up on the curb. I wouldn't be in here if my dad didn't press charges.

I was driving around and stuff, taking LSD, drinking, just trying to kill myself and stuff. Couldn't do it. Came pretty close though. Wrecked the car and everything.

So wrecking the car wasn't exactly an accident . . .

I wanted to.

How come?

I don't know, it's just . . . it's pretty tough, being a kid and all, you know. I mean I've been through stuff that, you know, thirty-year-old men . . . (Hesitates.) I've practically stayed on the streets since I was about five, all by myself, you know, even when my mom was home, 'cause I never got along with my dad. When I was about five, I was hanging around with people, you know, fifteen, sixteen? I had friends like that. I was trying to mature out of the house? When I used to go home, when I did come home, my dad used to throw me through walls, shit like that. Hit me in the mouth about six times. From that I have . . . (Frowns.) blind rage now. It's like every time I get angry or something, no one can stop me. (Laughs.) Mack truck, I guess you could say.

I try to control my temper. It used to be I just picked up people and just *threw* 'em.

That's what made me go to that Satan church before, you know? And then I realized, this stuff ain't doing nothing for me, so . . . Don't mess with it no more. It's crazy. I believe in God. Just want to get my life straight. And the counselors here told me, you know, believe in God, and stuff like that, do what's right, not what's wrong.

It's like I have an . . . (hesitates) out-of-body experience sometimes, too. When I'm on acid, it's like, you know how people trip out? It's like *normal* for me. You think things, you see stuff . . . (Softly:) It makes me never want to come back, you know? I want to stay there forever.

It's better out there than it is here?

Yeah! (Smiles.) It's like *different*, it's a different world, you know. You *observe* things more, I guess you could say. It's not good for your body, though. Tore me down pretty much, one time. 'Cause I was frying for four *days* one time. This last time. Took twenty-six hits of LSD, thought I could handle it. And I forgot, and just . . . pshoo . . . (shakes his head) I was just totally out of it. And ever since then, I've been having flashbacks. Like right now I can see a little bit of trails, you know. Like a shadow of a trail. I'm a little bit . . . trippin' off of that.

I've been doing it for a pretty long time now.

When did you start taking acid?

When I was seven . . . At the time, I thought it was like candy or something, used to pop it in my mouth every three hours! (Laughs.) And then when I got in here, it got all out of my system and everything, pretty much. And then when I did *this* stuff, it just total freaked me out. I mean I just . . . tchoo! Everybody's *faces* looked like they was falling off! I thought I was seeing my dead friend, you know, that's when I wanted to kill myself. I thought, "Oh, shit." I said, "Man, I should've helped my friend out and stuff," you know. You start thinking, thinking weird thoughts when you're on that stuff. I mean, all you see is like . . . (he's searching for words) it's like it's unreal! And you wouldn't think a little piece of paper could do all that. And like I realized what I was doing was messing with my mind, and stuff . . . once . . . you can't stop, you can go into a bad trip and stay there forever.

I used to have a lot of *good* trips, though, you know? You think good things, and you see good things . . . (Vaguely:) if you think bad things, and you get all worried, and you get panicked, then weird things start happening to you, and stuff. It's really weird, like even arguments, you remember things, and stuff, and then . . . and then sometimes I'll wake up in the middle of the night and think I'm on acid, just in cold sweats 'cause just *thinking* about it in my dream, come back and it's there, stored in my system now. My fat cells.

It's like you can hardly tell when a person's on acid. The way I can tell is 'cause my jaw'll lock? I won't talk or nothing, I'll just set there, my jaw'll be going and I can feel the muscle and everything just like lockjaw or something? That's the only way you can actually tell if a person's on LSD. Also by their pupils. But my parents didn't think, you know, at my age . . . They thought I was just a hyper kid. And they had me seeing psychiatrists and everything, they didn't know *what* was going on. They couldn't help me, 'cause they didn't know what the problem was! (Laughs.)

Did you ever try to tell them?

Uh-uh. I was afraid to tell 'em. Like my dad or something, my dad finds out, you know . . . Like this last time, he don't even know I take it *now!* He don't even know.

It's been hard to get off of it.

Did you ever go to a drug program, get help?

They didn't really know. All they thought, I was like drunk.

Pretty much everybody out here does acid. I mean—acid *rules*. They do crank up there, a *lot* of crank, and coke, I wouldn't touch that. LSD, 'cause I thought that was a safe drug, or something. Some crazy idea! (Laughs.) All my friends started when they were in seventh grade. It's so easy to get, you know. I can get any drug I want. But I only wanted LSD.

I used to go to *church* on LSD. (Laughs.) Used to feel real calm, and comfortable, you know? And you know . . . when you're on LSD, you feel closer to God, too. Some weird reason. (Laughs.) I used to just sit in church and just look at the preacher all day! (Laughs.)

I tried it in two different churches, the Satan church and a different church. It was like night and day. I felt like I was getting like a split personality, so I just started going to one. Didn't mess with that stuff no more. Scared me.

Did anybody try to help you out when you were getting knocked around by your dad? You must have been marked up . . .

I'd just tell 'em I got in a fight, 'cause I used to get in a lot of fights. So you know, they'd say, "Oh, he got in another fight." They wouldn't even ask, really. If they did, I'd tell 'em that. Tell 'em just somebody busted me in the mouth.

Cops beat me up this time, though. (Laughs.) I thought that was police brutality, but I guess they call it different, 'cause I was resisting arrest or something? And took a billy club to me. (Laughs.) Here, and my leg, you know, like I was standing up but handcuffed, that's tough! They got me in the car, banged my head against the car, that was a trip! They're mean. They're worse than Iron City, you can just ask some of these counselors here. They'll just do it for the fun of it. I mean *big* guys.

Used to get knocked around by *everybody*, though. (Quietly:) So I just took a lot of it and just held it in, didn't talk to no one. Psychiatrists, I just told 'em I'm normal and everything, I'm not, you know, I'm not *crazy* or nothing, nothing's going wrong, and I've got this perfect *family* and everything, and I used to draw pictures of it, I used to pull wool over their eyes, as you'd call it, saying yeah, this is how it is, with the little dolls and everything (smiles), and they'd believe it, and they'd say "There's nothing wrong with this kid." Or they'd just—"There's *something* wrong with this kid," that's all they'd say, "there's *something* wrong with him, think there's something mentally ill with him or something." So they put me in this special day class, this special behavior class, for six years ever since first grade or something. They'd try to pull it out of me, but I didn't trust no one and everything, so I'd just hold that stuff inside and everything?

They thought it was just *me*. They just put it all on me, and I . . . I got to thinking it was all me, too. So that made it worse. So then I wouldn't talk to *no* one. So I didn't know who to believe, what to believe, I was all confused and everything, so I was just trying to be . . . anarchy? Kind of like, just being rebellious towards everybody. So I just went along on my own, kind of like. Said, "F this," you know? (Laughs.)

And when I had LSD, I had flashbacks on that stuff, just remembering what people did to me and everything? So every once in a while—it's getting a little bit lighter, but it's like each time I take LSD it makes it grayer. I mean I can get real violent when I . . . (He's frowning, fists clenched on the table.) I can feel it, my behavior changes, my attitude, changes my personality, the first five hits I took it changed my personality. I wasn't quiet no more, I wasn't . . . it was like someone says something to me I just . . . I didn't *say* nothing to 'em, I just *threw* 'em! (Laughs.) Started breakin' 'em down and everything, trippin' off that. It would of happened sooner or later, if I didn't get it out then. It's pretty hard to tell people that I'm angry at them and stuff like that, and so, then when I'm on acid, it doesn't mean nothing, I don't *care*, I'll go through a wall if I have to to get 'em! I did that before. Went through someone's front *door*! Just grabbed 'em by their neck, threw 'em out, started beating 'em up, then ran.

I'm telling you, being a kid's hard. I mean, if I was eighteen, I would have a job already, or something. I could be going into the Marine Corps or something. Cause my cousin's a recruiter. So he wouldn't josh me around or nothing. Probably want to be a Navy Seal or something. Or a mercenary.

Why do you want to be a mercenary?

I just . . . (slowly:) took a lot of pain, you know? I mean, the average person'd be *crazy* by now! (Laughs.) So I could handle it better than the average person. Me, I'm *living* a mercenary life, practically! You know, dodging people . . . I did it for all my life almost, now. So you know, might as well just keep on doing it in a *legal* way. Just like—stay away from *people*, you know? Like get my angry—my aggressions? out on people who I'm supposed to de-terminate? You know, be an assassin? People that need to be assassinated, I'd just—people still do that, don't they?

Wouldn't you feel kind of bad about that, though? Like if they said, "Go terminate this guy," and you . . .

I'd be glad to do it! (Laughs.) It's like—I don't like to kill people or nothing, but something like that, you know . . . (Earnestly:) If it's just a job, it's legalized . . . I mean, if I was going into the Navy, it'd be the same thing. I'd have to kill people. You know? If we went to a war or something. Well, this is just protecting my country, doing it for a right —doing it for a good reason. No, I wouldn't feel bad about it. You can't feel bad about it. Just get it over with.

Dawn Olivetti

"It's not good to live past the age of twenty-nine"

She wears her hair shaved up close to her head on the left, long and floppy on the right; she looks like a kind of punk elf. She was born in Rivertown of working-class Italian-American parents, moved to Cherry Grove as a child, and for about the past six years has been living mainly on the streets, both in Cherry Grove and more recently in Hillview. "I'm like, OK, I'm supposed to live in Cherry Grove, but I mostly live in Hillview." She's been shuffled in and out of group homes and juvenile institutions since she was ten.

When I talked with Dawn, she had been arrested after running away from the group home where she'd been taken after a bad acid trip in the Cherry Grove Mall.

Like the end of October last year I got picked up 'cause I was tweakin' pretty bad.

And I started—I was seeing things like—you know that dude, man? —(earnestly:) nobody knows what I'm talking about, but that dude on the *peanuts?* He walks around with a *cane?*

Yeah, the peanut guy on the Planters can with the top hat.

Yeah! He was *talking* to me, man.

He was, huh?

I'm serious! (Laughs.) I was like, *whoa!* And then all of a sudden, he started making me *mad*. So I hit him? And like it was *weird*, 'cause I was fading in and out, you know, I'd start *tweaking* and then I'd . . . I'd still be tweaking but not like real *heavy*? And then like all these peanuts were falling down. It was weird.

What were you tweaking on?

Camouflage. You know what that is? It's a kind of acid. It's supposed to be like the best. And I took like twenty-seven hits. Because I had them on me, you know, and I was like "Whoa, why not?" 'Cause I was on the streets and I sold acid to make money. And like I didn't—the twenty-seven hits would be like fourteen hits, 'cause I worked up to it.

And then I just decided "Well, why not." And I did it. And it's like my body didn't *want* it that day.

I didn't even *care* that day. I remember I was sittin' there, and I knew it was in my pocket, and I was like "Man, why not, it might help." And I went for it.

It was in the mall. I'm serious. (Laughs.) I used to *love* that place, man. It ain't too cool anymore though, 'cause now the security guards started getting pretty bad and kicking me and all my friends out. So we don't go there that much. Occasionally, you'll see somebody there and you'll be like "Dude! What's up?" But not that much. About a year back, that was like a *hangout*. For all the people like me.

What's a person like you?

Like . . . all the *punks*. And we'd go kick back in Burger King, and just sit there. And then we'd leave there, and go, do you know where Wilson's [department store] is? And there'd be like these *chairs*, and we'd sit there. And then we'd have to leave 'cause they'd start complaining.

I was in Hillview. And somebody ran into me and they told me something. And this was after I already *took* it all. And I had to go out to Cherry Grove to take care of some business. And I went out there.

And (mysteriously:) I took care of it. And then since I was out there I decided to go to the mall. And I started *peaking*, man. (She puts on a wild, terrified face.) I was like "Noooooo!!" It was like I was sittin' there and there were like all of these people standing around me, dude, and I was like "Oooh . . . nooh!" (Laughs.) And you know I could've got away, too, man . . . But I couldn't *move* right, man, like I could barely stand. And I know if I was straight I could've got away in a minute. 'Cause once I'm ready to go, *no* one catches me. Occasionally, I get caught, but usually I can get away. I guess that was one time I was *meant* to be picked up.

I didn't do much for a couple of days. For about four or five days I just kind of *sat* there.

Sometimes I still feel like doing some acid. But not like a whole *bunch*; just like, you know, *drop* a couple. And tweak for a while.

This friend of mine, he took a sheet? And he wrote a letter to his mom? The same kind like I had, too. And he wrote a letter to his mom, and it was all sloppy, you know, 'cause you can't write that good, when you're dosing and everything? And he wrote, "Mom, I was meant to be a gopher." And he was found buried in his backyard. (Almost inaudibly:) He buried himself.

Uh, what do you mean "he buried himself"?

He *buried* himself, man.

You mean he buried himself underneath a bunch of dirt?

Yeah.

So . . . he was killed?

Yeah. And then this other guy, he just *licked* a sheet, he didn't take the whole sheet, he just *licked* it. He's kind of messed up. He thinks he's an orange? And like you'll say, like, "Dude, I'm thirsty!" and he'll be all "No, no, don't eat me, don't eat me!" And he'll start tweakin' out and he'll yell "Aaaaah!!" He does this to, like, *everybody*. And he doesn't *go* anywhere, he just sits in one place all the time. And then this other friend of mine, he gets lost *all* the time. You'll be walking down the street talking to him? and next thing you know you got to go back a couple blocks and *find* him, you know? It's terrible.

All these guys are friends of yours?

I know the guy that gets lost better. I know him pretty well. And then I know the guy that thinks he's an orange pretty good. And the guy who buried himself, I was just like *acquaintanced* with him. This was like about two years ago, two or three. And I wasn't there when it happened, but somebody, you know, they ran into me and they're all like "*Dude, this dude buried himself!*" And I go, "Nahh . . . un-uh" . . . But finally they convinced me.

But this dude that gets lost all the time, it was *terrible.* We're walking down Cherry Street and they had these lights in the window. And he stopped and stared at the lights. I went back and he's just like *staring* at them and I'm "Come on, we gotta go," and he's "No!" I'm like "OK, I'll leave you, all right?" I mean, man, these people are *weird.* (Shakes her head.)

I can deal with some people. Others I can't.

The guy that thinks he's an orange—does he have any family or anybody who cares where he is?

Well, he's pretty old now, he's in his twenties. So I doubt they're really concerned. (Laughs.)

(At the time of her bad trip in the mall, she'd been living on her own for several years, on the street or with friends.)

See, when I was little, my mom jammed to Chicago. And I never knew my dad, and like a couple of years ago I kind of sort of met him.

So I went out to live with him? (She stares at the table.) But it didn't work out. So as soon as school got out, he got me a plane ticket and I came back out here. So now I'm here.

See like—it was weird. OK. She got a divorce from her second husband because we had . . . (she pauses) *problems* with him. And then she found this boyfriend. And he did drugs. And she has this problem—every guy she meets she falls in love with. And she'll do *anything* for him. So *she* started doing drugs. And she started feeling like me and my brother were like making her feel *old*. Because we were like her *kids*, you know? So, she got a divorce. I mean not a divorce, she jammed! OK, I'm tweakin'! (Laughs.)

So she got tired of you guys because you reminded her she was old enough to have kids?

Yeah; I guess. 'Cause he was like fifteen years younger. So there was like a big difference.

She took me to Safe Haven. And see, I didn't know what was up. (She was ten.) She just goes, "Well, I'll be back in a week". So I'm sitting here expecting her to come back and I never see her again. Like a couple of months *later* I found out what happened.

What'd you do when you found out what happened?

Didn't affect me, I don't think. Because during the whole nine or ten years, however many it was, things like this were like *constantly* happening. And it got to where it didn't even affect me anymore. Well, she didn't actually take off before. She was *there*, but it was like she *wasn't* there? And there was, like, my stepdad. But like the only way I got attention from him was if I did something wrong and he'd hit me for it. But that was still *attention*, so I was like "Killer!" (Shakes her head.) I don't know—its *weird*; I think it was kind of screwed up in the head, but that's *my* opinion.

My grandparents live next to Hillview. And every once in a while, I'd go spend a weekend with them. And I used to be like *majorly* skinny. 'Cause, you know, I never ate. And I totally *munched* when I was at their house and they thought I was eating like this all the time! They couldn't figure out why I couldn't gain any weight.

How come you weren't eating?

'Cause I didn't know how to cook. I ate *crackers*, though, dude; I ate baloney. But, I don't know, she wouldn't cook. And I was like too scared to go and get something out of the kitchen. Like on my way to school there was like, two or three blocks down from my house? there was a store. And on my way to school I'd go by there and, you know, snatch something once in a while. And I'd eat that.

And when she did cook, it was like a sandwich. And I'd go like "Whoa, *killer!*" (Laughs.)

Do you think she worried about you not getting enough to eat?

She wasn't with it, man. She was just like *whatever.*

Was that because of the drugs she was doing?

It might have been. (Smiles.)

But I remember like my first couple years that I could start *remembering* things, you know? Like when I was five and six? And she was cool, you know, she fed me all the time and stuff? And then like when I hit around seven, it just all changed.

Did you ever ask her for stuff, or say "Hey, I'm getting hungry?"

No. I would never ask her for food. But sometimes she'd sit there, and she'd just *give* me stuff. And it wasn't like food but it like *substituted* for it, so it was cool. I wouldn't be hungry. Yeah, like *killer* . . . like she would give me cigarettes, or she'd give me some drugs sometimes. I was like about eight or nine.

How did you feel when she did that?

At the time, I don't know *what* I thought. Now it's like—you know, in a way it was cool. 'Cause a lot of parents aren't like that. And a lot of kids *want* their parents to be that way. But then in a way I feel like, well, maybe if she didn't do that, maybe I wouldn't have gotten into the problems I got into when I got older.

I didn't start doing anything *heavy* until I was like thirteen or fourteen. I used to, all I did was I'd get stoned, you know. But then it got to where it wasn't fun anymore, you know? And then I started doing like coke and stuff. And that was like *major* fun. That was like . . . I loved the coke, I don't know why. And then like I'd do acid once in a while. Most of the stuff I didn't do that much. The only thing I did a *lot* was like coke. I'd do that a lot.

Sounds like it wasn't too hard to get what you wanted around Cherry Grove . . . Why do you think so many kids are doing drugs out there?

I think some people might do 'em for peer pressure. And some people might do 'em because they've never done it and they want to find out what it's like. And then they end up liking it, so they do it. And then . . . let's see . . . there's other people that just . . . what*ever*, you know?

Like my friend? She like OD'd like three weeks ago? She OD'd and she's in Valley State [a psychiatric hospital] right now 'cause she was *dead* when they found her, and they brought her back to life, but she was in a *coma* for a while? It's like—I don't know, dude, it was weird. Like *we* did drugs, but she was *different*, and we didn't want her to do drugs. And we'd always be telling her, you know, not to do 'em. But she was determined to do them anyway, and I don't know why, she just *was*. (Softly:) She wasn't like *us*. She was like . . . special. See with us, we're just like *people*. But she noticed the little things in life, things that other people couldn't see. It's weird. Sometimes I feel like maybe its because we kept telling her "No." I know when they told me I couldn't smoke for twenty four hours? Dude, I'd go and buy a pack of cigarettes and smoke every cigarette in *front* of them. And, you know, it was just because they said no. So I had to do it anyways.

So . . . you wouldn't advise people to "just say no" to drugs . . .

(Much laughter.) Nooooo . . . I wouldn't.

I hate people, like, telling me what I have to do or telling me how I should've done something. Or else like if I did something wrong . . . you know they'll like totally jump all *over* me. But if they had any sense . . . (Plaintively:) I already *did* it, and yelling ain't gonna change anything because it's already been *done*. It's just like *now*: I told everybody, I'm gonna try not to do many drugs. I didn't say I wouldn't, but I told them I'd *try*. And now they're kind of like, if I slip, they're all like *"Whaat?"* . . . And I'm like *"God . . .* it was one mistake, OK?"

Are you scared that you'll get back into drugs in a big way when you get out?

Actually, right now nothing really scares me 'cause I just came back in here. But last time I was in here? I remember . . . It was like "You can leave," you know? I'm like "God damn . . . cool!" But then I was like . . . I didn't know if I could *handle* it, you know? 'Cause like it'd be just so much *freedom*, you know? And I kept telling everybody, "Man, you let me out of here, you ain't gonna know *what* I'm gonna do," you know? And it was just weird, 'cause I had to, like, control *myself*, you know? 'Cause I wanted *this* . . . and *this* . . . It was terrible. But I got over it.

(Only one drug really frightens her: heroin.)

I've managed to stay away from heroin. A lot of my friends are on that stuff now. And they're all like "Dude, you should try this!" and I'm like "No, that's OK, I've got my own drugs over here . . ."

It's ridiculous, man. You sit there and try to talk to them. Especially when you're wired and they're on heroin. (Laughs:) And you're sitting there trying to talk to them and they're just kind of laying there like *this*. (Head on the table, eyes dopey.) I just have to get up and leave—I say, "Look, I'll catch you later."

I've heard that heroin gives you the perfect feeling that you've always wanted. It just, I've heard it makes people feel like they're *floating* or something. You're just like *happy*. I guess that's why.

Do you figure maybe they're trying to get away from something?

Probably. (Quickly:) But I can't think of anything they'd be trying to get away from. They don't seem like they have any problems.

There was another thing we did that we had to go to Hillview for. And this I did with them. Crack. *Dude*, I did it one time, I'll never do it again. It was *terrible*. God, I tweaked all the way home. And it seemed like we were on the road forever. I mean I thought I was *never* gonna get home. And in reality we didn't get home till five o'clock in the morning. We left at midnight to go, you know, I don't see why it took us so long. I couldn't breathe the next day, and I already have asthma and I didn't need that stuff. (Laughs.) I could see me at home sitting there and all of a sudden I'd have an asthma attack, no inhaler, and if I did have one, I wouldn't know how to use it! But they seem to *love* that stuff, man.

What would you like to be doing when you're older?

My main goal, I want to go to England.

Why England particularly?

I feel like I *belong* there. It's the whole scene, pretty much . . . I want to go and hang out in the subways. Play guitar. Get in a band and just kick back. I like the Crucifux, and the Sex Pistols, but they're not as popular, and Metallica and Slayer and Siouxsie and DRI and DI, they're kind of new. The Tendencies. Hard-core stuff. I was *in* one, but as you see, I don't play in one right now. It wasn't working. 'Cause I mean like we'd be all playing, and I'd end up in here, and other people just wouldn't be serious about it. (Disgusted:) 'Cause, you know, they'd like come to practice, and they'd be all messed up where they couldn't play, or they just wouldn't show up at *all*, you know, for rehearsal. It wasn't cutting it. So I was thinking maybe I could just go to another country. Find me a band that's like *serious* about it, and play.

Or I want to work at Tower Records, or I want to like be, you know, one of those people that set up concerts? Or—I wanta be—I gotta do *something* with music. I'm *serious*, man. I mean if there was like absolutely no way I could do anything with music, I think I might go for electrical technology. But I'd rather do something with music.

If you could be the president . . .

(A long pause.) I think . . . I would let girls fight on the front line in the army. I'd *kill* to be on the front line. 'Cause if I knew that I could do that, I'd join the army right now. Actually, I might join the navy, but . . .

What's so great about being on the front line?

It's *killer,* dude! (She's excited.) You're all up there . . . Got your gun and they got *their* gun, and you're just like firing away at each other . . .

But you might get killed . . .

Yeah, but *they* might get killed, too. And like you would *win.* And we're all gonna die someday. And if I was meant to die, then I die. At least I could die knowing that I did it for my country.

You'd feel pretty proud then?

(She looks distracted.) I guess . . .

If there was a war, would you want to just jump right in and join it?

Yeah. I love adventure.

You're not a peace person . . .

Not at all. (Laughs.) More like anarchy.

Do you know people in the military?

Yeah. There's this one guy, but he always AWOLs from it, because he has to come back and take care of *us* for a while. 'Cause like we'll be on the streets, right? And I don't know what it is, but every time he leaves, we get into some kind of trouble. And he finds out about it somehow and he has to come back for a couple of weeks and straighten everything out.

And then he takes off and gets back to the ship again right before it leaves. Once it leaves, we're in trouble, 'cause he can't exactly come back then. While he's there, it's cool.

It sounds like he cares about you guys.

Yeah. (Smiles.) He's Dad.

An older guy?

Yeah. He's like twenty-three.

She says she doesn't really like to think about the future much, though.

It's not good to live past the age of twenty-nine. In fact, one time there was like ten other people besides me that were like that, and we decided that whoever got to have their birthday first, we'd all be in a house and we'd blow it up. (Matter-of-factly:) And that'd be how we died.

Why twenty-nine?

Well, see, like we're in a different generation, right? In this generation, thirty just happens to be old. See, in your generation, forty was probably old, right?

We used to say, "Never trust anybody over thirty."

Now it's never trust anybody under eighteen . . . (A long pause. She's looking down at the floor.) (Softly:) My friend killed herself like May 16. She shot herself right there. (She points to her temple.) She ran away from group home, and then she wrote her mom she'd come back, if she didn't have to go back to her group home. And she came back and things got heavy and so she ran away again. And I think maybe it was just like . . . you know, you just get tired of it sometimes.

Tired of . . . people hassling you? Getting on your case?

It's not so much the people. It's just that—I don't know—you're like—you're never gonna have a place where you can stay without people *yelling* at you. And—I don't know—you're just never gonna have what you want. And you just get sick of it, man. And you end up *doing* something.

Postscript

Three months later. She's back in Juvenile Hall: morose, depressed, on medication.

I *think* I turned myself in, but I'm not sure. 'Cause I'd been gettin' in trouble, is why. And then like I came here and I wasn't even *myself* for like six or seven days. I was just like uuuugh . . . They told me I made *no* sense whatsoever.

See, like, while I was gone, I found a new drug. I mean it's not *new*, but it's something I never did before. I've always like *wanted* to do it? But I've been scared to do it because it's so addictive. And finally it was offered and I was like "Oh, sure!" But it's like, now, if you laid it in front of me, I don't care how many people were standing there watching me, I'd take it. OK, I started like shooting heroin. And I fell in love. I mean I hate it, too. But um . . . it's like I *wanta* stop, you know, sometimes. And sometimes I'm like, *why* should I stop?

And I won't promise anyone that I'll never do it again. 'Cause one day I'm gonna be there and someone's gonna say, "Here." And I'll say, "Oh . . . OK."

She's hoping to be sent to a good group home, where she'll have some peace and quiet and will be away from the constant pressure to do drugs.

As far as I'm concerned, it'll be my last chance. If my life's going pretty good after that, then I'll know, and that's cool. If not I'm giving *up*. I have to be in a group home before I'm eighteen or else I'm out the door. And see, if I don't go to this group home . . . (pauses) if they release me today, I could like have everything I want within an hour or a couple of hours. By dark. I'll have what I want. And what does that get me?

I don't know—what does *that get you?*

That gets me bloody boots, bloody fingers, and no money in my pocket. And a fucked-up head. Or brain, put it that way.

Cindi Richardson

16

"You've got to help me here some"

Lucky I stole my mom's car and wrecked it. 'Cause otherwise I would never have been here and I would never have gotten the help that I'm getting right now. I'd be out there still using it. But in here you can't get to it; there's no way. And then finally, you know, it just gets out of your mind, you don't ever think about it that much. Like I used to be always worried, you know, "Oh, I don't want to get fat," like I would do it, one of the reasons, not to get fat, and just to be high with everybody else. You know, "My friends do it, I want to try it, too!" So I would do it, and not get fat, and now I'm in here, I've been gaining a lot of weight—it's like I don't care if I get fat or not, people have to like me as what I am, not as what I do.

She's dark-haired, gregarious, a nonstop talker. Born in the Midwest, she moved with her parents to Rivertown as a child: "It's OK, it's more of a wire town. Everybody that comes in here from Rivertown, they're busted for wire. You know, crank, speed, and all that? It's a little town, it's a small town, but that's where it's all busted at. Rivertown's a speed town. Anything you snort up

your nose. That's why all of us from Rivertown are in here." Her
stepfather's a chemical plant worker; her mother's been on disability
since she hurt her neck in an industrial accident. Cindi was picked
up by the Rivertown police after smashing her mother's Toyota
Supra into a telephone pole. Her mother pressed charges. She came
into the Hall with a severe methamphetamine addiction; she's been
drying out for a month.

It's the only drug they can get around there. It's hard to get weed since
it's been busted, you know, the ships coming in? Everything's getting
busted. And the acid ain't that good. So the only thing that's good is the
wire! (Laughs.) That's the best stuff to get, so let's get that!

But I finally admitted to myself and my family, like I admitted to my
mom, I'm addicted to drugs and I need help. And she's all proud of me,
she's all "Oh, maybe you're gonna be one of those few kids who grows
out of it." I'm just sick and tired of it. You can spend twenty *bucks* for
four lousy lines! And that high goes away and then you're thinking, "God!
I could have bought, with that twenty bucks, two pairs of *shoes?"* It's like
I never have *money,* and I'm swapping my *jewelry* for it, and it's like "I
don't want *this."*

Did your mom know you were using crank?

She knew, because I was living at home and I was doing it. And it
was Christmas, and I did about seven lines that night over at my boyfriend's
house. It was like an hour before we opened presents and we're sitting
there and all my relatives are there and I had a nosebleed for twenty
minutes.

And my mom *knew.* She's all "What are you snorting up your nose?"
and I go, "Nothing," and I was trying to lie to her, you know . . . And
then I started getting real *skinny,* and then one day I couldn't get it? I
could not get *no* wire or *no* money, and my boyfriend had it? So I go to
my stepdad and me and him got into a fight. And I was all "Well, I don't
got to stay here," and he says, "No you don't, get out of here," and I go
"I will, I hate you!" And I ran. And I blamed it because of my stepdad.
(Earnestly:) It was *my* fault! It was 'cause I couldn't get to my drugs! I was
putting it on my stepdad, but it wasn't his fault. I just wanted people to
see that it was his fault and it wasn't mine, I wasn't addicted.

We got along great until my boyfriend got me into the drugs. 'Cause I wasn't doing *no* drugs, and then he said, "Oh, just take one little hit off this joint," you know, and I said, "No, no." I was turning it down for a while, and then I said, "OK, *now*." I took a hit and got more and more into it. I did weed, I did wire, I did crack rocks, I didn't like that. I did a hit of acid. Half a hit. I didn't like that, I said, "No more of that!" (Laughs.) And I started drinking and I *really* didn't like that, 'cause I barfed a lot. The one that I really liked was the speed. I really got off on that. I wanted to keep that, and that's mostly what it was.

And like I was trading my jewelry. (Indignantly:) And my boyfriend was not doing *nothing*. You know, if he wanted it, it'd be "Cindi, here, trade *this*," you know? He'd say, (singsong:) "Babe, I promise that when we get *older* and we get *married*, I could buy you another one like that." And you know, dumb me, I'd say, "OK, yeah," you know. (Laughs.) So I would trade my jewelry, and then I'm "God, I don't have much jewelry left" . . . That's where all my jewelry mostly went. And he didn't do *nothing*. He would not trade *none* of his stuff. It's like "Let's use Cindi the *girl*friend, and trade all her *stuff*," and then I guess, when I was all out of it, "Let's dump her and go on to another one."

One time he bought an eight-ball, and he says we'll sell half and we'll make more, and I go "OK," like that. And we did almost *all* the eight-ball, and we gave lines to our friends and stuff, and we didn't make *nothing* off of it. (Laughs.) And it's like "Oh my God! Like we wasted an *eight-ball*!" An eight-ball costs like a hundred and forty, fifty bucks. And that's how much we wasted. We did it all to ourselves. And we were wired *every* night . . . It was like all the time, every day, line, line, line. And then when we came down, when we were all out, we came down *hard*.

And I was like chasing the bag. All Tommie's friends would come over, and then Tommie wouldn't have none, but his friends would? And his friends would leave, and I'd say, "'Bye, Tommie, I'm going where the wire's going, OK, you can stay." I'd come home at night, he would hit me and stuff, he'd say, "I didn't know where you were, you worried me." I said, "Oh, I'm sorry, I'm sorry," you know, like that, and the next day his friends'd come over with that bag again, I'd be *gone*, whooom! (Laughs.) I'd be gone so fast he wouldn't even know.

One night I went out with one of his friends and him and we drunk some beer and they had wire and weed. I mean it was local weed, it was real bad. So I did wire and I drunk beer. And I got so messed up, I had so much stuff in me that I wouldn't get into the car and Tommie had to push me in, and next morning I woke up, I had seventeen bruises on both my *legs* from it, I was like *whoa!* (Shakes her head.) 'Cause I had had this stuff, you know? Cause you can't really tell when you're high, you're all "Yeah!" You're in such a better mood. But then when it wears off, you're the same old person! It doesn't change your attitude. 'Cause I used to be "Oh, I'm so happy," I'd be in a *lot* better mood, nothing could make me depressed or mad, you know, I was gonna get to do what I wanted. But then when you come down, you're in twice a bad mood than what you would be, really. That's the only thing I didn't like, is coming down. But that's the thing you had to take if you were gonna do it. You had to be prepared to come down the next day. It's gonna catch up sooner or later. You're gonna have to come down sooner or later. (Laughs.) You can't *always* be up there!

I can't see him no more. The judge said no contact with him at all. (Scornfully:) And he wrote me a letter and he goes, "Oh, baby, you don't need a drug rehab, you're not addicted to it." He said that so I could go back out there and he could use me again. I know it. Like I told him, I said, I need help. He don't want to admit it that *he* needs help. But I know he needs it as bad as I do because he's been doing it longer than I have. And he's nineteen, and I'm sixteen, so you figure he's been doing it a lot of years before I even started! So he's probably really into it now. But he's all, he wrote me a letter: "Oh, I'll be *waiting* for you," and all this. And when I go home, I'm not gonna tell him I'm home. I don't want nothing to do with him, it's like get out of my *life*, he's the one that got me onto all this. So like, you know, why *me?* Why couldn't he go and get one of the other innocent girls?

I didn't even smoke cigarettes, I didn't do *nothing*. (Ruefully:) And then with that weed, it was all "Just take a little hit." And then drinking, just, you know, "little bit, little bit." And then it came to the wire, "Just a little bit." I said, "I like *this!*" And then I took that half hit of acid, he rode me across town on the bike, I jumped off, I felt like my *leg*, I was walking on air. I tweaked so bad I started *crying* . . . It was like "My God, I don't want no more of that." I just wish wire was like that too, a drug my system couldn't get used to like the acid. 'Cause if my system couldn't get used to that wire, then I wouldn't be in here. If only wire was like acid. But no, I liked it! My system's saying, "Yeah, come on," (laughs) you know, "Yeah, I'm all for it! Bring it out!"

One thing that I wasn't gonna get into was shooting up. 'Cause after the nosebleed, I started smoking it on foil. And then I said, "I'm not gonna touch a needle." But then *everybody*, they *say*, "I'm not gonna touch a needle," but when you get sick and tired of foiling it, smoking it, you'll go to your veins for it. You'll get into it that bad, too.

This is my first time being arrested, my first time being in here. Like when I came in I was so scared, I cried for like a week. I wanted to go home. I'm all (wails:) "I want to go home, I don't *like* it here!" When that cop put the handcuffs on me, threw me in the car, I was like "Whoa! What are you doing, handling me like that!" First time, you know, and I was *so* scared. But you know, my mom said, she's all "It's good that it happened to you now. Because if it would have happened to you when you got older, it would have been harder for you to quit. It's good that happened to you at a young age because now you can get all the help you need." (She looks puzzled.) 'Course I don't understand her point that much, but hopefully I will later on. Only if I could go back in time and listen to her and not do it.

Why'd you steal your mom's car?

Me and my boyfriend got into it, and we have a boat out in Harley, by Rivertown, and I went out there and stayed the night a couple of nights. 'Cause he was hassling me, you know, and stuff, so I went out there. And then I had to walk home on the railroad tracks barefooted that morning. I had no way into Rivertown. I called him and he wouldn't pick me up. He goes, (arrogantly:) "No, you can walk home." So I started walking on the railroad tracks early in the morning barefooted. (Laughs.) And that's a *long* walk.

But I walked. I was so mad, when I got into Rivertown, I said I'll break inside the house, take a shower. 'Cause they went on a vacation, two weeks' vacation, and they told us that we weren't allowed back in till they got back from their vacation. That we could not move back in till they got back. 'Cause they didn't want *us* to ruin their vacation. So, you know, that made me real mad 'cause I had nowhere to go 'cause me and Tommie got into our arguments. You know, I wanted to go *home*, and they said, "No. We don't want you to ruin our vacation." So I thought, "OK," and so I went home and I broke the window, got in, I took me a nice shower, and then I thought, "Well how am I going to get all the way across the other side of Rivertown?"

Thought, "Well, the Supra's here and the key is too!" (Laughs.) You know, the only thing I was going to do, I thought, I'll just *get* in it, I'll *go* to Tommie's house, and then I'll come back, I'll get Tommie, and I'll drive the Supra back and park it, put the cover back on it, they won't even know. And then Tommie can get me and take me back over to our house. And it'll all work out.

I only made it up the *street!* And I was *straight* when I crashed! (Laughs.) I didn't have *nothing* in my system! And I crashed. And like when I crashed, this lady's all "Don't worry, don't worry, nothing's gonna happen." And I tell her, I go, "I'm a *runaway*, I broke into my Mom's *house*, I don't got a *license*, I just wrecked the Supra." I go "I'm *busted*." And I go, "I gotta run, I gotta run." And she's all "No, I promise the cops won't take you, I promise." Soon's the cops got there, she left.

And it was *hard* when my parents came to court, and my mom was all "Why did you *do* that?" And like I couldn't say nothing, I just cried and cried.

'Cause like they're sort of like a wealthy family . . . getting a pool in January and stuff . . . Which I can understand, it was her car. And I shouldn't have took it. Like I told her, if I could go back in time, I would never have took the car. (Earnestly:) But you know, you only live once, and you make those mistakes, and that's how you learn not to make them again. You gotta make the mistake at least once to learn and know not to do it again. That's how I think of it.

You weren't living at home then? When they went on vacation?

Me *or* my brother and sister wasn't. 'Cause me and him had got into that fight, and I ran, 'cause I couldn't get to my drugs. So I took off. And I was living with my boyfriend four months? And then my brother and sister ran away. They were living out on the streets. My sister's fifteen and my brother's fourteen. We were all living out on the streets. *All* of us wanted to come home, and they said, "No, we're going on vacation for two weeks." Which I could understand, they didn't want to leave us home, 'cause they were afraid we were gonna steal. And they didn't want to *take* us, 'cause they thought maybe we'd run when we got up there and it'd be far away from Rivertown and we'd have nowhere to go.

But like I didn't have noplace to go, I wanted to come home, I didn't *want* to go back to Tommie. And that's the only place I *had*, so I went back to him.

When you were gone, and your brother and sister, too, what did your mom and stepdad do? Did they come and look for you?

No. They told us, "The door's open if you guys want to come back." But I was having such a good time partying, "Oh, I'm not gonna go home, why should I go *home*," you know?

Weren't they worried about you?

I *think* they were. (Hesitates. Quietly:) I just don't think that they wanted us to *know*. You know, it's like "I don't *care* what you do." That's what they wanted us to think, but you know, I knew they were worried about us. 'Cause *I* would be, if *my* kids ran and *I* didn't know where they were? I'd be very upset.

I felt like they didn't love me and want me. I'm all "They don't love me and want me, 'cause if they did they'd be out here looking for me." That's how I felt when I was on the run was like, my mom don't love me, if she loved me she'd be out looking for me. Which it *did* make sense. She knew where I was. She knew I was living with my boyfriend, and at what house. If she wanted to find me, she could have came over there and got me. Or at least she could've came over and *talked* to me. But I had to go talk to *her*. And she was saying, "Well, it's all *your* fault." You know, I'd go, "Well, for us to get this all together, Mom, we've both got to meet halfway." And she would say, "No, you've got to come the *whole* way. You're the one that goofed." (Plaintively:) You know, it's like "I can't do it on my *own!* You've got to *help* me here some!" You know?

But she knew what I was doing. She knew that I was into the drugs. Because I'd come over and visit her? Although I was kicked out, I still came over and visited. And talked to *her*, but I wouldn't be there when my stepdad got home. Because I was afraid to, you know, look face-to-face with him. I would *not*.

And like I'd go over there and visit her and stuff, and she'd sit there, "Oh, why are you so *skinny?*" And I'd lie to her, "It's 'cause I'm living on the streets." But it *wasn't* cause of that! It was because of the drugs! And I just didn't want to say anything . . .

And now that I came in here, I've gained so much weight! I went home, I can't fit into my pants! (Laughs.) Thought, "Oh my God!" I go, "Well, I need new pants!" I fit into *hers* now! It's like, whoa! But she says I look healthy. She goes, "It's better than being just bones." And that's true.

But like I feel sorry for my sister. She was in here, just for a week. First she went to Safe Haven. And she ran from Safe Haven and they found her and put her *here*. And Safe Haven said, "OK, we'll take you back." Well, over at Safe Haven she ran again. So she's in Rivertown living on the streets; when they find her she's gonna be locked up for a *while*. And then my brother, *he* was out on the streets, and then my parents came back from vacation, and my parents go, "OK, we'll take you back." You know. My brother was all happy. Well, he just ran a couple of days ago I heard, too. So he's back on the streets *again*.

He's into drugs, I know that. I think he's into the same thing that I am, you know? He's fourteen. It's hard to explain to your little brother, too, "You need help," you know? And he's thinking, "Well, *you* did it, so I'm gonna do it." You know? And that's not how you do it! Like my sister, we get into it, she's all "I get to do what you did, because *you* did it!" I go, "Well, I'm older and you're younger." I mean, how do you explain? . . . (Laughs.) And her and my mom start fighting. Like my sister, she's all saying "Oh, my Mom hit me and left bruises on me." It made my mom look bad.

Now that all her friends know that I wrecked the Supra, some of her friends say, "Oh, God, I can't *believe* you're going to go pick up your daughter and she wrecked your Supra." (Plaintively:) That's only *material* things that I wrecked, you know? There's a difference between material things and a *person!* That's what I wanted to tell her, but you know, I could just see it: "Be quiet, Cindi," and all that. They were all "Well, you know that was my pride and joy," and I was all like *crying* . . . That's the only thing I could do. I felt so bad, too. I went, "Cindi, why did you *do* that?" But I didn't mean to *wreck!* I didn't do it on purpose, "Oh, there's a telephone pole," (laughs) you know?

Your mom and your stepdad are really into material things?

Yeah, well, like Ricky *buys*. Ricky's the only one that's working, my stepdad, my mom's on disability—she had a back operation. And so like he buys *whatever!* You know, we own a boat, we have a horse, a horse trailer, the Supra, and then they're getting a pool, they bought a house, it's like, all their money would rather go on, you know, the material stuff. It's like all they ever do is buy, buy, buy.

And then when us kids wrecked it . . . (A long pause.) Like I wrecked the Supra and she's supposed to buy a new *Jeep*. So it's like the Supra really didn't *hurt* her that bad. You know. She was mad, but it didn't hurt her that bad, I don't think. If it had hurt her that bad, she wouldn't be able to go out and buy a new Jeep! Couldn't have hurt her *that* bad.

All her relatives are in Ohio. Her father lives nearby, but he hasn't come to see her in several years.

Like he don't want nothing to *do* with us. I don't see why he don't want to see us either. That's what I don't understand about it. He used to send us money and visit us on Christmas and special occasions like that, but now he don't do *nothing*. He don't even send us a birthday card, it's only sometimes. It's like—I don't know if *he's* into drugs or something, and like *his* life's going down the drain or something? I mean like he just don't have time for us kids, he has better things to do. But he has to see that, you know, my mom didn't have us on her own. He should be over there, too, helping out *her*.

He don't even pay child support. They got one of those, you know, citation things out for him, and they're not even doing it. It's been like two years. And they haven't caught him yet. If they really *wanted* to, they could. My real dad won't have nothing to do with his kids. He found out I was in here, because my boyfriend told him? And he goes, "Well, *I* can't do nothing." (Indignantly:) And he *can*, because he has custody over his kids still. And like, he just doesn't want nothing to do with us.

How come?

I think 'cause we're such a hassle! They gotta look back at all the mistakes they made on *their* parents. 'Cause I know like my Mom made a lot of mistakes. She popped up pregnant at the age of sixteen. Imagine what *her* mom did! It was like, Oh my God! . . . (Laughs.) Pregnant with me at age sixteen, I know her Mom *flipped*. But then *my* Mom has to look at me and say "Well, I made those mistakes," you know. I made worser ones than that.

But see, nowadays it's more drugs. That's what kids are more getting into, is drugs. Like *my* kids'll probably get into it real bad, but hopefully I can stop it before that happens. You know, "*I* went through that, you guys, and it's not a place to go." (Earnestly:) I want to teach them, you know, this ain't any life, this is *not*. And that was how my mom was trying to teach me, but I didn't see it. I was like "Shut up, you're always on my case." It was always "*Don't* drop out of school, *don't* get into drugs, *do* this, *go* to college . . ." You know? I was like "Why don't you shut up and get off my case!"

But she's trying to like *push* my life in that direction. You can't *push* your kid's life in that direction! You can't say, "You're going to college if you like it or not." That's that *kid's* life, not their parents'! And that's how she'd be with me, you know: "You're going to school. You're going to college." "You're gonna do this." I'd go "OK." You know.

She was working on glass containers 'cause she never finished high school. She never got her diploma or nothing. So I guess that's why she always told me, "You're gonna finish high school, you're gonna go to college." 'Cause she didn't want to see my life like hers. She had a back operation, she's supposed to go in again, they messed up, they forgot to take a disk out or something.

But when I was living out on the streets, it's like "Oh, my mom can't tell me to do nothing, I do what I want to." And it's good, too, you know, 'cause you get to party and all that, but then . . .

Like some nights me and Tommie didn't have a place to stay and we had to sleep in the car. (Disgusted:) And that got *ridiculous*. And then he wants to have a *kid*! Saying, "I want a *kid*!" And I'm saying, "Un-*uh*!" You know, I'm into *drugs*, I hate to see the kids that come out and . . . This is the kind of life I'm giving it? as me into drugs? No way! And then living in a *car*? I don't want to raise my kid in a *car*! You know? It's gonna be a bad life for a kid, I don't want to bring it in the world yet. But he didn't see that. He's all, you know, "Well, if we have a kid and get married, then I know I'll never lose you." I go "Well, I can divorce you, too." (Laughs.)

When we were living together, I could *not* talk to a guy. I had to ask him, "Tommie, can I go talk to that guy right there?" And I think it was mostly because of the drugs. Because the only time he griped if I was talking to a guy was if he was wired. But like if he was coming *down*, he was like "Get out of here, get out of here," you know? I could talk to any guy I wanted to, and he wouldn't think nothing of it. But if I went over and talked to a guy for five minutes when he was on wire and I came back, he'd say "Did you spread your legs for him?" And I was like "I was only over there for *five minutes*, Tommie, what can I do in five *minutes?*" He always thought bad of me when he was wired. Always thought that I'd go around and spread my legs for everybody. But when he was coming down, it was like "Get away from me, go talk to that guy over there," and he didn't care. So it was like when he was wired up, he was a great big old *macho*, I guess. Like "I've got an old lady and I boss her around," you know, wanted to show all his friends that he could. I was like "You don't boss *me* around, Tommie!"

That's the only thing I didn't like, was sleeping in cars. 'Cause like we slept in Iron City. It's like a bad neighborhood, some of the parts of Iron City's *bad*, and you'd be sleeping in Iron City and there'd be *black* people all walking around and stuff, there'd be black people selling rocks on the corner at three o'clock in the morning and stuff, and it's like you'd better watch out over in *that* area, they steal anything they can see! If they got a place for it, they'll just walk up and steal it. I guess it's the same in Rivertown, too. You know, if you're into drugs that bad, you'll steal them. But it was scary the couple times we had to, it's like you're on a street you've never seen, or been on, and it's like (head on her hands) "Oh, *God*," you know?

But it's hard, especially in a car you can't stretch *out* in, you're always scrunched in . . . Oh, God! Once in Rivertown they told us to leave and said they never want to see us in a car again. And then one in Iron City told us, "Well, you can't sleep here 'cause the neighbors are complaining." 'Cause they see a strange car. So we just got up and left.

He's nineteen years old and he won't work. He was telling me that I had to work to support him. I was all "Nuh-*unh*, I'm still going to school. *You're* the one that goofed up and dropped out of school, I'm not gonna drop out 'cause I have to support you, nuh-*unh!*" He *is* a druggie, you know. Like my mom always told me, "He's a *druggie*, he's a *lowlife*, he dropped out of *school*, he'll never have nothing." And I couldn't see that at the time. I was all "Well, I *like* him," and all this. And then it just kept more and more, and she kept on telling me he's bad, Cindi, he's bad news. And I could not see that.

I seen different. (Laughs.) Like "I don't know what you're *talking* about, Mom." She was right all that time. I mean he's *cute*, you know . . . (Laughs.) But then I started falling in *love* with him. But I don't think his part was love, for some reason. I think it was just "Oh, let's use *her*. She's young, she's never been in Juvenile Hall or nothing," and I think it was a game. I think he's been playing games on girls. But I didn't see that at the time. He's probably got another girlfriend already. You know, he's using *her* now. And it's *bad!* Some girl like me is gonna be put in here because of a guy like that again and have to go through the same things I'm going through right now.

Maybe when he gets older in life. Maybe when he starts *wanting* things. He's nineteen and he lives with his *mom* now, from what I heard. (Disgusted:) I mean like he don't have *nothing*. He has a car that's a *piece*—you have to stop and put water in the radiator, 'cause it's got a great big old *hole* . . . I don't know, it's like "Tommie, come *on*" . . . (Laughs.) Sooner or later he's gonna start wanting things and he's gonna learn "I'm gonna have to go out to get the things I want."

I got hit a couple of times. My mom knew about it, too. You know, but she like stayed out of it. She's all "Well, it's you and Tommie's problem." 'Cause she didn't know really what was all going on. I didn't tell her, "Oh, it's because of the wire." But she knew, 'cause I'd come home with bruises on me. And one time I came with a bruise on my cheek, and I lied to them and told them that we were down in the park and Tommie threw the football and hit me in my cheek? And then the school, my junior high school, they called them in on child abuse, because they thought my mom did it? I never told *any*body it was Tommie. If I'd told somebody it was Tommie, he's eighteen, nineteen, he'll get busted. They'll take him away from me! You know, and I'm all "I don't want that, I don't want that!" But now you know it don't make me no difference. 'Cause look who's suffering, *I* am. And he's still out there having fun. And I'm in here suffering, having to serve time. And it's not fun in here. I could be doing better things right now.

I do want to go to college. I want a good life. I want to go to college and become a veterinarian and then when I get older have my own business, like, you know, where *I'm* the head honcho and *I* tell people

what to do. And I want to have a life with a husband and own things
. . . I've always wanted to have things.

I've always wanted to have maybe only one kid. I don't know, it's like
I see how much me and my sister and brother give my mom a hassle, I
don't think I want, you know, three kids to give *me* all this hassle! (Laughs.)
It's like whoa! It's just too much. 'Cause I can see what my mom's going
through, it's like, *God!* if *my* three kids were to do that to me I would
tell them, "You get out of my life and never come back." (Laughs.) Only
she's hanging in there still, she's going "Yeah, you're welcome back."
And she's all "I've only got a couple years, and when you guys turn
eighteen, and you guys goof, I don't have to take you guys back if I don't
want you." You know? Which is true.

If I was president, I'd make for no drugs at all. I mean bust *everybody*
that's doing it. You know? Because there's gonna be kids that are growing
up like me . . . (Pauses.) Like what are they a use for? They kill people.
You have overdoses, right? And nobody gets cured by them. It's a waste
of people's money . . . Now when I see on the news that places get busted,
like those ships that come in and get busted, you know, I'm glad. But
when I was living on the street, I was like (horrified:) "Oh, *no!*" . . . I
hate to see the kids like me get into this. 'Cause it's not a good life.

They have all these programs, "Just say no, just say no." I seen those
and, you know, I didn't listen to it. I just ignored it and went on with
my own life. And I'd say that's what all the other kids do, too. They'd
say, "Oh, you know, the commercial." (Laughs.) And they'd go out and
try it theirself. I think that when kids see it advertised—"Just say no"?—
some kids don't know even what it means. Like I didn't know what it is
till I met Tommie and all, I didn't know that much was out there. Kids
see "Just say no" and they don't know about drugs, well, they'll say "Let's
go out and *try* it, we don't know what it is." It's like an *advertisement*, I
think, a little bit. Especially for all the kids that're like say sixteen and
don't know nothing about drugs? You know, haven't even heard about
it? Some kids don't even hear about it till they're eighteen, nineteen. And
they see "Just say no" to drugs, they're all "What's *drugs*? Well, let me
go out and try it!" You know, that's what gets you addicted right there.
It doesn't help!

But they should—I think in every school they should have a . . . just
like a class, and every kid in the school should go to it. And they should,
you know, show films of what happens to people, have people go in there

and say, "Well, I've been in Juvenile Hall. I had to go through it." And, you know, tell these kids that are just growing up, so they don't have to make the mistakes.

And these older people that are selling it to us little kids should know better not to. But all that they're looking for is the money! It's more money in their pocket, they don't care if that kid has an overdose or not, and it's sad because some kid'll go out there and have an overdose. I know if I was a dealer and I sold it to some little kid that had an overdose? I'd feel so bad. But some of these people, you know, "I got my twenty bucks I needed." That's just messed up, it's like it's not worth it. I would rather have a kid's life than twenty bucks. You know? But some people don't care! They'll say, "Oh, well," you know, "one less I have on my list."

I think it's sad especially that kids, their parents bring them on this earth, and they're into drugs. And then when they're little, the parents sit there and do it in *front* of the kids. That's messed up. 'Cause I have known people that do it in front of their kids. They was just *little* kids, and like they got a three-year-old, his name's Tyler? That I know? And he goes around and goes (she pretends to smoke) "Ssshoo! Want some?" Like a joint. And the dad sits there and *laughs*, ha-ha-ha! That's not funny! And he goes to school and goes, "Pshoo! want some?" And the teacher says, "Where'd you learn that from?" "My daddy." You know? It's all gonna catch up on the dad, watch.

Some people are into it so bad they'll sell their body for it. You know, "I'll swap you something for something." And that's just lowlife, I think, that is *way* down. I wasn't in it that bad.

Hopefully, by the time I have my kids they won't have to go through this. 'Cause I don't want this. Especially upon the kid. It's just a great big old hassle. Over stupid *drugs*. You don't even need them. I thought you needed them when I was living on the street. (Shakes her head, laughs.) "Yeah, I need it, I need it!"

I don't want to live all drugged out all my life, don't *own* nothing . . . (She's quiet for a minute.)

I don't care how fat I get now. If people don't like me, don't look my way. You don't gotta like me! There'll always be *somebody* out there that'll like me!

"Rocket Queen"

15

"I don't want to die, but I think I'm going to"

Me and this dude named Willis we cut school one day and ran over to this abandoned bus out in this field. And sittin' there, we were choppin' lines, and I'm all paranoid: "Hey, man, are you sure the cops ain't gonna come?" "Oh, no, man, I used to come here every day last year!" And I looked out the window and there were two squad cars sittin' out there, cops are gettin' out of the car, walking over to us: "The cops are here!" "*Nah*, are you serious?" "Yeah, I'm serious!" So he scoops up the wire into his hand, I grab my wallet, we take off running, and as he's running, he's got the wire in his hand and he's *lickin'* it as he's running and he's bustin' up laughin', and *I'm* bustin' up laughin', but we weren't bustin' up laughin' when they caught us and slammed us. Well, I don't know if they slammed *him*, but I know *I* got slammed.

He's intense, thin, drawn, with a shock of blond hair that usually falls over his eyes. Born in Rivertown, he has spent most of his fifteen years in a small semirural town, Harley, a few miles away.

Harley's main street is the highway running out of Rivertown into the countryside; lined with small strip malls, car lots, and gas stations, it roars all day with heavy truck traffic.

An avid rock fan, he chose his name from the title of a song by the popular hard-rock band Guns 'n Roses: "May be a little young," it begins, "but honey, I'm not naïve."

He's been in and out of county juvenile facilities since he was eleven, usually on drug charges, occasionally for robbery. This time he faces multiple drug charges: "It was cocaine, crystal meth, crank, and pot." He'll be sixteen in a few weeks: "It's my second birthday locked up and I'll probably be here for my seventeenth birthday, too."

"Let's just say the Harley police know me very well. We're on a first-name basis. And my mom is on a first-name basis with them.

"The other night cops came to my house, my mom's all 'Fuck you!' and yelling at 'em and shit? I tried to stop her from gettin' arrested. I was pulling her away, saying, 'Nah, man, you can't be saying that to the cops, I've tried,' and she's all, 'Fuck you, you can call the FBI, you can't make me do shit.' 'Yeah they can Mom, shut up!' (Laughs.) I got her in, I walked out, and I shut the door, and I was talking to the cop, you know, 'I'm really sorry, she's just drunk, I'll try to keep her down, sorry about the noise' . . ."

The first time I came to Juvenile Hall, it was because of drugs—well, not really 'cause of drugs, but it was drug-*related*. Walking through the field one morning before school—we cut about the first two periods of school because we didn't like the first two periods of school. And we were walking to school through a field in Harley, which was by my middle school, and we stopped to light a joint before school, and he lit it and threw down the match. And we started walkin'! And all of a sudden we heard this *crackling* and just turned around and looked and the *field* was on fire! (Laughs.) We ran and tried to stomp it out, and couldn't do that, so we just took off running. I guess some lady saw us and called the police, and they went down to the school and asked, you know, who came in from this time to this time. They knew right off who it was.

'Cause they *always* knew right off who it was. Whether it was us or not, they knew right off who it was.

After that I was in here four days. And I got out. And I swore like everybody else that I would never come back. I ended up gettin' arrested for cocaine abuse when I was about twelve and a half or thirteen. Plus it wasn't only cocaine abuse, it was for marijuana, too.

Smoked a lot of weed. When I was twelve years old, I overdosed on vodka. So the doctor told me if I ever drink again it could kill me. 'Cause I guess my liver was pretty thrashed. (Laughs.) So I try to avoid drinking.

I used to get drunk, smoke weed, I thought there were times I was gonna *die* 'cause my heart was beatin' so fast and I was just so *spun* on coke. Not with crank—I mean I can do a lotta crank and not really worry about it. But coke? Gets you going so fast, even though it's not for so long. 'Cause it feels like, it's not the same as crank, with coke you do it and you'll still be going the same, it don't feel like you're going the same 'cause you wanta do more to get back up to the same to where you were before? And then you do it, and then you get back up to where you were before, which now you're actually going faster but it *feels* like you're going like you were before, and then you start coming down a little bit and it feels like you came down a lot. So you do more, which gets you going even faster to get you back up maybe a little bit higher than where you were before.

I would do a lot of coke, a *lot* of coke. There were times when my nose'd be bleeding, I'd go to do more, my nose'd be bleeding even longer and longer, and it'd bleed and bleed and bleed and then when I couldn't get it to stop bleeding I'd be holding a napkin up . . . (Shakes his head, laughs.) Put it in my drink, I'd start *drinking* the shit! I had to get it in me *somehow*, you know, put it in water, put it in Pepsi, put it in, you know, *tequila*, which is my favorite, I love tequila. Oh, yeah, works just the same. Doesn't work as fast, but it works. It'll get you where you're going. Or I'd put it in a little like Zig Zag, or a little piece of napkin or something, swallow it? That'll do it. I'd smoke it. *That*'ll do it. (Thoughtfully:) Ain't never *shot* nothin', though, never plan to neither.

I'd wake up in the morning, do some crank, stay amped all day, or do some coke, stay amped all day, and then just get *wasted* on pot at night, so I could eat and go to bed. And that's the way it was for a long time. Starting first thing in the morning. When I first woke up. I weighed a hundred and twenty-eight pounds when I got out of my group home and like within a month I was weighing a hundred and two. So I was dropping some very drastic weight and everybody could tell. Everybody knew something was going on.

I was selling dope. I was selling coke, I was selling crank, I was selling pot. I used to get a gram, which is like four quarters, which really isn't nothing, I'm just using it for an example. But they charge you like sixty bucks for a gram and then you can make like seventy-five bucks—well, you make like fifteen, twenty bucks. Well, actually I was sellin' for twenty a quarter, so that'd be eighty bucks. I'd get sixty bucks, 'cause that's what I owed *them*, and then I'd *do* the rest, the other twenty, so I wasn't makin' any money, I was doing it all. That's how I got my dope, I never paid no money for it, not from *my* pocket anyways.

Though it's just a small town, Harley has a thriving drug culture. There have been several well-publicized crackdowns on metham-phetamine labs in the area, and large seizures of marijuana. But they've made little difference in the booming local drug market. He thinks fewer people sell drugs now than before, but "the ones that do sell are selling more."

'Cause it's fun. It's the thing to do. It's the eighties. Just like they say, man, it's sex, drugs, and rock and roll. (Laughs.) It is. That's how it is where I come from. In my town it's sex, drugs, and rock and roll. That's all there is. In fact, damn, I'm surprised that that little town ain't got a whole *shitload* of people in here! I'm serious.

I think it's 'cause it's such a small town. They really ain't got nothing else to *do*. Except for go to Rivertown. And Rivertown, what are they doing there? Sex, drugs, and rock and roll! I think just about anywhere you go now, sex, drugs, and rock and roll.

You know, like—you see people that are clean and sober? And it's like a lot of people: "Oh, they're stupid." But not me, I think that's really good. I wish *I* was clean and sober! (Laughs.) Just 'cause they're doing something *you* can't, why put them down? That's the way I used to think though, too, you know, "How could you *not* want to get stoned?" You know? Now that I see where it keeps gettin' me time after time, I can see how they don't want to get stoned.

Some people say it's just too hard to be straight.

Yeah, it's boring. It is *real* boring to be sober. It's boring, it's not fun. You know, they say you can have fun without drugs, which, yeah, you can, but you can have more fun *any* day with drugs. And I know that. And that's why it can be so hard. Because anybody that tells you that they've done drugs and don't like it is either lying to you or they're stupid. I mean I'm glad for people that aren't doing drugs, but, uh . . . (Trails off.)

Do you have a dream, something you really want to do when you get out of here?

In my life? (Smiles.) Being as big a band as Guns n' Roses, but I mean that's just about impossible. No, I'd say if I got dreams . . . I'd like to just essentially get over my drug addiction and do something creative with my life. Like become an electrical technician, something like that, something along that line, be a machinist, for [the power company], you know, something that I think I'd be good at. 'Cause I like working with electricity and wires and stuff like that, I guess from all the car stereos I ripped off, I don't know! (Laughs.) I like to fix things. And I've got a two-hundred-and-seventy-five-dollar gold ring that I made, and I like making jewelry. I fixed a lot of necklaces and stuff, bracelets. And I like that. I'd like to do something like that.

And maybe when I get older do something to help kids in here even though . . . (He stops, frowns.) I don't know . . . I'm afraid if I did help kids in here it'd be like people who've tried to help *me*. And it wouldn't do no good anyways. (Hesitates.) And I hope someday I make it before I end up dead, because I was doing some serious shit.

Like, uh, inhaling inhalants, you know, gasoline . . . I was addicted to that for a long time. Every day. I'm scared to death I'm not gonna have a chance to grow up. I want it so bad now I'm afraid I'm gonna die real young. In fact, I'm afraid I'm gonna be dead before I'm seventeen or eighteen.

That's not very long . . .

That's not very long at all. It's scary. (Softly:) 'Cause I was . . . I mean I'd go through two or three cans of hairspray a day. And that's not saying how many cans of mousse, or shaving cream.

I never did that . . . what's it like to do hairspray?

Well, take off the lid and you shake it real good—only with Aquanet, that's the only one I've found, the *old* Aquanet cans with the little white buttons. You know, the big round cans, the normal Aquanet cans, not the new ones. They're the ones that've been around for a while. And you take 'em, shake it up, turn it upside down and you press the valve, hairspray'll come out. And after a while the hairspray'll stop coming out and air'll come out, and you inhale that. And after a while, you just start . . . seeing things . . . and totally leave reality.

When I was sniffing gasoline, I went out of reality a few times. I was just lucky I'm not dead. I was sniffing gasoline one time, walked into my house, and we had a big wall clock hanging on the wall. And all of sudden my nose grew into like a big carrot thing but it wasn't a carrot? And I turned my head this way and it hit the clock and the clock swung and went all the way out and then went back down, and then I swung again and my nose hit the clock again . . . And I don't know, it's just . . . I try not to do it no more. When I go home, I don't sniff gas, and hairspray ain't something that I do—maybe once in a while—'cause I know how bad it is and I know I'm gonna die from it. And I guess I'm addicted to that, too.

I never done it with nobody else. It was always something that it was just *me*. I think my friends kind of got suspicious though when I was running down, you know, two or three four times a day to buy another can of hairspray . . . (Laughs.)

What were you feeling—what kind of state of mind were you in, when you'd go get a can of hairspray?

(Thoughtfully:) To tell you the truth, I don't even know *what* in the world ever made me start. Nobody ever told me if you held a can of hairspray—it was just logic to me, that if you held a can of hairspray upside down, all the stuff was gonna go down and the little stem would be up at the top and just air would come out, and everybody I've ever talked to has never even *heard* of that! But, uh, what made me do it? That's a good question. Guess 'cause—I wasn't getting tested for it, it wouldn't show up on my tests. It made me high. It was what I would imagine heroin would be like, PCP. It took me higher than any fry* I ever did. Oh, yeah. I've done four-way windowpane, I've tweaked really hard, but doin' *that* I tweaked a *lot* harder a lot of times than any drugs I've ever done. I've never done heroin, PCP, or anything like that. But hairspray . . . inhalants is definitely the most potent thing I've ever done.

Four-way windowpane?

That's when they take a hit of fry and dip it four times so it's four times the strength. In fact, the first time I ever did fry, it was that, so I was just (Laughs:) *whoo!* Melting into the ground! We were out fishing at the Rivertown power plant cause my dad works at the power company, my stepdad. And it was late at night and this diesel was going over the Rivertown bridge, and right when it got up top, that whole bridge just *melted!* I went Whoooaaa! . . . (His eyes are round and staring.) And my dad's all like "What's going *on*?" . . . I'm glad it was dark that night, 'cause if he would've took one look at my eyes, he would've kicked my ass from here to anywhere.

I got out on a temporary release, not last week but the week before. I got out and I didn't want to do drugs and I didn't *need* to do drugs and I prayed I wouldn't *do* drugs, but I did drugs anyway. And that really bothered me, 'cause I didn't want to do it, but then I did it anyway. I figured that was just pure stupidity.

I just hope I can do it. I'm gonna give it a shot and a half.

It sounds like you're trying to do it by yourself . . . is there anybody out there you feel you can lean on, to help you get through it?

Yeah, I got one friend I can really, really, really count on, that's my friend Ray, my best friend, we're like brothers. He's getting married. I'm best man at his wedding as a matter of fact, but I'm not going. I'm locked up. (Disgusted with himself:) Just turned eighteen, I was locked up for his *birthday*, too. He's got a stepkid. He's happy.

---

* LSD.

*But he's only eighteen—what about adults, like your family,
other people you trust?*

I got my Uncle Matt in Cherry Grove. And I got my great-grandma,
but she's not doing too good. She's gettin' up there, she's not doing too
good at all. Got my Uncle Jay, who's not doin' any better.

I had a girlfriend that was nineteen years old. Shit, I feel if I was still
with her I wouldn't be where I am right now. I *know* I wouldn't be.
'Cause it was right after we broke up that I got in trouble. It was me, Ray,
Darlene, and Michelle, we were just all buddies, you know, it was *us*.
Real good friends. We did just about everything together, you know? We
used to go on adventures together . . . I could tell you some stories about
stuff we've done. It's funnier than shit. And Darlene's going in the army
now. (Quietly:) It's strange how we all went our separate ways. Michelle
lives in Hillview now, I'm in Juvenile Hall, Darlene's going in the army
for four years, and Ray's gettin' married . . . It's weird how things change.

Me and him are still best friends. Me and Vicki are like best friends.
But they're doing what they *want* with their life, *I'm* going in the Hall
again. Like the same thing over and over again. (Shakes his head.) I don't
know where I'm goin'. You heard that song by Whitesnake, "Here I Go
Again"? Well, here I go again! You know, this is how it happened with
the *last* group of friends I had. Really good friends—they went their
separate ways and I came *here*. That's why I want to change so bad, is
because I'm tired of things going good for everybody else, you know, and
not good for me.

I'm scared to death to go to this drug rehab they're gonna send me to.
Scared shitless it ain't gonna work, and I want it to. Hope it does. I want
to be at home. And I just hope it works. I want to do drugs very badly,
don't get me wrong, I mean I'd love nothing more than right now to just
do what I could. But I can tell the impact it's having on my little brother
'cause I'm settin' a bad example for him.

*His biggest regret is "not giving more time to my little brother,
not spending more time with him."*

'Cause I don't think I got much time left. I grew up without a dad
pretty much, *he's* gonna grow up without a dad, and I wish I could've

been there, even though he's just a little kid. And to help my sister out. I think those are my two biggest regrets in my life.

And my mom works a lot. She got her job 'cause she wanted to get out of the house a little bit, but her and my dad broke up, so now she has the job 'cause she *has* to have the job. So she leaves my brother alone, a lot more than she left *me* alone. And that's another reason I wish I could spend more time with him, because I felt sorry for him, I really do. I guess having an older brother like me don't help.

What's an older brother like you?

You know . . . a thrash. Thrash? A thrash means to me somebody that don't care enough about their life or about their family to stop doing something that they know for a fact is killing them, and they know they're gonna die from it at a very young age, and they're not gonna have the time to spend with their family. 'Cause they're gonna be locked up probably for the rest of their *life*. I hope I live to a ripe old age, but since I don't think I will, I'd say the rest of my life. That's what I consider a thrash, someone who don't give a fuck about nothin' or nobody but themselves.

I don't know how I'm gonna do it. My mom's not helping much. But I just hope I can turn it around. I really do. Sometime. (Laughs.) I think if I got my hair cut so I could see where I'm walking, that'd help a lot, too. My mom's probably either gonna put me in a foster home, or she's gonna put me up for adoption. She won't come visit me no more. I'd ask her if I could come home, get another chance. But I ain't gonna ask for it.

Me and my mom used to be really close, and then she met my stepdad, which she's not seeing no more. But that's when things really started to change. She kind of went senile, I guess . . . lunaticking? She started drinking a lot, she started throwing stuff at him, she started throwing stuff at *me*, for no reason, just to *throw* stuff, I guess. That's when I started getting in trouble, was when she started throwing stuff.

What kind of stuff?

Oh, man, I've had to duck from beer bottles and cans and ashtrays, whole pots of spaghetti and whole bowls of salad, you know? (Shakes his head.) I'm talking about *pots* of spaghetti! She's woken me up in the middle of the night and beat me up and shit when she's drunk. She's come after me with baseball bats . . .

Baseball bats?

Yeah . . . her new boyfriend Jack? Which I really like, the first guy I really liked yet, he's a really good guy, he knows what's going on, he knows where I've been, 'cause I guess he's been through it before. I guess you could say he's a thrash, too; a no-good *adult* punk, I guess you'd put it. (Laughs.) And he's a good guy. My mom came after me with one baseball bat—she opened the closet door and grabbed a baseball bat, started to come after me. And he said, "No, you'll kill him!" And she goes, "I *know!*" (Laughs.) And he took the baseball bat from her, she turned around and grabbed *another* baseball bat and ran at me again! And I just got out the door, right when I saw her swinging the bat at me, and I just shut the door right when the bat hit the wall. And a couple days later when I walked in there, I looked, and where she hit the wall, there was a *dent* in it, about a good inch-and-a-half dent, and all the paint was knocked off. She thrashed that wall pretty good—I'm glad it wasn't me! (Laughs.) Tell you what, I definitely would have broke a bone. If she'd of hit me.

It's not only bats, she comes after me with *vacuum* cleaner tubes—she's came close with one of those, but (smiles) I ran fast, you know. She's hit me with *beers*, she threw a bottle of liquid heat at me, hit me in the face with it! She's hit me with ashtrays . . . just about anything else, though, I can dodge, I'm gettin' quick now!

But what's that about? Why do you think she treats you that way?

I think either she's having this stress, 'cause she does have a lot of stress, or she thinks I'd be better off dead, or maybe she's just tired of seeing me get in so much trouble. And feels she'd have to kill me if I'm gonna change. I don't know.

She works a lot. And she had my brother and sister to take care of. I was never home anyways 'cause I was always out doing my thing. It took a toll on her after a while. She used to be a real cleaning fanatic, now she's just like "Fuck it," she don't care no more, I guess. (Softly:) I don't know, she just changed. She works in a deli, which don't sound like too much, but I've been there before to help them out. And I'll tell you what, the place gets *packed*, and they get bitchy, they get rude, they're real assholes sometimes. In fact, one day a cop came in there and was really being a real jerk to my mom, and I told him straight up that he could just sit down and shut his pig-ass mouth or fuckin' *leave*. He just looked at me real funny and left. (Laughs.) I shouldn't have said that, but I did, because I was gettin'—you know, it gets *hot* in there, them cooking and stuff, and I can see where she's stressed a lot, you know.

She has trouble making her house payment and stuff, which we just got evicted. We have to be out either by the next thirty days or by the end of June. I don't know . . . She works under the table, making about five dollars an hour in the deli; she gets my Social Security check, which is five hundred dollars a month—well, its four thirty-something, four thirty-six or something like that a month. My sister's, which is the same, and hers. Now that adds up to over a thousand dollars, plus she makes about a hundred, something like that, a week. I don't know what happened to all the money. Seems to me she ought to have been able to afford, you know, five hundred seventy-five dollars, or however much it was . . . plus food and the other bills . . .

I think for a while there, a while back, she was getting pretty deep into a lot of crank and a lot of coke, which I can't say nothing about that, 'cause I think I was gettin' in a lot deeper than she was. A *lot* deeper. (He's quiet for a long time, looking off into the distance.)

I hope I . . . I hope I live, I don't want to die. But I think I'm going to.

Saffron Bailey

"I'm all drugged out"

The day I came in here for my court, I got all my friends, got high right before court. Went in court high, but didn't nobody notice. (Laughs.) High on cocaine. It was funny.

I have *dreams* about it sometimes. I wake up in the morning being like *this* (she gestures, her hand in front of her mouth), like I'm holding a pipe. And I have dreams that I'm smoking cocaine and stuff, and I have hallucinations because I guess I *don't* have drugs! And they give me medicine for that: Haldol, Cogentin, or something like that?* But they've been giving me that medicine since I was ten years old because I was seeing things and going crazy. Alcohol and drugs'll get to you! (Laughs.) When I go on the outs, instead of them, I take *regular* drugs. Then I come in here, I take *these* drugs. (Smiles.) I'm all drugged out. These drugs, my drugs . . . *Something's* in my system. (Laughs.)

She's a soft-spoken, personable white girl who speaks with a heavy black street accent. Her family roots are in small-town Appalachia,

---

* "Antipsychotic" drugs.

but she has spent most of the past five years on the streets of River County, mainly in the black ghettos of Iron City: "On the street, walking around all night long, going to the shelters." She speaks slowly, as if nearly asleep; she suffers from hallucinations and severe depression, and she's on medication most of the time. She's been bounced back and forth from Juvenile Hall to several crisis shelters in the county and nearby; most recently, she was picked up in Iron City in a police raid on a freebase cocaine party.

Me and around six guys was in this like room? I don't know what kind of room, it had a hot-water heater and that's all, in these apartments. And we were all in there 'basing cocaine, and the police came in there and busted us and was pointing guns right into our *faces* and stuff. And I was so *scared* . . . They threw us on the ground. And then, everybody was over eighteen except me. They said, "Did these guys make you *do* anything?" I said I wasn't doing anything. 'Cause they didn't see any pipe or nothing in my mouth, they just found the stuff. And nothing was *on* me. And they said, "How old are you?" I said, "Fifteen," and they almost died. And then they took me home and said, "She better not leave this house tonight." And it was only eight o'clock, and I was mad, so I changed my clothes so the police wouldn't notice me and (laughs) went right back outside.

She's been doing drugs since she was ten. "What happened, I seen everybody using drugs and drinking so I started drinking alcohol a lot, like beer at first. Now I drink Cisco. It's a kind of wine, but it gets you real drunk? And most teenagers drink that. And then I started smoking weed. And that lasted till I was around thirteen. And then when I was thirteen, I was in this group home, and had went and snorted some crank and stuff? And then they put some cocaine and some weed to make a gremmie? And that was the first time I did that, but then when I got fifteen last year?—we smoked some coke, based some coke, and smoked some crank off some foil. I never shot up or nothing like that, but I was getting into cocaine a lot. It was like every day."

And I think that kids take drugs to cover up for . . . (hesitates:) the things that happen. They get raped . . . sexually abused . . . mentally abused, parents fighting, you know, parents hitting on them, doing things like that.

It's not like I *need* it or nothing—I can go days and days without smoking, drinking, or anything—but then it's just the fun of it. There's some bad times too, though.

I had a bad time . . . (She starts to drift off, catches herself.) I had gotten real, real drunk and high off cocaine, I had smoked a lot of cocaine? And this guy . . . he had tried to make me ho' for him, and so we was in Iron City and I was trying to escape from him. So I was *acting* like I was gonna ho', and I was just gonna get in anybody's car and tell him to take me home. So I got in the wrong person's car, this young guy's car, and I should've knew better than to get in a *young* guy's car, 'cause, you know, they're *crazy* . . . (Laughs.) And then he had raped me and I was so high and I was so scared, and then *he* tried to make me ho'! (Laughs.) And then I got out and got into *another* young guy's car, but the next young guy he bought me a hotel room and left me there with a whole bunch of cocaine. So I was high, I smoked myself to sleep. Most of the time cocaine keeps you awake, but if you put it in weed, it makes you kind of sleepy, so I put it with some weed to make sure I went to sleep. I woke up the next morning, I was *sore* (laughs) and I was wondering *how* I got in this hotel room . . .

When I was ten years old, my mother had left me in Iron City all by myself. And she went away for almost a year and I had to survive on my own, so I was stealing clothes to get like little hotels, and stuff like that? And get my own food and stuff.

We was living in Hillview, and she had a boyfriend and he always used to hit on her and stuff and she used to take drugs. Now she's a Jehovah's Witness, but she used to take drugs and she used to tell us kids to stay out until five in the morning and stuff like that, let us stay out all night long with the other boys and stuff? Sometimes we didn't eat. We went over to this crazy house—well, not really crazy, but they had kind of the mentally insane people, insane-asylum house or something? And we used to go over there and go to the stores for some of them and they'd give us five or ten dollars, so we'd go eat at a hamburger stand or something.

But she left, I guess because he was hitting her and stuff. She just up and left. One day I came home from school and I never seen her again for a long time.

After your mom split, did anybody help you out?

No. Nobody. Well, her boyfriend, sometimes; he'd give me something to eat or let me stay at his house. The mean one. And that was about it. And my friend's mother, when she was alive, she'd help me some and stuff. But nobody hardly.

And I was stealing stuff. And I got caught stealing sweat suits, and then I went to a foster home. And then my first stepfather, his mother got, you know, authority over me, guardian over me? And I lived in with her . . . (Softly:) And then one day my mother called her and she asked her, "Have you seen Saffron?" And my grandmother said—I just call her my grandmother 'cause that's the only grandmother I know, but I know I have another one in West Virginia—said, "Yes, she's right here, do you want to talk to her?" And I just took the phone and hung up in her face.

Most of that time I was living by myself or with my friend and her mother, which was also a dope addict? And she overdosed on dope and stuff. And most of the time, I was stealing sweat suits and selling them so I could get some money to eat and sleep places and stuff. Sweat suits got up from thirty to seventy dollars. 'Cause Adidas and stuff, at the time they cost forty or more dollars. (Laughs.) Hillview Mall, that was the *place*. That's where I first got caught. That's why I went to the foster home.

And then one time I went right down here to this big store down here, this big store that they closed up? A supermarket? And I went in there and I stole all this stuff and put a vest over it and I walked out of the store. And the boy said, "Ma'am, this is not a laundromat!" (Smiles.) And I walked out and I put *that* down and I went, I got another vest, and I filled up and put my dress over it, and he said, "Ma'am, I told you, this is not a laundromat!" and I said, "You stupid fool," I said, "I'm *stealing* your stuff!"

And he looked at me, and I had on all these sweat coats and these sweatpants, I had like *six pair* on, and then he said, "Well, I got to go tell my manager; don't run." I said, "I'm not gone run!" I *wanted* to get caught then because I didn't feel too safe being on the street by myself then. (Quickly:) Somebody was after me and stuff. So he went, and they said, "Hold it, don't run!" I said, "I'm not going *no*where." It was funny. At first, he said since I was so helpful and cooperative, and I told him everything I stole and everything, he was gone set me loose. And he said since they got all their property back . . . and I said, "But you didn't!" (Laughs.) I lied and said he didn't, but he did. But I *said* he didn't, so he locked me up and it was OK.

Who was after you?

This guy named Kenny? He's twenty-eight now. And he's put me in the hospital before. I knew him ever since I moved to Iron City—I was about twelve or thirteen when I moved to Iron City. And at first, you know, he was like my boyfriend? And then when I broke up with him, he became mean, and that's when I told you he tried to pimp me? Last time I seen him he busted my lip and almost busted my jaw open, and . . . you know . . . he just beat me *up*, period, and put me in the hospital. And I had to go down to the police station and take pictures and stuff and he went to jail and now he's out again. He knew I lived in Eastville in Iron City, but he doesn't know I live in Hillview yet, and I hope he never finds out.

Every time he tries to make me ho' for him, he gets me out to the ho' show to prostitute for him? And he gets me *out* there, but then I leave him! I leave him right there. I get in the car and I tell him to take me home. And Kenny'll be out there all by himself. I mean (laughs) he should *know* after all these times I'm gonna keep doing that. He should just leave me alone. But he won't. And he knows that he can be put in jail because I'm only—well, I'll be sixteen this month and he's twenty-eight. It's a trip.

When I was thirteen, I had a boyfriend named Ricky, and every time he got jealous, 'cause if I looked up and looked the wrong way at a guy, he'd hit me. One time he tried to make me work for him just to test me out, and then he beat me up and stuff and then never again did he ever try that. And then Kenny, and . . . just *people*, I mean I got hit from people that I don't even know, for *other* people, you know? (Laughs.) Like "*Pow!* This is for so-and-so," and the person don't even *be* there, and I'll be there not knowing what to do. And then two of my best friends, two girls, jumped me because I had some drugs and they wanted them! So

I've been in gang wars fighting over drugs. I'm not the fighting type. If I have to fight, I guess I have to.

I got hit from my *principal*! When I went to the Catholic school. When I cut school in the third grade. I got hit with a wooden shoe, like a hard wooden shoe. And she's hitting me with it, and I almost got her tooken to jail, 'cause I was screaming and the police was there and it was like child abuse, they thought. I think I got mentally abused by other people, sometimes just people screaming and yelling . . . when people scream and yell I get so upset . . . but *physically* abused maybe, now that I'm older, from me being streetwise I get physically abused too much, (vaguely:) mentally abused too much . . . it's just hell.

It was a Catholic school, and if your mother give them permission to hit you, then they have permission to hit you. And in third grade, I mean she would *hit* me. (Laughs.) And I screamed and hollered, and then I got home and got hit with a *comb*, just a comb, and I got hit by three or four people at home! (Laughs.) My aunt, my uncle, my grandmother, *and* my mom—I don't remember if my stepdad hit me or not. And it was like I got a whippin' *all* that day. It was a trip. And all I did was cut school one day with a next-door neighbor that went to public school. And the only reason they found me was because I had a Catholic uniform. It's like there's not too many people that cut school in Catholic school and so . . . Only girl in the Cherry Grove Mall that has on a Catholic uniform. They said, "Are you this girl?" I said no! But I looked the same. And they took the picture the day before I did it. I said, "No, that's not me!"

Then when I got into fifth grade, I started cutting school more, and cutting school *more*, and I flunked the fifth grade and never went to the sixth, never went to the seventh—went to half of the seventh—never went to the eighth, and got skipped to the ninth. From being old enough, being more mature and being too streetwise . . . (frowns) they didn't want me around the younger children. And plus, if it comes down to it, I'm smart enough to, but most of the time I don't want to use that. I'd rather be more streetwise than schoolwise.

Did you learn much when you were at school?

I learned stuff, but my mind was on different things, you know. Sometimes I'd come to school drunk. And I went with the principal's son, and I think that's the only reason I got passed. And all the time I was cutting school in the ninth grade, I was at the principal's house (laughs), that was what was funny about it. See, the principal's son had already graduated from high school, so he would fake sick to not go to college, and then he'd call me up and say, "Come on over," after his mother left and went to *my school!* And I'd say, "OK, here I come." And I'd say, "Mom, I'm going to school now." And went over to his house.

I'm gonna be in the twelfth grade. I got skipped up a grade when I was in the eighth, 'cause they said I was too mature and too streetwise. And I think that's the only reason. But I'm a good reader and stuff, so I passed the reading comprehension twelfth-grade exam. And I'll probably go to NA or AA; try, at least. It's gonna be hard, but I'll try.

And, I don't know, I just want things to be *quiet.* I'm not gonna stay outside so much anymore. I'm not gonna go all these places where there's all these hoodlums that I'll be with.

I'll just walk down the street and somebody'll be "Hey baby!" and I'll be "What's up?" And we'll be talking, and they'll become my friend. And half the guys that I know, they say, "That's my girlfriend"—everybody thinks I'm their girlfriend! And then they get into "Aren't you who girl-friend, are you his or mine?" And I'll be like "Neither!" and they'll get in big fights. And I get into it, and they try to hit me and all types of things happen . . . (Drifts off.) It's a trip.

I'm scared I'm gonna take drugs again, cocaine mostly. I'm not too worried about the alcohol, 'cause I can drink every now and again and leave it alone. But cocaine, I'm scared. And I'm scared I'm gonna not go to school and mess up for some reason. And I'm also scared that I might see Kenny. I'm scared of that man. I'm scared to *death* of that man. And I just don't want to see him.

I talked to the police and I talked to everybody, but they said till he hits me and they *see* it or something, they can't do nothing about it. I was in Eastville and the policeman was right *there,* and he hit me and nothing happened, because it was a all-black neighborhood and the po-liceman was white and he didn't do nothing. It was like he was scared that they was gonna *jump* him if he did something, which *could* have been true. But still, he's supposed to help *me.*

If you were the president . . .

I'd take money out of the bank and give it to the people like in Ethiopia and stuff. I would do that. And I would—if I was president of *any* country, not just this country, I don't know, president of the world? Some of these countries that got racial things? I would change that . . . Though I don't like Chinese people. 'Cause I hate—early in the morning, I remember this when I used to go to Catholic school, early in the morning I'd get on the bus and they'd be "Ching ching yong" and I'd be all "My ears! Oh!" (Laughs.) When you just wake up, and you don't speak that language, it's not a polite thing to wake up to.

I'd be rich. (Laughs.) I'd put Kenny in jail, for life.

I'd give people more money, because I know when they have kids and it comes around Christmas and they only get one present, that's kind of sad. 'Cause I've had that happen to *me* before, only one present. It was a nice present, 'cause when you're ten years old and you get a Walkman, it's nice, but . . . (Smiles.) Now I want a Moped.

Do you think you're going to get one?

No.

"I couldn't eat, 'cause the food was moving"

I tried PCP when I was nine or ten. I don't really remember the effects, but I remember doing it again when I was twelve or thirteen. And it also caused me to get into a severe fatal car accident. Almost killed me. I spent ninety days in a mental hospital for that.

Half Hispanic, half black, with tight cornrows framing a striking face, she has the poise and beauty of a model. Before her parents split up, she lived with them in one of the intact lower-middle-class neighborhoods in Iron City. But she's been "on the streets, mostly" since she was twelve. "I'm gay, I live with an older woman, and me and her have been having a relationship close to two years now. There's a fifteen-year difference in our relationship. But I know that she loves me a lot and I love her a lot, we been through a lot together. And drugs is one of my main problems right now. And I'm gonna try to get it together, and she is, too, for the sake of each other, know what I'm saying? So I'm supposed to go to a drug rehab. And I don't know what the outcome is gonna be, of course, but I just hope something happens, you know, something good."

When I graduated from elementary school, I was a top student. But first of all, my mother had a cocaine problem. She started using cocaine, freebasing, in the early eighties, I'd say. OK, this split my family, this right here, OK? My mother went to treatment, her job had paid for her treatment, and then she did the program, she made it, she got out, she was trying to get her shit together. My father was still using, he would not quit using. And the people told my mom, you know, "well, if your husband's using, that's gonna bring you down." So they convinced her to get a divorce. She got a divorce—my dad refused to sign the divorce papers for like three years. So this brought on a lot of changes in my life.

'Cause I started my puberty when I was, I'd say, eleven. You know, I started growing up and going through changes. And when I was younger, I used to always *wish* that my parents would get a divorce, and so when they did, it was a shock to me. And I thought it was my fault, so I blamed it on myself, you know? And my parents played me the middle—it's "Go tell this bitch I said *that*," and "Go tell that bastard I said *this*," and that's when I really was messed up, that's when I first ran away from home. I was eleven or twelve.

But when I was graduating from elementary school, I had gotten a scholarship, savings bond, two hundred dollars, I was on TV—for black history month, couple of schools had programs for black history month—and I went over there to say some speeches, Martin Luther King speech, it was over the radio, I was in a magazine, and all this stuff. When I was younger. And once I hit junior high school, it was a total complete change-around.

Seventh grade was my hardest year in my life for me, OK? I had got into a lot of things. Mostly drugs and alcohol. OK, alcohol was my main problem in seventh grade, and marijuana. And I used them daily and I found myself blacking out in school, found myself being not interested, found myself getting into fights with my mom, because one minute I wanted to be with my dad, one minute with my mom, I didn't know, I was confused, they were playing me in the middle, and I was going back and forth between Hillview and Iron City.

And I just found myself bouncing back and forth, and on the streets a lot, in all kinds of situations.

Other times, I was out on the streets of my own choice. But they had tooken me out of my home because I was a problem child. My mother and I had started getting into fights physically and stuff, and so I had went to foster homes, group homes, and it didn't work out. So they sent me over here. I started getting into these little gangs. And me and this little gang got together. (Matter-of-factly:) And we went down, and we decided we'd get drunk and beat up on this lady and take her purse. So we did. And that's the first time I was in here, like three or four years ago.

Also, I was pregnant during that time, and I lost my—I didn't *lose* my child, I mean I had her, but she was taken away from me, the courts took her away. Because I was so badly involved in drugs. So I'm sixteen right now, I'll be seventeen in November—I was supposed to have a chance to get her back this year, right, but unfortunately because of my past drug history and because I've been in mental institutions twice, they won't give me a chance to get her back. So I had to legally give her up for adoption to some nice people, these white people, they live in Michigan. They have a nice home and everything. I heard she was doing real good.

She should be four years old in June.

I was twelve. I was, you know, out there in the streets doing my own thing, got caught up with the wrong crowd, and I had got raped. And see—I've been gay all my life. So I've always had a lot of problems with males couldn't accept it, you know. And they said, "Well, you know, you're too good of a looking female to be gay," you know, "and I'll just stick it *to* you, and then you'll just learn." But little do they know that that's just something that makes a woman draw farther away from it.

In 1986 I started freebasing cocaine. I was with a girlfriend of mine —I had been to a placement, fell in love with this girl, and me and her ran, we lived together for two years! (Laughs.) And for our age it is really shocking, how we made it, OK? We had our own apartment, this was down in Valley City, it was really a trip. And I started freebasing, that is how I got introduced to that.

That is a dangerous drug . . . cocaine, crack, is a dangerous drug. My mother used it back in the early eighties, before they sold it on the street? My father and mother, they'd buy their own coke and rock it up themselves. Nowadays, you get out there and you buy your shit, you don't know *what* you gettin', you know. I've smoked some *bad* shit before. (Laughs.) But after what happened to my mom, and I seen her when I was younger, I said, I won't *never* do cocaine in my life, you know.

And I ain't never said never again, 'cause I started doing it, and I started liking it, and that was when I started out again with the PCP.

I was doing at this time marijuana, LSD, alcohol, PCP, *and* cocaine. OK, I was doing *all* these things, mostly to a daily basis. I was doing any and every drug that I could do. I was experimenting with hero-ine at one time, which I'd *never* do again, and I can say that for a fact. (Laughs.) Because the high was nice, but the sickness was . . . (Shakes her head.) And I've seen a lot of people in and out of different institutions . . . And when I was in the mental ward, I seen this *baby* who was going through withdrawals and it really scared me. And I said, "Well, I'll never get on a drug that makes me go through that, never," you know.

So my cocaine habit got more progressive. I found myself being able to quit, but not for long. I'd want to go out there and use again. So finally I got so tired of being on the streets that I got in trouble and I got sent to the Hall.

So I went to court and I told the judge I had a drug problem, I need help. So I went to this drug rehab, in 'eighty-seven? I ran from there, because I didn't need to be in a program for a whole year.

So I got myself out there, and this time it was selling drugs *and* using drugs. Last time it wasn't that, but now it was selling drugs *and* using drugs. To keep up my habit, supply my high, and whatever.

I had a girlfriend who was in sobriety, and she was clean, and she was younger. And I mostly had relationships with older women all my life. She was dallying with herself between, you know, whether she was bisexual or whether she was homosexual. And I couldn't accept her going out with guys and going out with me, too. You know. Plus, we always tried to practice safe sex, and she wasn't using condoms with these guys or what-ever, and I was *really* scared, you know? Especially with the teens, in my generation, there's a lot of diseases going around. And I just said, "Hey, man, you know, I can't deal with it." Because with my old lady, the one I have now, I know I don't have to worry about catching a disease, because me and her, it's monogamy, it's me and her, you know, there's no one else involved in our relationship.

It was kind of hard for me, being gay. Getting accepted. I brought my girlfriend to the sophomore dance, and that shocked the *hell* out of every-body. (Laughs.) And I said, "Hey, I have no shame on my game," straight up. Because I am a young gay person and there's no doubt in my mind that I'm gonna be gay for the rest of my life. (Grins.) I was in my school newspaper and everything. And everybody was all shocked and shit. I used to be a closet queen, quote unquote, for a long time. I was bisexual for a long time, only for a cover-up, because I didn't want to be rejected, OK?

It was time for the proms and all that, you know, high school dances were coming up, so my dad said he was gonna rent me a limo and everything, for that night. So I got a tux, and she got a tux too, 'cause I mean I'm not real feminine, and I'm not real masculine, I'm just, you know, *me!* And I don't believe in that. You know some people think, well, who's the man, who's the woman? It doesn't always have to be like that, you know. Because in my relationship now, of course since my old lady's older than me, I listen to her, and I do like she says, but then, we give each other feedback, she'll listen to me, because you can always learn something, from somebody, you know. So I brought her to the dance. I did it. I had a really good time, I really did.

But then I had a relapse. I had smoked some weed—I was sober for like five months, smoked some weed, then I had started drinking again, and then I went back to freebasing again, and the whole works. I lost my girlfriend. But she was too young for me anyway. She was.

I used to also be very suicidal when I was younger. I used to want to kill myself. Because I was always blaming myself for my parents' actions, and for my *own* actions, you know? Oh, I *hated* myself, I wanted to die! Now I wouldn't try it if my whole life depended on it, you know? I would not try to kill myself. Life is too precious. I love my old lady too much. I have too many things planned for me. And I just don't think suicide— I know suicide is not the answer. I also know that you're not gonna go anywhere till the man upstairs decides it's time to go, you know? (Laughs.)

Because I tried to commit suicide a lot. The time I was in that car accident, OK, I have these two scars right here (points to her neck), these, this scar and this scar, and *this* scar. These cuts almost killed me, OK? Here's a huge piece of glass right here, one huge one went *there,* and a very, very large one right *here,* which caused an abscess that was *huge.* And I was—OK, I was on PCP, I don't know *how* much PCP I did, I just know I did a *lot.* So I didn't remember nothing. It took me *seven days* to come down, that's how much PCP I did, OK?

I stole this Lincoln Continental—don't ask me whose it was, 'cause I don't know *how* I got it, I just know this is what the police report that I read seven days later said. I didn't know *who* I was, I didn't know what *year* it was, I didn't know *where* I was, I didn't even know what was going on, really. I didn't understand *nothing*. I didn't.

I was spaced out for a good two weeks. I had amnesia for about a week. During this seven days, I was still under the influence of PCP. PCP was still in my brain, still affecting me. I still was hallucinating, I still was tripping out. I couldn't eat, 'cause the food was *moving* and shit? It was really tripping me out.

OK. Then I finally read this report, the report astonished me. It freaked me *out*. It said that I was going ninety miles an hour down a one-way street. I ran into a telephone pole. The top half of my body went through the windshield. I pulled my *own self* out of the windshield, pulled out a cigarette, and started smoking! (Laughs.) Then I pushed the car, the report says I pushed it like *three blocks*! And you see, that's what PCP does to a person, it builds up your adrenalin totally, you become superhuman. You do. You have superhuman strength. And I just freaked out. 'Cause I seen guys trip out on PCP, but I never even really realized, you know . . . (Shakes her head.) I read this, I was going like "No way, no way!" But when I read it, I was still bandaged up, scarred up, I had stitches *here* (points to her side), stitches *here*, stitches *there*, and I had a big old thing wrapped around *here* (her arm), and a big old thing wrapped around *there*, and big old things on my *head*, I had *glass* in my head so they had to take the glass out, bandages everywhere, things on my *leg*, and I was like "Damn, the fuck's going on here?" And they're all "Well, you were *really* fucked up." They said I was talking things that didn't make sense, I was talking sentences that didn't make sense, you know. That freaked me out.

And then that's when I had to go to the mental hospital. I was tripping out. And I thought I was *never* gonna get my sense back, and shit. 'Cause I remember one night I woke up in my room in Juvenile Hall and there was a ant on my bed and the ant was *this* big . . . (her hands are six inches apart) and I tripped out. That's one thing I do remember about being under. I don't remember nothing about that *night*. I just know that afterward being under the influence was what freaked me out. Really, *truly* freaked me out. None of my experiences with LSD have ever been like my experiences with PCP. Ever. That was outrageous. It really was. And *that* I would have to say was total suicide. *Some* kind of suicide. Evi*dently*.

I tried to kill myself one time when me and my mom, you know, was really getting into it, we were having physical fights almost every day, she was calling the police on me. I have been sent to the Hall twice for battery against my mother, I have been sent there one time for breaking and entering to her house, trying to get my clothes . . . (Hesitates.) So one day I came home from school and no one was there, and I knew my brother was gonna be home from football practice late, and I knew my mom was working late, and so I cut my wrists. And I really wanted to die.

Because I found this out: when you *want* to die is when you don't tell no one. Suicide people, they're quiet, they don't tell no one "Oh, hey, I'm gonna kill myself." They don't leave little notes for people to notice. That's when they're saying "Hey, help me. I want to be helped." But me, I didn't want anybody to know nothing. So I go in the bathroom, I straight *up* started slicing my wrists. Until I just fell out. And my mom came home from work and I was in a pool of blood. Doctor said five minutes later and there would have been no chance for me, 'cause I would have lost too much blood. So that was my *first* suicide attempt. Then another time I took all these aspirins, these *Nuprin* pills, you know, for menstrual cramps? I took a *bunch* of 'em. Made me sicker'n a dog, I said, "I'll never do *that* again!" (Much laughter.) I mean I couldn't eat for like *two weeks*, I couldn't even drink *water*, I mean yuuuchhh . . . throwing up *every*thing! That's when they sent me back to the mental ward over there.

I was over there for a while. Then I was seeing a psychiatrist—my mother *called* her a therapist, but the bitch was a psy*chi*atrist, OK, I hated her *guts*, I didn't ever want to *see* her, I told my mom she was only wasting her money. So I threatened to kill my psychiatrist, right (laughs), and got sent to Juvenile Hall for *that*. 'Cause I hit my mom and knocked my mom into my psychiatrist, and my psychiatrist told a lie and said I tried to kill her. But I was trying to kill my *mom*, is who I was trying to kill! (Laughs.) OK? So they both worked against me, you know.

So then I had this major grudge against my mother for years behind that. I still have a major grudge on my mother. I mean I love my mother, I'm *trying* to love her, but she's making it *difficult*, you know, she really is . . . 'Cause it's kind of hard to forgive her, 'cause my mother could've helped me keep my daughter, but instead she . . . (Hesitantly:) See, the judge was gonna send me to a home for pregnant girls where I could've went to school and lived with my daughter. And I could've gotten my *shit* together. And she would've been with me the whole time. And I really wanted to do it, but my mom went against that. Fuckin' bitch . . . (Laughs.) Anyway . . . I don't know why.

And then she said, well, I was raped and why would I want to keep a child when I was raped. (Angrily:) So *what*, it's a part of *me*, it's someone that I know is gonna love *me*, you know? And I went through a lot of trauma on that. I still do sometimes, you know, because she's my daughter.

My mother knew, anywhere I was in the streets, my mother knew. I always let my mother know. She accepts me being gay, my father doesn't, because I'm still more, quote unquote, Daddy's little girl. He'll never accept me growing up, he'll never accept me being gay, there's just a *lot* of things he will not accept. But yet he can sit down and smoke a joint with me. He can sit down and *drink* with me. But my father, he has a cocaine habit too, he still uses now, and that's one thing he will not let me do in front of him, is any kind of cocaine usage. But he'll let me smoke weed and drink. He rationalizes his behavior a lot, and I feel like both of my parents are very hypocritical to where's I'm concerned. That's why I don't choose to live with my parents. It's like this, I feel like this: my father has a lot of people coming into his house who use drugs, right, and *he* uses drugs. So when I come home from school, I'll have to *smell* drugs, you know, and *see* drugs, but yet he doesn't want *me* to use that type of drug, you know? I don't think that's fair. I think that's totally hypocritical.

And then my mom is kinda edgy about me and my old lady's age difference. I said, "Well, mom, you and my dad were around the same age when *you* guys got together." "Well, you're young, you don't know what you're doing." Yeah. OK, mom. Cool, you know. Whatever. Time will tell. She always says, until I'm twenty-one—well she's gonna ask me if I'm gay when I'm twenty-one, and if I say yes, then she'll accept it. And if not, then I'm just quote unquote experimenting with my adolescence. (Sarcastically:) Like *yeah*, mom, right. OK. Long experiment! (Laughs.)

I wasn't going to school. I *could* have, I just never got it together. My mother was covering for me a lot—my P.O. called, my mom would say I was home when I was not. But my P.O. was lazy, he wasn't keeping up on me, really, 'cause he could have gone to any school and found out I was not enrolled. But my old lady really wanted that for me, she wanted me to get in school. My old lady, she's very educated, she's had four years of college.

And I found out another thing also. A lot of people that are out there on the streets using are very intelligent people. There's a *lot* of intelligent people. I mean a lot of the black people—it's mostly black people use cocaine, freebase cocaine—but *half* of them people are very smart. Most of 'em have graduated from high school, I mean *most* of 'em—a lot of 'em have college degrees, a lot of 'em are just starting to use cocaine, you know, where they're losing—their family is messed up now, they're selling their last little things like their car or whatever, they rent their car for drugs and stuff, and it's really sad. You know, to see stuff like that. But when you're out there and you're using, you don't care. All you care about is where that next hit's gonna come from. Or where, you know, where that next *high* is gonna come from. You're not thinking about the next person. But then sometimes when I'm sober, I can kick back and look at those people and just trip out on them, and say, "Well, *damn*," you know, "what am I doing here?" you know? It really makes you think, and wonder.

But I really would like to go back to school. I really do not want to be considered as illiterate or uneducated, because I am not, I really am not. And I more or less *chose* to be in the life I am now. I could've been, at my age, I think I could've graduated high school by now. With my knowledge, my intelligence I have now, I know I could have, but I just chose to be—I let myself be out there, you know, when I moved into the streets.

Why do you think you made the choice that way?

(Thoughtfully:) I don't know. I always think about that. (A long pause.) I think for one because I was tired—I felt as though I was being a people pleaser all my life. When I was younger. I was always doing things to please my parents, make my parents happy, and proud of me. But I wasn't making *myself* happy. Or making *myself* proud. You know? And I wanted to see what it was like. I wanted to see how the other people felt, you know. There was always a class clown, you know, and I was always wondering what that class clown felt like. And being on the other side, being on *both* sides, being on the A-student side, and being on the side of you don't give a *fuck*, and that type of side, you can see through people, and what the hurt is, and what they're going through? You know?

And there's a lot of people out there that are *hella* smart, they could be something in life . . . (Another pause.) But I think most problems start all from home. I do. I think home has a lot to do with how people feel about theirselves, and how they're influenced, and what their potentials are, and goals are in life. Me myself, I think I was influenced a lot by my family, too. My father always wanted to push me and push me. But yet see, he never would really *appreciate* anything I did. Although deep down inside he did, he wouldn't let *me* know it. He would never let me know it. He'd say, "Yeah, that's good," but he'd never say, you know, "Yeahh!" Or he'd never really, like when I did something really good, my mom she might take us out for ice cream, something like that.

Society seems to think that the majority of people out there, well, they're lower-class people, poor people. That is not true, that is not true. There's a lot of people out there that, hey—I've seen a lot of *older* people get into freebasing, I mean I'm talking *senior citizens* here. Yes. And that is a shock, I would believe. Then I've seen a lot of people, mid-thirties, late twenties, they have nice jobs, they go out somewhere, a girlfriend or boyfriend introduces them to freebasing, then they get into it, and then they never can quit. 'Cause cocaine is a serious problem. It really is. I used to think that if AIDS didn't kill the world, cocaine was going to. Because I just found out some really startling statistics that two-thirds of, um, this population, we use one-half of the world's cocaine supply, period, *that* freaked me out. One-half of the cocaine supply is going to *us*. That is something *else*. That startled me, I said, "Wow!". . . . That really shocked me, that was a shocker.

Being out there using, you meet a lot of people. Come across a lot of people that you become really *close* to. There was a lot of different experiences I've been through. I mean there was never a dull moment in my life when I was out there, I can tell you that. And I met a lot of interesting people. Some people that touched me in one spot, just really touched me and really shocked me. See, since me and my old lady be dealing, then you really meet a lot of new people. Also we *use*, too, so we meet a new person, the next person might refer them to us, they'll come and buy their drugs from us. And I'll get to know 'em, I'll ask 'em a few questions, and then they might become a regular customer of us. And then we'll know 'em for years, and they'll be good friends with us.

I remember a couple times this lady, I mean she looked like she had just got off *work*, you know, (amazed:) and first thing she did, went to the rock house, buy some cocaine: "Give me some rock, rock!" And so I seen her and I asked her, "How long you been smoking cocaine?" She said three months. I said, "Baby, I'da quit." And she's all "Well, how can you tell *me?*" And I said, "I'm just telling you my advice." She said, "Well, how old are you?" I said, "How old do I look?" She said, "You look about nineteen." I told her I was nineteen, I said, "I've been smoking cocaine for three years, and you're thirty-two and you've only been smoking for two months. So think about it." You know. Really. And she been smoking cocaine ever since. She's been buying it from us.

That's another thing that brings a person down. It's also an environmental thing. If you live in an environment where there's drugs out on the street, where you're confronted with drugs, where you have a lot of pressure from drugs, or, you know, your old using buddies, old using friends, come up to you and ask you, "Hey, man . . . you gone take a hit?" You know?

I was gonna tell you about this. My coach here in Juvenile Hall, he said, "Well, all you have to do is say no." I said "Yeah, sure, suuuure!" (Sagely:) But after you're *addicted*, it's not so *easy* to say no! And he said, "Well, if you can be so strong, and say no . . ." I said it's not that easy. I said, "I'm sure, Leon, that you were a teenager once and hey, you might have been one of those strong ones, but there's not that much percentage of *strong* ones, quote unquote, these days because of the simple fact that there's a lot of peer pressure, and drugs in high schools these days, you know, the percentage is high. You have to think about that." The statistics, they show it. Facts are facts, you know. I mean it's not easy to just say no. People are gonna ridicule you, and a lot of people cannot endure shit like that. Especially a lot of teens, because they want to be accepted.

But me, I'm just a strong person, see. I was a leader in junior high school. People followed me, I didn't follow anybody. (Proudly:) I would be the one saying "Come on, let's go smoke a joint." Or "Come on, let's go drink out in front of the school." "Come on, let's do this and that." No one could ever say "Come on" to me.

I used to put people who use—who only *smoke* cocaine—I used to put 'em down. I used to call 'em baseheads, you know. I mean, the things that women do, to supply their high, are just amazing. Seriously. (Laughs.) Because cocaine is so addictive that pretty soon the habit will get so bad that you will do *anything* to get just that one hit, you know. And being on both sides of the track really trips me out. At times me being a user *and* a seller—I'm more accepting, I feel more comfortable using and selling than I did just selling. 'Cause when I was just selling, I was just with the sellers.

See, the sellers, the dope dealers, are *my* generation, these days dealers is my generation. You're talking your eleven-year-olds, your twelve-year-olds, your thirteen—people my little brother's age, your fourteen-year-olds, fifteen-sixteen-seventeen-and-up-year-olds, you know. I mean I know a couple guys that sell drugs in Iron City who are college graduates, who could've *went* somewhere, but no, they're selling drugs, they're riding around in BMWs, and Mercedes-Benz, they're riding around in Mustangs, 5.0's, you know? But they could be *legally* doing that. But me, since I'm a user, I'm not gonna always have all these material things, because I'm gonna keep my high up, also. So I'm not gonna go around with the flashy rings, and the flashy clothes, because (suddenly harsh) some days I'm not gonna *give a fuck* because I'm a user, too.

I wrote a lot of poems about that, about being on the using side and being on the dope-man side. Dope man's *king*, dope man is worshiped. In the drug area, he's God. Dope man is God. He's God because he has the coke, he's God because he has that hit, he has what you want. Has what *I* want, so to me he's God. When I get to my last twenty dollars, I'm gonna give it to him, you know? No matter what. When I want that rock, I want that rock. And do you know how fast a twenty-dollar rock goes? Twenty-dollar rock of cocaine goes *so* fast. And the drug only makes you want more.

I don't have a religion. I believe in God, I believe God loves me, I believe I am God's child, I believe God put me here for a purpose—I don't know what the hell the purpose *is* (laughs), but I know I'm *here*, I know there's *some*one up there, I don't know *who* He is, but I know He's there. He's got to be.

I wonder a lot about evolution and things. It really makes me wonder. Because when I was younger, my kindergarten teacher used to try to teach us evolution. But I was brought up in church. My father being a black male, he's Baptist. My mother being a Hispanic female, she's more Catholic. So she didn't ever really practice religion, but my father did. He used to always talk about church, but when his mother died—my grandmother died in 1980—that really changed my dad, too. Because his father died when he was a young boy, and that brought on a lot of changes. I think he started more heavily into drugs then. He was more or less in a sober stage until this happened. I remember a lot of going to church and stuff like that. When I was in sixth grade, my sixth-grade teacher she was a Jehovah's Witness and I started studying with them. And I believe in that religion, strongly, I believe that that is my religion if there was to be a religion for me, that would be mine. Because I know that there's a lot of things according to the Bible that I'm doing wrong with my life.

But I feel like this: I feel like God's gonna love me no matter what I do, you know? I feel like everyone should be able to worship God in their own way. I feel like we all have our own little temple of worship of God in our own hearts.

I forgot to mention to you that I had recently started using crank, OK, to keep me from using up all my coke? Because my old lady would leave me with the dope, right? And she'd get mad because I'd smoke more than I'd sell! You know, so she'd get mad. So she introduced me to crank. And I started doing crank. And *she* does crank. She doesn't do coke that much, she's not into cocaine that much. Her main thing is crank.

But when we're together . . . (Hesitates:) I can say this. I *do* have a lot of fun using drugs sometimes with my old lady. When it's just me and her, we're kicking back, we're in the tub, we're smoking a joint, we're drinking a bottle of wine, we're cool. You know? But I mean—when it gets to the other hard drugs, it's more serious, you know? So I started snorting crank, you know, and I found it better. Crank is like cocaine, the euphoria is the same, but it's not as great as the cocaine high. And the fastest way to feel that euphoric feeling is through IV, slamming, and through smoking cocaine and crank. Smoking cocaine and crank, you get the same high, but see crank lasts longer than coke. The high lasts much longer. You can stay wired off of crank for *way* longer than you can with cocaine. And that's one reason why people choose crank over coke. And that's a thing that I found out, too.

I really want to get married to the lady I'm with now, though, I really do. I'm really in love with her and I know she's really in love with me. But I want to wait till I get eighteen so there won't be no problems, none whatsoever. So I have a year to go. So I'm sure we'll make it through that year. I know a couple of other gay couples that're married. And I also want to have a child for me and her, you know. And I know that I'm not rich, so I can't have sperm transplants, so there's only one way to get pregnant. (Laughs.) Unfortunately. Since I'm not a millionaire and I can't afford that, you know. I do plan on having another child, though. So we can have our *own* family. But I would like to get my education started, get a career going before I have a kid. Straight up.

Even though I use, my life is not all based around drugs. I also have a lot of fun, too. I mean sometimes we might take a night off, we'll go out for pizza, or we might decide to go somewhere fun, go to the beach, we do a lot of fun stuff. I just think that I kind of missed a lot of my teenhood. 'Cause I was kind of forced to grow up fast, you know? I did a *few* things that teens do. But then I was too busy, really, drinking, using, to do the things that people my age do.

I plan to get married to her when I get eighteen. I mean I'm just so happy. No one's *ever* made me feel that way, no one's ever, you know, really treated me that way, and I just know I love her and I know she loves me. And no matter what my parents say, or *anyone* says, you know, I *know*. I might be young, but I know what I'm doing. I have my mind made up.

And so now, from here, I'm supposed to go to another drug program. I might be going to one in Rivertown, called New Family? My *mother* went there! (Laughs.) It's a year program. But I'm gonna have to tough it out this time, you know. 'Cause I look back over the years and I realize I'm gonna be seventeen next month, and my teens are going. They've *gone*, practically. And it really shocks me. And I've also heard about this theory they have, they have this one theory about how the government's trying to get all the kids, the teens, my generation? drugged out, so they can take over, the older people, easier, and run the government, and make it a communist government? I heard some shit like that, and it really freaked me out. And I also realized that by the year 2000 the world's gonna be full of computers, 'cause it already is now. And if I don't go to school and get on it, I'm gonna be nothing, because even the *street* jobs are gonna be taken up by people—(laughs and shakes her head) pretty soon you're gonna have to have a G.E.D., or at least a high school diploma, to do anything in life, you know, if not more. College degree to sweep the streets, you know?

So I'm really—I'm a good artist, I like to draw, I'll show you my pictures out there—I love to draw. I wanted to go to art school, but in one of me and my mother's spats, she spent up my money, that I had saved up, to go to art school. That really hurt me. That *really* hurt me.

Kathy Mulligan

"I started slamming when I was about eleven"

She's so thin she looks almost like a stick figure in a child's drawing. She was brought to the Hall from the county emergency youth shelter and is waiting to be placed in a group home. "I've lived on my own for a while. Actually, I've been in and out of my house since I was about twelve—just leaving, and getting put back here. My parents and I clash, our personalities really clash." She's from a big, lower-middle-class Catholic family, has lived in Cherry Grove all her life. She's been a heavy user of cocaine and LSD since she was "around nine or ten," and of heroin since she was eleven.

"There's eleven kids in my family, and there's six above me, and every single one of 'em's grown up with a problem. I mean everybody! They're all dropouts, every single one of 'em, none of 'em have graduated from high school, one of 'em had a kid at an early age, Danielle, and she's married now. Terry hitchhiked to New York when he was sixteen, ran away, Donnie was dealing, Rick was dealing, and Diane dropped out, and then there's me, and I'm having a lot of problems.

*"And then there's four behind me. And they're still raising 'em
the same way they raised all of us! (Laughs.) You know? They're
doing something wrong, and I say, 'Mom, won't you listen to me,
that you're doing something wrong. Why not just change a few
things, and see how it is with Tammy. If that doesn't work, change
a few things, see how it is with Robin, but everybody's gonna grow
up the same way, if you don't, you know, do something.' "*

I started slamming when I was about eleven.

My brothers never did it. They'd *smoke* it and everything. But
my brothers' friends, they were all doing it. And I'd been smoking pot
since I was about nine, and um, snorting cocaine every now and then,
behind their back. I'd take some of theirs! (Laughs.) And they never knew
I was doing it. And I'd snort, and I *loved* it, you know, I loved it. And
when I saw them sticking a needle—I used to *hate* needles, I was terrified,
I cried before they'd even get within a mile of me, if I knew I was going
to get a shot? "Oh, no!"—you know.

And then after a while I started watching them. My big brothers, and
my little sister, and me, and my other big sister, and my retarded brother,
we'd all go camping. And I'd watch 'em. And I was a brat at the time,
you know, I'd run around and get in trouble, and Diane'd say, "I don't
want to watch her, you guys take her with *you*," and they'd go and I'd
have to go with 'em, and I'd watch 'em. And they'd just do it behind here
(points to her rear), and so that's what I thought you were supposed to
do, so that's what *I* always used to do. They'd do it in their ass, or anyplace
they could do it without doing it on their arms or nothing.

And I got into it right away. Just started doing it *all* the time. They
never knew what harm it did to me, though, they never found out. My
brothers still don't know I use.

The needles I got were from the hospital. I'd go in for a checkup with
the doctor, which I arranged, and I'd get all the syringes, I'd just sneak
'em in my purse. (Grins.) And I had my own, all the time, you know,
no problem, and I never shared. Which was something, 'cause I heard
my brothers talking about [AIDS] all the time, and I got freaked. "Oh,
so that's what happens, huh?"

I remember the first few times I slammed, I got sick. My first time I
ever slammed, I was like—I sat up, you know, I felt like I was gonna
faint, I doubled over, started pukin' all over the *ground*, just a big old

rush, and I didn't know *what* was happening, I was *freaked*, I was *scared* . . . That was heroin, the first time I ever shot up. And I was just freaked. I mean I was *hallucinating*. I hadn't tried acid yet, but I had done a lot of pot and I'd snorted a lot of coke, but I'd never done any heroin and this was something *far* beyond what I'd expected. And the thing was, I was tweaking out on *everything*. I just closed my eyes and laid back and my body felt like it was falling into the bed, you know, and everything was just tripping, I don't know, and that just scared me. And I thought, "Well, if I can handle the first time," like they say, "I can learn to handle the next, and the next, and the next," you know, (laughs) "and it'll get easier."

And so I kept on doing it, and the next times were never like that, 'cause it was cocaine the next time! And so I thought, "Oh, OK," and then I tried heroin again, and it tripped me out like the first time: "Oh, *shit!*" 'Cause I did the same thing, I puked again, I didn't know *what* was going on, I didn't understand, and I was too humiliated to ask anybody. I'd feel like I didn't *know* anything, you know, if I went up and said, "Well, what's—what happens when you do heroin, and what happens when you do cocaine?" And they'd go "What do you mean, you don't *know?*" And so I was always reluctant to go and ask somebody.

I slammed heroin for about two months, which I didn't like because it scared me, but everybody on the streets was doing it. And I slammed cocaine. And I slammed crank a few times. But it was cocaine I was mostly into, and I would freebase it. And I would snort it. And smoking pot I love, I'll always love it till I'm an old lady (laughs), but that's no big deal, you know? Smoking pot, it's like you can't even get addicted to it, it's just something that's there for a good time, but the drugs, like powder, crack, and everything else, that's the stuff that gets into your system, and you feel addicted to. The pot you only feel addicted to if you've got no . . . power of result. But if you have control over yourself, you can never get addicted to it.

But it wasn't heroin I was shooting up at first, it was cocaine. And cocaine really wasn't that hard to find. Crystal meth and everything was around, and cocaine and everything. And I didn't really know the difference, except, you know, when I slammed it, there was a burn, and there was a big difference between crank and coke. And I didn't even know pretty much what I was doing, it was just "I'm cool," and "I'm older," " 'cause *I* do *drugs!*" I felt I was in with a more mature crowd, and living on my own, of course, I thought I was an adult, and just having older boyfriends at the age of eleven, twelve; nineteen-year-olds, twenty-year-olds, and it was just all, you know, all wrapped together. If I ran *away*, I was older, I was more mature and I was cool. If I did drugs, I was *in*. If I went out with older guys, I was accepted, and I was loved, you know?

I was an addict, cocaine addict, and alcoholic for about a year and a half. Until actually I found out I was pregnant, and then I just stopped everything like *that* (snaps her fingers), went through serious withdrawals and everything, was going to NA and AA, trying to go to work on my twelve-step program, and I came in here and got out again, and then I got all wrapped up again, had to go through it all over again.

Two and a half months I didn't do any drugs. That was a little phase. (Laughs.). I miscarried. Bye-bye! (Laughs.) I think it's all for the best. All you have to do is look at my past and see what I've done. To bring him here. That's not something I'd be very proud to tell my kid. When I had the miscarriage, I said "*Man*, you know? I could've done all those *drugs*? and it wouldn't of even mattered!" It's the wrong way to think (laughs), but it's just the way I was. My brain was all messed up.

But I remember I started getting into acid *really* heavy and I was taking about eight hits a day, and it was just like four-way and orange sunshine,* it was getting really trippy. And . . . (hesitates) one time I went on a bad trip. A really, *really* bad trip.

She attacked her boyfriend with a knife: "I tried to stab him 'cause I thought he was Satan and (laughs) everything . . . I mean I thought I was in Hell, the whole bit, you know. Really tripped out. We were down in Rivertown by the tracks? Down by the marina? And we were with this chick named Firecat, and she gave us this weird acid, you know? All sitting around a candle, down by the tracks, and we're all sitting around like we're in a séance, or something like that. And I started trippin' bad and then I wouldn't talk to nobody, and I was like over in a corner by myself, you know? And Mickey came up: 'Oh, are you having a bad trip?' I'm going, 'Yeah! Get away, don't talk to me or else I'll freak out,' and then I started freaking out and crying and screaming, etcetera,

---

* They are varieties of LSD.

and, um, he started grabbing onto me and trying to hold me, you know, really tight, 'cause I was all over, really crying, and after that experience I've never tried acid again."

And when I OD'd on cocaine, I had to go into the hospital and get my stomach pumped, and I was hyperventilating and shit. That was the last time I ever did cocaine. So . . . (Thoughtfully:) You know, it's like I had to have a bad experience before I could quit anything. Weird. It's like *here*. If I could get out, I'd come right back. I don't understand. Like I remember the first time I was in here, I'm all "I'm *never* coming back again." Next time, "I'm never coming back again." I was saying the same thing. Now: "I'm never coming back again." Like, Kathy, don't you ever *learn*? (Laughs.)

I remember when I was just hanging out at my house—oh, man . . . (Grins.) I had a trippy bedroom. One day I had nothing to do and I got *so* wired, and I go, "I'm gonna fix this room up so killer?" And I put up all these psychedelic colored woven blankets around my bed and up on the ceiling, and then on the walls, and you'd go in there it'd be just like colors everywhere, you couldn't get away from 'em. And I put candles sticking out from the walls, really trippy, and I used to go in there and turn on. And I remember I'd go in there and just lay up there, *totally* bored, and I'd say "What's there to do? Get stoned." You know? It was the first thing that popped into my head, was get stoned. I'd go in my room, lay up there and get stoned, kick back, and be tweakin', and then I'd go, "Damn, what're we gonna do? Fry!" You know? And I'd call somebody, and I'd go "Give me some fry," go all the way to Hillview, get some fry, and come back, just because I was bored, that's a major part of it, I think.

You've never tripped before? Aw, you should do it, just for the sake of it, 'cause it was, *ohhh* . . . (A wide smile.) Actually, I think just about every grown-up I ever *knew* knows about that: "Oh, acid, I remember *that!* Colors, happy trails . . ." (Laughs.) There's a saying: Don't follow your hand, follow the hand that follows your hand? You know, you see trails, and colors shoot out from your fingers . . . You're looking at that refrigerator there, you'd get up and start dancing with it! Tape recorder'd start talking back to you, I'll bet you anything! (Laughs.)

Something I haven't done since I had that bad trip, though. But I remember all the *good* times I had with it before, on the beach, sittin' there fryin' . . . and if I ever go swimming when I'm frying, it's like I start *drowning*, I can't control the feeling of water engulfed around me? Just trips me out, I go, "Oh, shit!" You can kill a person, you put 'em on that stuff, sometimes it trips 'em out so bad.

I remember the first time I ever, ever fried was at a little elementary school, and I got lost out in this big green field. (Intently:) I got *lost*. And it made so many colors I couldn't find my way out, so I lay down and watched the grass grow. And grow. And *grow!* And colors and waves and turns and oh, shit! (Laughs.) *Tripped* me out. You can't stop smiling, cramps your cheeks, they start hurting, 'cause you can*not* stop no matter what. If you said, "Your mother just died," you'd go "Ha-ha-ha"! (Laughs.) 'Cause you can't stop laughing, you know? It's trippy.

She started running away from home and living on her own when she was "around twelve."

We were brought up as Roman Catholics, and we weren't allowed to dress the way the other kids were. I mean we had to wear *dresses*. And we could not wear makeup. I mean not that that's such a big thing . . . but growing up, it is. In the public school system. And what happened with me is, we all went to Catholic private school until that one closed down, and then after that they just all of a sudden changed us to a public school, and I was scared and timid and shy, so I looked hard to be accepted. And the people that accepted me were the *bad* crowd, you know? And that was how I got hooked in, because I wanted so hard to be accepted and I looked for it, and I searched for them and they found me. And then I got into the smoking, and the drugs, and etcetera, etcetera, and I just continued, and now I'm stuck here.

A really secluded life. My parents were really, you know, overprotective, they kept me away from all the outside world. And I was a really good kid until I went to that public school, that's what brought me down. And I mean I was kept away from *all* the bad things. I don't know how they did it, but I think they did it wrong. They didn't *teach* me about anything, they didn't let me see any of the bad stuff, and as soon as I was there, I was, you know, I was *ecstatic!* I was like whoa! you know? (Laughs.) It hit me, and I just got completely enrapt in it.

After she ran away from home, she lived for a while at a video arcade and pool hall near downtown Cherry Grove. She slept on the pool tables.

It was the place I hung out at, it was like my *home.* I was there every day.

The owner helped me a lot, too. I mean I was in there day and night. I'd go in there around ten o'clock and I'd hang out and watch the MTV until about three in the morning. And I'd talk to people. Pick up on guys. I met new people every single day, all day, you know? Mexicans trying to pick up on me, "Hey, señorita!" (Laughs.) I mean they can't even speak *English,* how . . . (Laughs.) And at about three o'clock when they closed, I'd help 'em, I'd sweep up everything, then I'd clean the pool tables and they'd let me play pool till about six in the morning, and then we'd sleep till about ten or eleven when they'd open again. That was like my daily routine. And he helped me a lot. But I didn't really have any mature adults around. You know. It was mostly a bunch of either older teenagers, or early twenties, sometimes late twenties. But they all were really close. It's like they all really cared about me. I was like everybody's little sister.

There were these two guys that went to the Arcade, they used to drive around on these big old black Harley-Davidsons? And they were my bodyguards, they adopted me as their little sister, and I used to get up at eight o'clock in the morning and they'd come to my house and pick me up on the Harley and go down to the beach, you know, and play volleyball on the beach and stuff, drop me off about six. They always took care of me, took me around, up to the hills to get stoned, you know, and they were really nice guys.

Like one time somebody, an old ex-boy friend, came back, beat me up, and stabbed me in the back. And they went and—I don't know where, but I have never *heard* of the guy again, I mean I haven't heard of him recently in about almost a year now! (Laughs.) So I don't know what they did to him, they must've (laughs) run him out of the state or something, but they hurt him pretty bad, I guess. Let's just say if they heard of anybody hurting me . . . (smiles) I'd feel secure.

I know what his intention was. Well, see, he was an alcoholic, and I left him because I couldn't stand him beating me up all the time and burning me, with cigarettes, and etcetera, etcetera. Just . . . (Pauses.) He had his own little ways of hurting me, and I left him. And when he came

back, he called me a bitch and he's saying, "All you care about is yourself."
And I said, "I couldn't handle the pressure of living with you." And he
said, "Well I'll make sure that another guy will never look at you again,"
and he stabbed me, with the intent to paralyze me from my neck down,
so I would never be . . . (hesitates a moment, laughs) never have another
boyfriend again, you know? And that's pretty terrible. He never did it,
but I was in so much pain that I passed out when he threw me out on
his front lawn, and I woke up on his front lawn. And I went straight to
my bodyguards! "Help me, I'm gonna die!" And that was really awful. I
haven't heard of him since.

I even knew this couple kids out on the street, six or seven years old,
and I kind of, I was like their mommy! They called me "Mommy!" They're
still out there. And I don't know where they stay at night, but they're
around during the day. Those kids are *this* tall, you know? (Her hand's
about three feet off the floor.) Out there on their own, their moms are
in *prison*—well, I know one of their mom's in prison, I don't know where
the other one's mom is. But they really stick together. Sometimes they'll
go out, they'll rip off a bunch of things, you know like some store, go in
and steal a bunch of candy, and come to me, they call me mommy,
which really . . . oh, you know . . . brings tears to my eyes. Because
these poor children. Without *nothing*, you know. (Softly:) Shit.

It's really neat to have that feeling, though. That they look up to me
like that. 'Cause I've taken care of them—a lot of times I've gotten 'em
places to stay . . . They're too young, way too young. I mean (laughs)
I'm young, but *those* . . . you know?

I used to take 'em to the beach a lot. Because the beach is my favorite
place in the whole *world*. If I had a choice of anywhere, live anywhere,
it'd be the beach. And I used to see 'em down on Twelfth and Truman,
they used to hang out on the corner there, you know, panhandling together. And I'd say, "Hey guys, how 'bout we go to the beach?" And
they'd go, "OK, Mommy!" And I'd pick 'em both up and walk to the
beach and I'd play Frisbee with 'em or whatever, and I'd get 'em some
food. You should've seen these kids *eat*, too, they ate up a storm, they'd
eat me out of my own purse, you know, all my money would go! (Laughs.)
I'd go, "Shit, I gotta go find some more money!"

One good thing is, I was never hungry? I never—I was out on the
streets a few times by myself, but I don't know, I was always fed well.
Pretty much. Though when I came in here, I weighed like eighty-seven

pounds. I mean I was bones sticking out everywhere. Now I look reasonable, but . . . (hesitates) I was *really* bad when I first came in here.

It was stress, I think. It was just . . . everything. With all the stress I
was going through, I just wasn't hardly even hungry, you know? And I
was really energetic, I was up and down all the time, always going here
and there and walking, to the beach and everything, and that kind of got
me really skinny, I don't know why.

Were you hassled a lot, out on the street by yourself?

Oh, yeah, many times, men took advantage of me. Numerous times.
I mean a couple times a guy would—I'd meet a guy, know him for a
couple days, you know, and then that night I'd say, "Hey, can I stay at
your house?" And, "Yeah, sure!" I'd say, "No strings attached, right?"
And he says, "Nah, don't worry about it, you can come and I'll leave
you alone." And then ten minutes after I get there have me in the bedroom!
(Scornfully:) And I'd say "Hey, wait a second, what *is* this, you know, I
am *not* here for you guys' sexual fantasies." Nobody can be nice anymore,
let you have a place to stay, just for one night at least, and let you go.
They expect something in return, every single person. Except for a few,
I've met a few.

And so I'd have to leave, and then I'd be on the streets again. You
know? That night, because that person couldn't leave me alone. I mean
I don't mind if I'm expecting something out of him, in return, I mean
like a relationship, if I like him, and I think it's gonna last for a while,
but you know.

I had people taking care of me, I had a couple gangs taking care of
me. And my friend Juster, who's like my brother, let me live in his
apartment with this old, *old* man named Fred, who's ninety years old?
He takes care of him because Fred doesn't got no place to stay and can't
do *anything* anymore, he's just *completely* out of it. So I took care of Fred
while Juster worked, and I was pregnant and so Juster took care of *me*,
you know? We were all helping each *other*, actually. And I helped Juster
stay clean off of his drugs while I was pregnant. We helped each other,
actually, went to AA together, and brought Fred with us (laughs), we
actually were like a little family, it was fine.

And then just three days before I came in here this time, I got raped.
I walked up to the beach, and I found forty bucks, two twenties rolled

up, so I had some money, and I went back to the park and this guy grabbed me and pulled me in the car and raped me. And nobody's *done* anything, and I've been here three weeks. It's like they don't care. And you know they just left me here, with like *nightmares* at night, and just, you know, freaking *out*. Whoa!

And that guy that raped me gave me chlamydia. Sexually transmitted disease? And I got rid of that in a few days, but I was *scared*, and the day I went in here, next morning I went and got three blood tests, pelvic exam and everything, and I had *one* thing, and it was curable. I was thanking God it was curable, 'cause I didn't know, what I had, you know? "Great, this black guy *rapes* me, and I don't know," you know? It was scary. The feeling of not knowing, for three days, too . . . and I'm sitting there going, like "Shit, what am I gonna do if I've got a *disease*," you know. Because you know I was pregnant, too.

But you still feel drawn to being out there . . .

Oh, yeah. I can take care of my*self*. I've done it before. I mean if I have no choice, if I had to go on the streets again, I know I could survive. And my family life's, you know, never gonna work out.

Her sister says her mom won't speak her name in the house: " 'She doesn't talk about you anymore because everytime your name's brought up she starts crying.' She's getting gray hair, ulcers, because of me. Ulcers, she's so worried. And I don't know, it's just every time I go, everything seems to be OK for like a month or two, and all of a sudden I just jam again, and I don't know what it is, it's like calling me out there or something! (Laughs.) You know? The outside world's saying, 'Hey, hey!' I'm all 'No, not again, please!' " (Laughs.)

Oh, I have scared feelings, yeah. I mean I get uneasy about it, thinking if I get out of here and get in a group home and it works out for about a year and all of a sudden I feel like running again, what am I gonna do, you know? Shit . . . (Quietly:) Because right now I've got all these people out there that I know and that love me, and I look up to them, you know? And I expect them to help, I don't know why. But if I got out of here, maybe in about a year, and I went back, maybe they wouldn't be there.

And what would I do then, start all over? That's what it would be. So I don't know . . . (she looks distracted) what happens to you . . . if you went to start over.

What about the drugs?

Right now I don't even have a want or feel a need for any of it, narcotics. Which is funny. The last time I was in here, and the first, and second, and everything, I was like, you know, "Drugs . . . drugs . . . drugs!" And now it's like my body's cleaned out of it, my whole system seems to be cleared. And I don't even feel a need for it anymore. That's children's stuff. Like "Get away from me, I'm too old for that!" (Laughs.)

Too old for drugs?

Yeah! It's like, the younger ones, they experience it, they go through their phase, some of them do go on to their adulthood, but some also they grow out of it, like me, I grew out of it. You know, smoking pot every now and then is just no big deal with me, but the slamming cocaine and everything, that I was doing, its just—nah, nah, that's . . . preschool! (Laughs.)

I mean I know kids right now who are nine years *old* slamming. Whose *parents* have gotten 'em into it. Like this one girl, if she did something good in school, her mother got her an eight-ball. You know? And that just trips me out, because my parents would have *never* done that, but I still got into it, so people do it for different reasons, I guess.

But I know a lot of young people right now that are out there slamming dope. Not as many slam as snort, you know, but . . . Like this little kid Justin, I've known him for two years. He's *this* tall (laughs), *little* kid, you know? And he's like, I'm like *his* mommy, too, and I've seen him out there, when I haven't been around, I'll go up and he'll be snortin', doing a line and stuff? And he's *so* young and he's just so . . . innocent-looking, you wouldn't think. Well, he's a little skinhead, with bangs hanging down to about *here*, just two bangs, wears these boots, big old Docs* or whatever those guys call 'em, and hangs out, you know, riding his skateboard, with these big old wide *eyes*, always tweaking and everything, and then he's

* Doc Martens, a popular brand of boots.

just so young for it, you know? And I think, "I can't believe I did that when I was that age," you know? I was *that* young, and it just saddens me to look at it now, look back on it. It's a trip.

He has his ear pierced, he's got a little tattoo, upside-down cross on his arm—it's like he sees what they do and goes right and does it, you know.

Would you do something different with your own kids?

I would raise them to *know* everything that's going on out in the world, and I'd let them make as many of their own decisions as I could, without letting them harm themselves really bad. And then I'd raise them, you know, in the *world*, so that when they grow up, they're gonna *know* what's bad and what's good. They're gonna be able to make their own decisions, and they're gonna be the *right* decisions. After a while. Everybody makes mistakes, and every single person in this world, every child that is growing up, is different, and you have to search, you have to reach *in*, you have to find out, that person. Everybody's special, everybody's different. But they treat people—I mean there's certain people who'll treat me as though I'm *dirt*, but there's something special about every person. And there's gotta be something special about me, I don't know what it is, but certain people like me, and then other certain people despise me. You gotta love your child, you gotta raise them different. I don't know.

I know my parents took me away from the *whole* outside world, and when I found it, I reached out for it, "Come get me," you know? (Laughs.) I was a little child who didn't know anything, wanted to learn. I learned the hard way. I mean I learned some lessons I wish I never had to learn.

I mean if I could've learned a different way about drugs, I would've done it.

PART 3

THE INTERMITTENT BLAZE OF FOLLY

We may cultivate this most precious possession, or we may disregard it. We may either smother the divine fire of youth or we may feed it. We may either stand stupidly staring as it sinks into a murky fire of crime and flares into the intermittent blaze of folly, or we may tend it into a lambent flame. . . .

—Jane Addams, *The Spirit of Youth and the City Streets*

The Hall, like every other institution of its kind in the United States, sweeps up a wide spectrum of troubled kids. For the most part, their offenses are mundane. "The typical delinquent admitted to a detention facility," according to a recent report from the U.S. Department of Justice, is "male, over the age of 15, and charged with a property offense." More juveniles are behind bars for property crimes than any other offense: they've broken into houses or stores, stolen cars, vandalized schools. They make up the largest single part—nearly half—of the army of adolescents now in detention across the United States.

Others—about one in four both nationally and in River County—are there for violent offenses, and their numbers rose in the late 1980s despite a drop in the youth population as a whole. Some are behind bars for gang-related violence: River County's gang scene isn't as developed as it has become in many big cities, but, like the drug trade with which it often overlaps, it's increasing, especially in the Hispanic neighborhoods and among some Iron City black kids with ties to gangs in the larger cities in the area.

The other prominent group in the Hall are those with no place else to go. Until the mid-1980s, you didn't see many street kids in River County: even most of the poorest kids in Iron City still had some place to live. But by the end of the decade, there were many kids living by their wits on the streets of the county, not only in Iron City but in the white-working-class areas in Rivertown—where officials recently dedicated the city's first shelter for the homeless—and in Cherry Grove. Some hide in the parks in Rivertown or sleep in cars; others drift into the bigger cities in the area, and often back again. They wind up in the Hall and in the county's youth shelters when they're caught breaking the law—it's usually for stealing food, clothes, or alcohol—and occasionally they turn themselves in, in search of food, shelter, or medical care.

Jeremy McClure

"They don't do it in Beverly Hills"

Lean and rangy, his mop of blond hair askew, he could have stepped out of a Walker Evans photograph from the Depression of the 1930s. His grandparents moved to Iron City in the forties— lured, along with thousands of other migrants, white and black, by what were then booming shipyards, steel mills, and refineries. He lives with an older relative in a poor neighborhood that's now mostly black. "There is some whites around, but it's mostly black people. It's pretty hard for a white person, in Iron City. But I get along pretty good. I'm cool with everyone here, black or white. I don't act like a black person, I don't act like a white person, I don't act like anyone, I just be me, 'cause I'm used to them, they're used to me. I don't listen to that rocker music—Slayer, and them. I listen to Beastie Boys, Cool J, and all them. I mostly get along with everyone. If I don't smart out anyone, I'm pretty cool over there."

I live on the rowdy side. I mean there *is* a better part of Iron City. There is nice homes in the hills, very nice homes. All people live there, black, white, Chinese, it's a nice neighborhood up there. But I live on the lower part, in a nice house, but where I live the neighborhood was good a long time ago, that's when my parents—that's why they bought it, right, they bought the house for that. But it just changed. You know —people gotta do what they gotta do to earn money. So you know, if it's illegal, it's illegal.

There's a lot of kids out in Iron City at nighttime. Just looking for trouble. Just staying in groups. You know, if one person's alone, they'll beat him up, take their money. Just *mess* with 'em. Like take their shoes, throw it on the roof . . . Everyone! Grown men! Men are *mean* around Iron City. They'll rob you, shoot you . . . If a white dude's walking along, some black dudes might get him. Or maybe some Chinese people? Might get some Filipino dude. (Amazed:) Everyone wants to fight everyone!

It's too much, you know, just criminal like. Everything's always happening—dope, robbing houses. The wrong people to be with. I'd rather live in like Cherry Grove, River Heights or something. It's quieter, kids are more *calm*. They might use dope, but it's more calm, you know. It's a nicer neighborhood. I was there late, it's just quiet, maybe kids are out, but they're having a good time, nothing's going on. It's a nice little neighborhood, I'd love to live there. I like staying at my sister's house in River Heights. They have parties and stuff, but it's just fun. You roam around at night, you're walking, you know you're not gonna get *hit*, or beat up? There's a *chance* you can, but, you know, it's quiet. You feel safe.

Why do you think all of that stuff goes on in Iron City?

Why? 'Cause . . . I guess provety. Money, moneywise. That's about the most thing I can think of. If they had money . . . (Trails off:) They don't do it in Beverly Hills! (Laughs.) Only the people that don't got money does it. It's just, everyone's out to get money, or, you know, the *fame* of owning a lot of stuff—being the head person or something? That's what I feel about it.

What about in your family, is money a problem?

No . . . not to go out and get a brand-new car or something like that, but to get like clothes, to eat—we eat like, God! (Laughs.) I mean I eat as much as I want. Food, we have a house, three bedrooms, two bath-rooms, but it's just in Iron City. A lot of crime is around and we're always afraid someone's going to rob our house or something. 'Cause they do it around our neighborhood a lot. Yeah, but it's alright, we don't have problems with money that really much. I mean, we're not *wealthy* . . . (Hesitates.) The things that I'd really *like* to have, y'know . . . I don't have *them*, but I mostly get my way . . . 'Cause I beg for a little while, at Christmas . . . something like that.

And I got an aunt, you know, she takes care of me real good, and I don't live with my mom or nothing, so I get my way with her a lot. I live with a guardian, it's her like godfather, and we're alright, he's working at National Oil, we're alright. I guess my mom—well she was too young or something, alright? I had the chance to go back a thousand times, but I just stayed there. And ever since, I've been there. And I got dogs, pigeons, all type of stuff.

He's been to the Hall several times before, mostly for theft and burglary.

I guess it's when my guardian mother died . . . grandmother? Then I got set loose a little bit. You know, I got looser, and I got *madder*, and wilder, and I stayed out longer. It might've been over that, and it might've been 'cause of—she's the one mostly kept me around the house and stuff. My grandfather, he mostly let me go, you know? And I guess I started goin' out with my friends, drinkin', eventually stealin'. But not for the . . . (Pauses.) Maybe not for the money, but just to have the money in your pocket right *then* and not have to earn it or nothing to get it to you? Just to have it in a whole *bunch*. Eventually, we started, you know, all kinda stuff, stealin' . . .

Especially bikes. Right, OK, we got a nice expensive bike I used to race, like when they do them flips in the air and stuff? And we used to do that. My bike was stolen about *three times* in Iron City, so I guess I got mad, and me and my friends, we went out and got *other* people's bikes. But pretty soon I gave it all up, you know, and then I went to Juvenile Hall up here a couple times, about three times, over little garbage like that. And then I gave it up, right, and then I bought a motorcycle. And then it broke down, then I went out and stole one.

Then I started goin' in factories, gettin' money there, smokin' weed, drinkin', stayin' out late, you know, runnin' from the police, throwing bottles at the police station.

Throwing bottles?

Yeah! Just for the fun of them chasing us.

You liked it when they chased you?

Yeah, that was fun! There would be about fifteen of us, twenty, in a big old *pack*, you know, not out to fight or *kill* anybody, not to rob an old *lady*, but just to go out, get drunk and have fun! (Grins.) We'd throw bottles and hit the police station. Get up and just *run*, everyone just scatter, we never got caught. All the police cars, they would come from everywhere, you'd have to know how to hit fences and jump on *roofs* . . . get your hands tore up by barbed-wire *fences* . . . (Laughs.)

That's how I mostly started, you know, doing the crime, is friends, really. It depends on who you hang out with, to me. If you hang out with the wrong kind of people, you don't *have* to, but eventually you're gonna lead up to it. 'Cause you want to have friends. And them's the only kind of friends that you can find. And they *are* friends . . . they're good . . . but it's just the things they do to have fun. You know. They'll go play football with you and all that, but (casually:) when it's time to *do* somethin', we do it.

And I became like the clown of the pack, always havin' fun, and if someone dared me to do something, I'd do it. And in here they know about me, they call me Murdoch, from the A-Team? The white guy, the goofy one? Alright. I'm good for that.

I like to have fun. Always having fun. If you ask anyone in here, I'm always clowning around, having fun. I'll do *anything*, mostly. I can do everything: fish, hunt, whatever you want to do! Play games, whatever. Go anywhere! I'll usually join in.

He's a fine all-around athlete, but he never did sports in school: "I never really got into it, you know? I wanted to, I signed up and all that, but the grades, I guess mostly . . . I don't know how

I got good. I played baseball at the Farm, and I really . . . I found out that I had a talent that I didn't even know I had. I mean, I can do anything. I play every game, I'm good at it here. Some kids don't like it, some do. The jealousy, you know. But any game, dominoes, you know, whatever you want to play, I'll play." But he has trouble controlling his temper: *"I could get angry about anything. Anything could make me angry. Could happen to anyone. But I can take it to the limits more. 'Cause I got a bad temper. You know, I throw stuff around, not as to hurt anybody, not as to break anything, but sometimes I have broke stuff. Hit the wall, kick the doors, everything."*

When you steal stuff, or try to get the cops to come after you, is that about being angry?

Nah . . . that was fun. That was all fun. Stealing maybe, if you had more money in your pocket, that's *more* fun. To go out and spend money, maybe on girls, you know . . . If you got a lot of money, you could *eat* all the time, 'cause at your house, your parents just didn't know, but if you go out and buy a pizza, with your friend? It's gonna cost about ten dollars! For a couple pizzas? And I'll eat about ten pieces, eight, and . . . Go play video games, you know how much money goes down video games? And go get *beer* and *candy* and spend like . . . (Shakes his head.)

I remember I robbed this factory before, me and my buddy from the army. He's cool, but, you know, he just did it with me. Every year we did it when he came back. First time, we was roaming around—me, him, and a kid that used to be here in Juvenile Hall. Actually, we're pretty cool, you know, we're nice, around adults and everything, we were just going out and having fun, stealin', having fun, that's it. When we was walking around, we seen the guy counting money, this big ol' boat factory where they paint it, build it and stuff? I came back, and you know, they didn't have an alarm. We went in, no dogs, there was a man up there asleep, and snoring away. We was *laughin'* and makin' noise, and being stupid, and we found some money, right? Everyone just started *snatching* it, but we divided it up equally, and one kid stayed out front because he didn't want to come in, so we never shared no money with him! (Laughs.) We never told him about it till later. But then I started searchin' around, found a envelope full of hundreds, fifties, it was about eight hundred dollars, 'bout four hundred apiece, four twenty.

Every day, just not goin' to school, just . . . it was a life. Spending twenty dollars a day. Fifty. On my dogs. I bought dogs. Pits. Yeah, pit bulls. And I bought all kinds of *collars*, food, chains . . .

Every time, we'd get around, we'd just find some way to get a lot of money. It'd just *come* to us. And then we went to Wilson's [department store], you know. And we found out there was a way to steal shoes. Not wear 'em, take 'em back to another Wilson's and say "My parents bought this for me." Then we'd get two hundred dollars. Every year we'd hit Wilson's up. One time we got lucky. They was following us and we knew it. Alright, we'd ditch 'em. You know, the little security guards? We'd ditch 'em inside the girls' bathroom, stuff like that! (Laughs.) And we'd go around. And pretty soon there was another guy stealing suits. And we was about to get caught right there, but they turned around and got *him!* (Laughs.) They was chasing him and we just flew out the door. I got a hundred and eighty dollars, my friend got almost two hundred and something. Just sellin' the shoes back. Eighty-dollar shoes, ninety-dollar shoes.

And we'd go along the [railroad tracks], in River Heights, open up cars, find some money, or either start the car up and drive away. Never had no auto theft, just drive around, (he grins, clutching an imaginary steering wheel) eeerk! Get out and run.

And when he went back to the army, you know, it was boring for me. My friends started getting mad at me 'cause I never came around. 'Cause he was my best buddy. And then me and my *other* friend, we started robbing houses. For the quick fifty dollars, sixty dollars. And the fun, too. My friend was kind of serious, you know, he wanted to be quiet, and I was *laughing*, goofing off, throwing tennis balls against the wall, playing with the balls and stuff, messing around with little kids' toys, playing with their little four-by-fours . . . (Smiles.) And I was having fun, it was a big fun to me, to do that. But then we got money. But then we quit. We thought about getting shot, killed . . . so we quit.

Killed?

Right! They would. They would, in Iron City they will. 'Cause I know, if someone come to rob *my* house, we got shotguns in the other room. I'm just gonna grab a gun, y'know, and either he's gonna get outta my house or I'm gonna blow him, you know, *out*. He's gonna *go*. 'Cause I know how to shoot a gun, I go huntin' and stuff, so he's gonna go. (Casually:) It's mostly like that everywhere in Iron City, people around there really don't play around. You know. They're serious. Sometimes, you know, if you just *talk* stupid, talk can get you killed. And I've been around a lot of that.

You smart off. Or over dope. If you start selling dope for someone, then you start smokin' it, and smoke it up, then you gotta have it, so you start smokin' *their* dope, you can't pay it back, that'll get you *hurt*. That's mostly around Iron City. To me, that's what I've seen.

And then I was mostly not going to school, staying in the house all *day*, sleeping. Go out at night, come in about four, five o'clock in the morning. Stay in the house till three o'clock, four o'clock. Come back out. So I rode around at nighttime. Alone. That was bad. And I had a nice bike, six-or-seven-hundred-dollar bike, I used to race with? And that was bad. *Everyone* wanted it. So what I gotta do is get a car. So I don't have to be walkin' and stuff, riding my bike. And just, you know, go out with the right people, maybe get a girlfriend . . . (Trails off.) But, you know, not get in trouble no more.

We used to race over there. About thirty of us. We probably had about thirty thousand dollars' worth of bikes, all together of us. We'd come from Hillview all the way back to River Heights. I've rode over fifty miles before. Every day. Get your name in magazines, *BMX*, you know? I really enjoyed racing. I was fast. (Grins.) And I could jump real high. I used to compete like that with my friends. Freestyle. I could wheelie, on my back tire, five or six blocks.

You want to keep doing it?

Nope. Too old. Got rid of it. Sold my bike. You get bored with stuff like that, you've got to get out of that. And it's hard watching your bike. (Disgusted:) We got four of 'em ripped off, four-hundred, five-hundred-dollar bikes.

He's been in the Hall for eight months this time around. His probation was revoked because he wasn't in school. He was then stuck with extra time for fighting and "smarting off" in the Hall.

Not goin' to school. That was my last offense. School's the one that hit it off. I got five months for not goin' to school. A hundred fifty-one days. And I've been here eight.

I never went to school on the outs, either. I had problems at school.

You never went at all?

No, I went. I went to a lot of grades. But when I was little, fourth grade, I never liked to spell? So all the way through, I never spelled. And I still don't spell that good. If I want to spell, I grab a dictionary. I mean I can spell to write a letter, but no *economic* word or no big ol' *humongous* word. So I never did it. And then when they asked me to do a spelling test, I'd just sit here like *this,* (hands folded) just sit there and cover my hands, and I wouldn't do it, and they'd get pissed, and *I'd* get pissed, and I'd leave. And finally, I just quit goin'.

Did you ever ask them to help you out with the spelling?

Schools ain't *like* that. They don't—there isn't really no help at school. They just give you assignments, you do it or you don't do it. So that's how it is. I guess if you went to an *expensive* school . . . for all boys or all girls, something like that? *They* might give you help, but schools I've been to? The only school where there's an opportunity [was] for bad kids, the police made you go there, the law? And I mostly learned how to do a lot of math there. Lot of history. I remember a lot of history and English. But the rest of the schools . . . (Shakes his head.)

I wouldn't do no homework. Why would I want to bring homework *home* when I can't do it in *class?* You know, I'll go out and party with my friends, drink and stuff.

The schools, I'm just gonna tell the truth, they're really no help in Iron City. If you're smart . . . if you really wanna learn when you're little, you gotta grow up all the *way* doing that. So basically you gotta get into school *first*—and just have a good mind on your shoulders. If you don't got it, you know, you're gonna get into crime, drugs, or all that. And if your family's into it, too. If your family's into it, you're gonna be brought up the same way. Straight up. Unless you can change it. There's some people who can, but most of 'em can't.

How did your family deal with the school problem?

Well, when I was little, I used to get whuppin's, room time—well (laughs), that's what it's called *here*—go stay in your room, don't go outside? But, you know, then they couldn't spank me *all* the time, I'm gettin' a little bit too big! (Laughs.) About twelve, thirteen, I quit gettin' whuppin's, you know, with the belt, 'cause they seen they was doing no good. They'd just talk, talk to me all the time, right? First they'd talk to me—if I'd get kicked out again, I'd get in trouble, and a whuppin' was the last resort, 'cause they didn't think you had to, but if I'd smart off . . . Most times I got it when I deserved it.

He had a big belt. (Laughs.) And most of the time it was just over school. And, like, attitude problems. Or from anything. Like if they said, "Are you drinkin'?" and you *hadn't* even been drinkin', they'd get upset! Or the cops would come to your house thinking you burglarized a home . . . (Pauses.) And sometimes you're scared because you—I *have* done it before.

I went two years of ninth grade. I should've been in the tenth. I should be in the twelfth, right now, I don't even know *what* grade I'm in. See, I been locked up eight months. I been to *these* schools.

What do you think about these schools?

(Scornfully:) Aw. *This?* I hate it. This one don't cut it at all. This ain't *nothin'* here. I never learned nothing in here. You don't learn *nothing* in here. You don't learn nothing. It's easy, three hours a day, from eight to eleven. That's what, three hours? Three and a half? Thing to do is be quiet. If you're quiet, you're good, you'll do good. Just make like you're doing your work. I came here, for real they said I need help, at school. I ain't got no help there, that's where I need it. To go back on the outs and do good. 'Cause if I go back and get kicked out, I got to be sent right back in the Hall.

I'm gonna blame it on this place. I'm gonna try to tell the court this: "Well, they never set me, you know, to go out there and do better." I'm not learnin' sh——*crap* at this school. I ain't learning nothin'. Not one *thing*.

They should work with each kid and find him at his level, see what he can do. And *help* him, you know, to build up his encouragement, to work in school. Make it a *fun* way. If they have to give 'em a little prize, let them out of their room? You know, if you give these kids late-ups here, whoever gets the most—whoever tries? And when they get over a certain percentage, they try real hard? I bet you these kids'd be learning more. 'Cause I know *I* would. No one wants to be in their room. And that's one way to do it. I feel that.

Or they could spend their time, you know . . . (Earnestly:) If the teacher can't help us, then they should have a private tutor. For each kid. Work with the kid each day, each separate kid, whoever needs help. Smart ones, go about their work with the teachers. Dumb ones, the dumb ones should be with a person, you know, maybe two in a class, that can get along with another teacher, so he can get help, 'cause you know he's gonna have to get a job later on.

And you know, the only thing you're gonna do . . . (Stumbling:) If I don't . . . I'm gonna have to go in the army, you know, if I don't . . . If I just keep on getting in trouble, I'm gonna go out, take my G.E.D., and just get in the army. And probably make a life of it, you know? I'm gonna have to do *something*.

You can ask *all* these kids, they don't *know* what they're gonna do. They *say* they're gonna be all *this*, and all *that*, but you know . . . There's only a couple of them that's going to be. There's only a couple that's gonna be what they're gonna be. People who've got money, that's what they're gonna be.

If they don't have money . . .

They're stuck.

Do you have an idea of what you'd really like to be doing?

I'd like to work carpenter. 'Cause, you know, you start in that, all you have to do is learn to read a tape measure. And I've been doing a lot of stuff. I build all my stuff, pigeon cages, saw, work in shop, you know, I go out and I hang Sheetrock with a guy . . . It's fun to me. Hammering and stuff. It's not that hard work. It's hard, but it's nothing—(frowns:) it's not gonna *kill* you, you know? Like working in a *fume* place, you know, gasoline always around you, or something. Liquid. So that's what I'd kind of like to do.

And if I couldn't do that? I'd be lost, probably. 'Cause I don't know what else I'd like to do. Not unless it's an easy job. Like *this*. (He gestures around the room.) I been thinking about this is just about the coolest job any person could have. Being a counselor? It's the coolest job you could have. To me. It's simple! They might say it's hard, but it's *so* simple. Besides the paperwork, it's so simple. To watch us. To play dominoes with us and play pool. Come here every day and get good at pool. They eat with us. Listen to the radio. It's just like home! You know? Use the bathroom . . . Good money, watch these kids . . . So this would be a good place.

Or police officer. It's good. I kind of like that, too. Though I guess that's a hard job. 'Cause (laughs) I've seen the police come after *me*, when I've been in, you know, someone's backyard, and you *know* they're petrified, 'cause they're walking slow, that someone's gonna come out and *shoot* 'em, with a gun. Every time you see a cop in Iron City, they've always got their hand on their guns, or dogs, 'cause they're petrified. A lot of cops get killed.

I'd really rather be a carpenter. But . . . (he hesitates, concentrates) there's really not . . . I don't think there's gonna be that much *room* for 'em, in a while. It's just slowing down, to me. They're finding like new things, new ways to, um . . . they're probably gonna build the houses easier, where they just connect *bolts*. I don't think they're gonna be using hammers and, you know, wood, that much. Maybe wood for the inside of the house, but you see how, you know, they needed workers for buildings? Now they got machines to put up the big old . . . it's got people directing it, foremen, really, so that'd be cool. I don't know. It's just gonna come that way.

But I got my heart set on going in the army for a long time.

You think that's going to be your best shot . . .

Yes. For a lot of kids it is. You know. You get trained in there, well enough to take care of your*self*, alone. You can build up money to go to college. You can save money, and you're living there. And get a car. And get yourself on the way. Maybe move away, to a nicer neighborhood. Get married, something. Well, naw, I don't want to get married! (Laughs.)

Why not?

(Quickly:) If I can't support *me*, how'm I gonna support someone else? See?

You're afraid you wouldn't be able to support somebody in the future . . .

Right. Maybe. You never can tell. Because the future comes. Might hit the lottery or something! (Laughs.)

But the job situation worries you?

Aw, yeah. Well, everyone! Just 'cause we're kids—well, I'm almost gonna be eighteen in a little while—just 'cause we're kids, you know, everyone's thinking about it. 'Cause you know . . . I'm almost out of school, what am I gonna do when I'm out of school? Have a *paper route* or something? God! That ain't gonna cut it.

So . . . school is . . . (A long pause.) Everything's 'bout money to me. You can get by with school if you got money. 'Cause if you go to a rich school, they'll mostly . . . If you pay, you start donating money? I know a kid's dad donates money there, he ain't that smart, but he got *out*. And he's gonna get a good job, I know he will. In a way he's pretty smart. In a way.

What about when you get out? You want to go back to school?

I'm not. I don't really want to. I have problems in *every* school. The only way I can do it is night school. If I can't get night school, I don't know what I'm gonna do.

I don't want to come back. Pretty soon I'm getting old enough where it's gonna lead into a bigger jail. County jail. This is a play game, right here. (Disgusted:) This ain't nothin'. But pretty soon it's gonna lead to something worse. Staying out of trouble, you know, is my . . . big . . . hero at the moment. (Laughs.) 'Cause I don't want to come back.

If I could make you president of the United States . . .

I don't know, I'd probably be too worried about war! (Laughs.) Yeah. Of course. Well, I'm not maybe *really* worried 'cause there's *other* people who worry about it. But in a way, *everybody's* worried about it. I'm sure they are. 'Cause, you know . . . You read in the magazines—I can read and stuff—about big nucular bombs and stuff, and what they can *do*, and how *big* they are, and what they're *filled* with, so, you know, makes you think, 'course it does.

But if I was president? I'd try—people that pay taxes? Give it to the schools. Find where they need the help at with the kids. Give it to the town. For the police. Police need a lot of money for more policemen. And . . . try to fix up the town. Where there's provety, you know, bad houses and all that? Fix it up. And if it's in a desperate need, you know, make a certain place where maybe they can get more money to pay their rent. If they're using dope, put 'em in a place like a jail, for dope. Till they can get their act straight. That's the only thing I can think of.

Maybe we will *make you president.*

Yeah. (Softly:) When ten years happen, hope I'm doing *something*.

14

"Maybe one of these days I'll come back and be a real person"

I kind of live everywhere, really.

Small, frail, very pretty, she has a series of deep slashes up one forearm from wrist to elbow. "They're old . . . What do I do that for? It's like if I get depressed over a guy or something." Another smaller set of gashes on the underside of her arm, near the wrist: "These are kind of new. I was pissed off 'cause I was in this fucked-up place." She's feisty, intense: as we talk she taps her foot, raps the table, tosses her long red hair out of her face. She was arrested for being drunk and disorderly in a Rivertown city park after running away from Safe Haven, a local shelter for runaways.

I was drunk in public. OK, I came back to Safe Haven, right? I was waiting to run away. And so a friend of mine came back to Safe Haven, too. And we ran away together. It was me and Jennifer Sams, you know her? Blond hair? Big tits? And we got drunk and everything. And so the Rivertown police—fuckin' assholes got nothing better to do than fuck with the kids. We weren't doing *shit*, you know? We weren't disturbing the private, I mean the public peace, or anything like that. But they're still gonna pick us up, of course, when they see us. So they brought us here and I been here ever since.

But when I get out of here, they just better give it up because they ain't gonna keep *me*. They should have learned by now they aren't gonna keep Ginny Swenson. 'Cause I'm gonna do what I want to do. I've been telling them that for the last four years, and I been *doing* it. But if they haven't learned yet, they'll learn one of these days.

She was born fourteen years ago yesterday in Rivertown. "My family's in Idaho . . . Montana . . . around there. Washington. About four years ago I came out here to live with my dad and everything and it didn't work out. So he left. He's somewhere off somewhere, I don't know where. So now I'm kicking it here. I came here from my mom's house to live with him. Well, actually I kind of left him and then he left. And all's he said was 'You better take care of my fucking daughter.' "

He wanted me to go with him, but I didn't want to. 'Cause I hated him.

How come you hated him?

Cause he's a *dick*. I mean he drinks and everything, badly. And he acts the fool when he's drunk. I think he's in Arizona. Or in Washington.

Does he try to stay in touch with you?

Probably tries, but probably just can't find me. 'Cause after I left, he kept trying to come and get me, and after a few times he finally realized I wasn't gonna go with him, and he finally gave up. Smart. (Laughs.)

And your Mom . . .

She knows where I am, basically. (Casually:) You know, she knows I'm still in the *state* and everything. But she just doesn't want to talk to me. And stuff like that. She's a bitch. I ain't sweatin' her.

Off and on, I live on the streets. Sometimes like if I get sick of being out there, you know, or if it gets too rough or something, then I'll come to Child Protective and they'll put me somewhere. Safe Haven or something. And then when I get ready to leave again, I'll leave, go back out on the street. That's like my *life*, out there on the street.

But it gets pretty dangerous, doesn't it?

Yeah, it does. I've been through a lot of the most dangerous things. (Shrugs:) Don't really mean nothing to me, though.

It doesn't scare you so much . . .

No. Doesn't scare me. (Pauses:) I've been raped . . .

That doesn't scare you so much either?

Not really. I mean . . . (Laughs.) I know that's terrible, but . . . (Earnestly:) It's one of those *challenges*. I mean if you're gonna be out there, you have to prepare for whatever's gonna *come* to you, you know what I'm saying?

I like it. I really do. (Smiles.) You probably think I'm crazy. But I do. It's challenging, you know? And I like that. It never gets boring, you know? You meet a lot of different people. Some good, some bad. Definitely some bad. (Laughs.) It's pretty cool, I like it.

I don't like to *go* to people for things. I like to try to do it myself. You know? because I just—I don't like that.

You don't like being dependent on other people?

No. I don't.

So where do you stay then?

Sometimes in the park. And once in a while at a friend's house. You know, depending on if they're like "Why don't you come over and party for a while?" And then I'll probably go crash there for the night or something. Here and there. Sometimes I don't go to sleep. At all. Food? I'm not the type. I don't really eat that much or anything. But if I do, I just kind of like steal it, sometimes. Or like . . . um . . . (hesitates, embarrassed:) Before, I've like done things with people for money. You know.

It's not really prostitution, because I don't go stand on the corner and fuck *anybody*. But like I'll meet someone, like a guy or something, right, talk to him, he'll get what he wants, you know, if he gives me what *I* want, you know what I'm saying? And it works out. But some guys: "Fuck you bitch, I'm gettin' what I want and that's it." But some of them give me something, too. I make it, though, all right.

You don't worry about not getting enough to eat?

No. Because food ain't nothing to me anyway, really. I mean all I need is just a little bit a day. 'Cause I don't really like food.

What about if you get sick or something?

Then I come back to Child Protective. Till I get better or whatever. And then I leave again. I know that's pretty bad. That's like—I don't *like* to do it, but I don't really have no other choice. They're like a hotel, or something! (Laughs.) Some things, as much as I do want to be independent, some things I have to be dependent on. I mean I know I can't take care of myself a hundred percent, you know, 'cause like when I get sick and stuff, I come to them. But I try to do most things, almost anything I can, on my own. But if it gets to be terrible, then I come to them. Like if I get a cold or something or, you know, I feel kind of sick, I don't come to them till it gets *bad*.

Sometimes I'll stick with them a little while, you know, try it, and then I say, "Fuck it," and leave. It's *hard!* (Laughs.) I mean in a way a little part of me wants to change, you know, make something out of myself. And the other part of me says, "Nope, I gotta get back out there."

She also trades her body for dope, but she doesn't consider herself really strung-out: "Not yet. Hopefully, I won't be. I feel OK about it. I mean I don't—I can take it or leave it. The ones that are strung-out just don't know how to handle it. Don't know when to quit it, you know what I'm saying? Like if they're . . . fast, if they don't use their heads."

I like it, too. I *love* it. I like coke. Coke and alcohol. My alcohol I steal though. Like Safeway? It's really easy to steal it from there. (Proudly:) I haven't got caught yet, though.

I'm pretty smart. I pretty much know what's up. I've learned. Like when I first started out I was stupid, you know? But I've learned, in the past few years. How to kind of—know people? Even though I haven't known them? You know what I'm saying? And shit like that. How to judge people, all that kind of stuff. How to get what I want. I mean I still have more to learn, probably. But I make it OK now.

See, a couple of my friends in Hillview are dealers. You know, coke dealers and everything. And I can get coke from them. And you know, sometimes . . . (Pauses.) I can fuck someone for some coke, or something like that. (Laughs.) I know that's terrible . . . but it's true.

You feel bad about doing that?

No. To be honest with you I don't. (Smiles uneasily:) Seriously.

Does it ever make you mad, about your parents leaving you?

Not anymore. It used to. But now it's their fucking loss.

That's when I started drinking, and stuff like that. Doing it—you know, having sex with boys, stuff like that.

(She was ten.)

My mom got disgusted and everything. And her husband, also, we didn't get along. Well, he drank too, they were both drinking a lot, and he was just an asshole. So I said, "Fuck it"—came out here looking for my dad.

He was drinking a lot, too. Cause when I came back, he celebrated with a case of beer! (Laughs.) It was kind of my fault he started drinking, though, 'cause he had stopped, I guess. Supposedly. From what I hear. He had stopped for a while. And when I came back, I said, "Well, Dad, let's get some beer," you know, "celebrate, I'm back!" You know; I hadn't seen him since I was—they got divorced when I was three and then I saw him once when I was seven. So it was like "Damn"! (Laughs.) So he's all "OK"! So him, my aunt, my cousin, and me were all fixing to have a good old time and everything, get drunk. And then like all my friends around that neighborhood, they're all like older, like *hella* fuckin' partyers, party day and night, even on weekdays. And *he* started partying with them too, and everything.

Like the ones across the street, they'd have big parties in their garage, and he'd go over there a lot. Me and my cousin would go over there, my Dad would go over there a lot. Crazy bastard. (Laughs, shakes her head.) But they liked him. Cause he partied and drank with them, and stuff.

And then finally things got out of hand. So I said, "Fuck it. Fuck *him.*"

I'd go over and stay with my boyfriend. My boyfriend *then.* He was twenty-two. I was twelve, and part of the time I was thirteen. My Dad would chase me, and off and on I'd live with him. Like he brought the police there to my boyfriend's house. And then like after I was with him for a long time, we broke up. And then when I'd run from him, I'd go . . . (stumbles) and, ah, probably stay in the bushes. I could go like to *friends'* sometimes, but like—I didn't want to ruin my welcome, so I'd like stay there one night, "Thanks a lot," you know. Stay out in the bushes and steal food. And I didn't stick around Rivertown for long. 'Cause I got sick of Rivertown. It gets boring after a while.

Is there anything that really does make you mad, that you wish you could change?

Yeah. To be honest, I wish that these fuckin' Child Protective people and these dumb-ass authority people would just leave people like me that wanta be out there doin' what they wanta do the fuck *alone.* The people that *want* help, just let them come and get it, don't *chase* after the people. If somebody wants help, they're gonna come and ask for it. Basically. (Emphatically:) And if people *don't* want it, they should just leave them the fuck alone. That's what I'd want to change. I don't think that's right.

You don't think they have a responsibility to reach out, try to take care of you?

Well . . . yeah, they do. But some people don't want that. Like me. You know? I've been trying to tell 'em for the fuckin' past four years, "Leave me the fuck alone." I mean, yeah; that *is* good in a way, if they try to reach out, but in a way it's not. Just depends on which way you look at it, you know, what point of view. Am I making sense to you at all?

Yeah.

She likes to write poetry, about "love, mostly." "Well, it's not basically love . . . It's like hurt, you know what I'm saying? Like a guy you met or something, and something happened, and you got a broken heart about it, and that shit?" "Does that happen a lot with you? Getting a broken heart?" "Not as much as it used to. 'Cause I'm not letting it. I'm not as—I don't know if you want to call it naive, or what, as I used to be."

You don't let people take advantage of you . . .

No.

Her brothers and sisters are "around Idaho and stuff like that. Around Kansas . . ." Her older sister has been in touch with her from time to time: "She wants me to quit."

Maybe one of these days. When I get older . . . (Thoughtfully:) I'm sure I probably won't be doing this *forever.* I mean I don't intend to be a *bum.* I just want to be . . . I like challenges. And adventures and stuff?

Is there another kind of challenge you could get into, that might make you want to do something different than what you're doing now?

No. I don't think so. Have to be something good . . . (vaguely:) modeling . . . I'd have to fucking get my act together and go to one of these group homes and stuff, but I ain't ready for that yet. I may never —I mean it may be just a dream that never comes true, but maybe one of these years.

She hasn't been in school for "a couple of years."

I think the last grade I probably completed was possibly sixth grade.

Ever feel like you'd want to go back?

I don't know, to be honest. 'Cause I'm still not done exploring the world, you know? I mean (laughs), I'm still ready to *go.* I just want people to leave me alone and just let me do what I'm gonna do. 'Cause I'm gonna do what I want to do anyway.

Does anybody hassle you about not being in school?

If they do, I just tell 'em to fuck off. I mean they *do,* sometimes. But, you know. It's my business. It's not *their* business.

If I was *out* there, I'd be happy. I really would. I know you won't believe that. Being locked in, I don't like that feeling. (Quietly:) Like the other day I just felt so locked in I just fucking *cried* all day. Like, God, get me the *fuck* out of here. Especially if you're used to being where you want to be when you want to be there and how you want to do what you want to do and all *that* shit?

She's felt suicidal many times.

I tried once when I think I was about eleven. I OD'd. Pills. Said, "*Fuck* it." Now if I wanted to kill myself, I could easily do it. 'Cause I have my drug-dealing friends out there. I could kill myself with no problem. But I'm not gonna do that. I'm not *done* yet. I'm not doing that shit no more.

(Yesterday was her birthday.)

Did you have a party?

No! In this shithole? (Laughs.) Fucking—they gave me this puny-ass, disgusting, ugly old plain-ass stationery, this stinky-ass perfume. Some pretty good cake, though. But I planned on going out there. I planned on being out there, getting fucked up, for my birthday. Party with some friends. But *no,* had to end up in *here.* But that's OK. (Laughs.) I'll have a belated party. Get fucked up. *Seriously* fucked up. More fucked up than usual. I mean *fucked up*. I'd probably get wasted off my ass. I know I would.

Being fucked up is pretty fun . . .

Sometimes. Sometimes I can't . . . (hesitates; slowly:) keep my mind together . . . so something happens to me.

Do people try to rip you off?

Rip me off for *what? I* ain't got nothin' for nobody to rip off.

Good point.

I don't sweat that. 'Cause if anybody tried to do that, my friends would just *shoot* 'em. They're big-time—big-time dealers. They're the big boys. Not the *little* boys that are selling twenty-dollar rocks on the corner, you know. Thousands of dollars a day and shit.

I was walking down the street with a couple of my friends and they're all "Hey, babe" and all that stuff. They were driving a BMW, and that was the night of the Pebbles concert? Started talking to us and everything? Gave me their number, partied with them. So if anything like that happened, I could just tell them what's up and they could have two hundred people after the motherfuckers. I swear to God. I'm not lying. It's true. That's how into it they are.

If I made you president and you could do anything you wanted . . .

I'd say, "Motherfuckers, you can all go free." I don't give a fuck if they're here for murder, there's still murderers *out* there—big-time ones, too, worse than these little ones in here. And I'd say fuck these Child Protective-ass people. I'd make it legal for people to run away, I'd make it legal for people to live on the street, shit!—(vehemently:) legal for fucking *drugs,* 'cause if people are stupid enough to do them, then they're killing *themselves,* the drug dealers aren't killing them, so you know, it's their choice. People say the drug dealers are killing people, they *ain't.* People have to . . . it's their choice if they want to do it or not. I'd make that shit legal, I swear to God I would. And . . . I'd get me some money, get me a house. (Laughs.) Noo . . . But anyway.

Even though she prefers living on the street, she's had some bad days. The "weirdest day" was about a year ago when she had just turned thirteen.

I was in Hillview, right? and I was just walking around the street. And it was really weird. This was the day I got raped. I was walking on like Hillcrest Road, walking around out there, and these guys just stopped and "Ooh, babe, what's up," and all this stuff. And all this shit, and I said, "Not much," and everything, you know . . . and to make a long story short, we got some peppermint schnapps and drove back up to Hillcrest Road, and we're kicking it drinking and everything, and they got—you know, they fucked, and everything.

And then later on that same night, I was just walking around and everything and there was this guy, this white guy, I guess he was drunk, and he just started chasing me and everything, right? I mean, he's chasing after me, and shit, and I'm all "What the fuck?" And he's like "Say, wait, stop, I just want to talk to you for a minute" and shit, and I go "Leave me the fuck alone!" And then these guys just kind of said, "Hey, leave her alone," and then he just kind of like left me alone after they told him to leave me alone. And I walked off. And it was like . . . shit like that was happening, and that happened just all in one *day*. I mean that's not that *much* really, but it was a pretty weird day. It's weird, it's weird even just thinking, you know, talking about it.

What's a real good day?

Almost *every* day! (Smiles.) See some of my friends and everything, kick it. I'd just, you know, get fucked up, steal a bottle from Safeway. I meet, you know, new people every day, too. So it's like I have people everywhere.

I love it out there. That's all I've got to say. I *love* it out there. Yeah, I do. And I don't think I'm the only one. I just love it, oh, *God* I love it. I wanta get the fuck out of here and go back out there. And I'm going to. And these fucking people can kiss my ass.

Maybe one of these days I'll come back and be a real person . . .

You are *a real person.*

Well, you know what I mean.

Postscript

The next time I saw Ginny, she had been put on medication because she'd been disruptive in the unit. "Did you ever hear of thorazine? I went off the other night. I was just pissed. Sick of this place. And the other shit, I think it's that stella stuff* . . .
They give you fifty milligrams a day. I love them though, I swear. You probably think I'm crazy. I used to get so high, whooooa! It was killer! *People on the outs are trying to shoot up thorazine! Only difference between shooting it up and doing it orally, or whatever the fuck that is, is it gets to your blood faster."*

---

* Stelazine, another "antipsychotic" medication.

"They can't arrest us all"

They got me into drugs when I was about eight. My mother and my stepfather.

He's graceful, slight, a natural athlete, with long, flowing dark hair, "part Italian, part redneck." Like a lot of kids in the Hall, he hasn't been locked up for committing a specific crime, but for violating the conditions of his probation: "Not living at home. Dirty urinalysis. Failure to show up at meetings at the probation office. Things like that." He's been arrested before for robbery and vandalism—destroying public property.

"The rest of the family's never really been into drugs. I come from a family that one aunt is a nurse, another is a teacher, and another aunt's a model. And my mother's like the only one that's just stuck, not doing anything. My mom, when she was a kid, she was the rowdy one in the family, and I just—I don't know, I just inherited being the rowdy one in the family, I guess. I've been in trouble with the law for, well, not really quite a lot of time, but just on and off."

They had me transplanting weed from a grower into coffee cans, because they had like a *garden* inside the house. It was a long wooden box with dirt—soil and stuff—with *weed* growing in it. *I* didn't know what they were. I was young, vulnerable, she told me it was tomato plants. I didn't know what tomato plants looked like anyway (laughs), so I agreed with her. And then when I was about eight, their friends came down from Oregon with two big Hefty Steel-Saks full of weed, just all these *buds*, and the guy was sitting there and they started smoking it, and my dad said, "You want some of this, you want some?" Said, "Sure," you know. Took a hit, and I was, you know, *loaded*. And I liked it. I thought, "God, this is *neat*." And I thought, "This is pretty fun." I was laughing, you know, having a good time, had *everybody* laughing, and I just kept on it ever since.

Then my mom started working two jobs. My stepdad left us, she started working two jobs, and she started doing cocaine. And then like she'd get drunk and she'd give it to me and my brother. I was about ten or eleven. He was about twelve. And then when that got too expensive for her, she started doing crank, and then she got us on *that*, got us doing that. "Here," you know, "you want some of this? Try some of this, try some of that." You know, you just *did* it, you didn't think there was anything wrong with it. Like, "Gee, *Mom* can do it, her *friends* do it, everyone in the *family* does it, can't *we* do it?" And we just kept doing it, and then pretty soon it wasn't Mom giving it to us anymore; we were looking for it. Somebody would give it to us, or we'd go find it.

Usually, I have a lot of girlfriends, and a lot of them are like "You
· wanta go party or something?" "Well, I don't know, stay here for a while." "Well, I'll go get some of this and some of that," you know. And they would buy a lot. The girls I go out with, they just buy it and give it to me. So I usually don't end up paying for it. I haven't bought any drugs in the last two years! I've, like, if my friends only had ten dollars and wanted me to get a quarter, I'll throw in five, ten, fifteen, or something. But I won't go *looking* for it, fiend for this, fiend for that, "I need some of this." I won't rob people, steal from people, steal people's stuff to get drugs.

How did your mom feel about giving you drugs? Did you ever talk with her about it?

Every time I tried talking to her about it, she was like . . . how do I put it? "Well, it's *your* fault you're doing the drugs!" You know, she didn't want to take any of the responsibility for it, of giving it to us in the first place. "Well, if you wouldn't've, you know, took that first joint, or whatever, if you wouldn't of smoked it, then you wouldn't be doing it now." It's like, well, *you* guys are doing it all over the house, have stuff everywhere, how are we supposed to *not* do it? (Ostentatiously:) "You have your own mind. We can't force you to do anything." You know, she was like that.

And then the society and environment and everything I grew up in, it's how *most* of the people were. All the kids my age, you know, most of *them* were doing it. It's the way I've always grown up, I guess.

I had a job where I was a laborer for a construction site. I was running around cleaning up things; pull a tractor over here, drive a truck over here, just drive it over for them so they could load it, and they'd take it wherever. And I was getting paid about eight dollars an hour, made fairly good money. And like I'd get paid and I'd go home, and I'd be at the house and my Mom would come by. "Oh, we're going to do this. We'll be back in about twenty minutes." I'll say, "No, I'm not going to stay here, because I know you're just going to take off. I'm not going to stay here." I'll try to leave. My stepdaddy's real big, he's about six-six, six-seven. He's like "Are you going to stay here or are you going to leave. You've got two choices. If you leave, you're not coming back to this house. Period. So you can stay here and watch the kids while we're gone for a little while." It's like "Oy, of *course* I'm going to stay!"

And if I stayed, they wouldn't leave me any money! I'd go open the refrigerator, it's like "Uh, what about the *food* for them?" "Well, *you* just got paid." And I'm "Uh, well, it's my *brother and sister!* Aren't *you* the parents, aren't you supposed to support all three of us?" "Well, you just decide what you're going to do." And they'd leave, and it's like—I'm not going to let my little sister and brother go hungry. You know, if all I had was ten dollars, whatever, I'd buy ten dollars of food for them, and I'd just let them eat and just, you know, do without myself.

And I love my little brother and sister a lot, and I'd end up putting them to bed, cleaning up the house, straightening up my mother's room, my room, the kids' room, everything, picking up after them, doing a lot of the housework and everything, and, you know, spending up till two or three in the morning just wondering when they'd get back. They'd come back about three days later: "Oh, well, we were in Oregon looking at a house." "*Oregon?* Well, I was stuck here and I only have like fifteen dollars left from my paycheck that I had two hundred dollars!" "Oh, well, I don't know what to tell you . . ."

You didn't hear from them all this time?

No. And like my mom, she wasn't too good about paying me back. My stepdad, you know, we never really got along, 'cause like the second day I *met* him, he picked me up off the ground, choked me and swung a hammer at me and stuff, tried to hit me with a hammer. He'd pay me back, though. He'd pay me back a little of the money I'd spent. Plus, I'd buy more groceries for the house and stuff so that *I* could eat later, too, so I could come back and still eat . . . (He's quiet for a while.)

Everything just started getting to where I didn't want to have to deal with it. It wasn't my problem really, but I still, you know, put up with the responsibilities. I'd have my girlfriend or something stay there and watch my little brother and sister while I'd go to work, come back, and I'd tell her thanks for everything. She'd stay there till eight or nine at night. Her mom would come and get her.

You feel like you kind of had to be a parent . . .

Uh-huh. (Laughs.) I'd think, like, this must be how *they* feel, my parents feel, when *I* take off for two or three days at a time! They'd wonder where I am, why I haven't been around, why I haven't contacted them, if I'm dead or alive or in a car wreck. I'd be worried, 'cause I *do* love my mother, and I'd be worried like, if she's up in Oregon, I mean, there's a lot of winding roads and stuff, a lot of trees. So they could go off the road and into the forest somewhere and not be found for a week, and I'd be thinking like "God," you know, "they could be dead." I'd be real worried and everything. And I'd be thinking, "God!" and entirely reverse the situation, you know; like, "Where are my *kids* at?" (Laughs.) You know, "Where have *my* kids gone? I haven't seen them for three days now. What's goin' on here?" I'd think like, "God, this must be like how Mom and Ray feel."

And a lot of times, when my little brother and sister—one of them was what, five, and the other seven—so they were like "Haaagh!!" Real noisy, and a lot of times I'd be like (totally exasperated:) "Ohhh, aaaack!" I'm about to drop-kick them *both* out of the top-story window here and just (laughs), you know, go get *me* some food and *forget* these kids. And I'd have to put up with it. I'd have to put up with it. I'd finally get them to get to sleep and I'd end up getting just *loaded*, just loaded as I could while they were asleep so I could put up with them when they woke up.

And then finally I just moved out. My mom, I just told her, "I can't handle this anymore." I moved in with one of my friends. It was going good until the cops came over, kicked in the door, brought me here. They said because I violated probation.

He's candid about his own drug problem, his heavy use of crank and cocaine. But he draws the line at dealing.

My mother sold crank, my brother sold it, and a lot of my friends have sold it. I won't sell it. I'm not going to—you know, if I'm going to do drugs, that's *my* life I'm ruining. I'm not going to try selling it to everybody else, try screwing everybody else's life over. You know, if that's what they want to do, that's *their* choice, but I'm not going to help them. That's how I see it. They can go to the next guy, the next man for their dope, not me.

He wants to quit drugs altogether.

I'm not gonna do it. I'm not gonna do dope at all. If I do, I'm just going to end up back with the [juvenile authorities]. And I'm not going to do it. It's not worth it just to feel good for an hour or two and get a headache and go to sleep. It's not worth it to me. I've been doing it for a long time. That's what keeps me coming back time after time. That's the problem. That's the thing I've got to stop doing. It's either that or it's years of my *life*, either give up a few hours' high or a few years' pain and misery sitting in a cell somewhere, not knowing what's going on outside, not being able to see any *girls*, not being able to do things, go places, have fun. Then when you get out, you'll probably be worse than when you went in!

Most of the kids who go come out worse, because all they do the whole time they're there is talk about robbing, stealing, killing, raping, and everything else, you know? The first day out, they don't get laid from some girl, they're just gonna take it into their own hands and they're going to *make* the girl. A lot of them will do it. They go, "I'm not going to get caught, *she* don't know me." And they always end up being busted and right back up for rape. And it's not going to be me, coming out worse. 'Cause I'm having enough problems *now*.

He dropped out of high school a year ago. He wants to go back, but his mom isn't helping, and he's not getting any help from the schools or the probation department either.

My probation officer doesn't *want* me to go to a normal school. He doesn't want me to go. He says I'll get in too much trouble. I know most of the people, you know, at Rivertown High School. And he's afraid that I'll get in trouble, get in more trouble than I would if I was going to the county school, like the little County Day? Where you go from eight to twelve? (Snorts.) I'll get in more trouble *there!* I got more time in the day to do *whatever.*

And like I *wanted* to get back in school? I went down—and like I stayed out all night one night, getting drunk and everything, and about six o'clock in the morning: "Oh, God, I've got to go to school!" I had to go down and get signed up and everything. And I still made it! I could have just stayed there, the appointment gone and everything, but I took on a responsibility. (Proudly:) I didn't call anybody or anything. I *walked* down, I was clear on the other side of town, too. I went all the way clear across Rivertown, whoosh, went home, showered and everything, got in the car, went down there, got enrolled, and they said, "Oh, well, we don't have an opening, sorry." I said, "What do you mean? Someone told me I have to be down here this morning, get in, 'cause you had an opening." "Oh, I forgot to tell you, they gave the opening to somebody else, 'bye!" So I left.

So my P.O. asks, "So why aren't you in school?" So I said, "They gave my opening away." "Oh, well, just wait until there's another opening." So I'm waiting. And he arrested me for not being in school. (Laughs.)

I'd like to be an oceanographer, like studying underwater life, the animals, everything. I started, it was in seventh or eighth grade, I did this thing on Halley's comet, and found out that a lot of space and everything has a lot to do with the ocean, the tide and everything. And I just started getting into marine biology and everything, and the two of them, why they just started getting to me. It was like I was being *pulled* toward them. And I just started talking to this one teacher, Ms. Bernstein, one of my eighth-grade teachers? I just started talking to her about it. She was the science teacher, and I was ahead of everybody else in science. They were all staying in algae and *fungus* and all this stuff, and I was already into marine biology and everything. They were still studying land biology, and I was already in the water.

She started telling me, you know, "If you want to get into this, it's going to take a lot of math." And then she ordered to my math teacher to get me doing harder math. She asked to see my math. I showed it to her and it was all *right*, all the problems were right. She thought, "This work's too easy." She said, "It's really boring, huh?" I said, "It's *real* boring. So she ordered harder math for me, got me doing a lot harder math. There's the thing. I've been doing math good, and I just got into oceanography and astronomy and it all came together.

Me and my brother won this grand-prize thing at the 7-Eleven where you scratch off one of those little cards, the little Hulk and everything? And it was like eight thousand dollars, a TV and stereo, and all this other stuff, and they'd throw seventy-five hundred dollars each into a scholarship. And we won it. And plus my whole family is always like putting money into a scholarship for me and my brother. 'Cause nobody in our family's ever finished college, except one aunt. She's the manager of a credit union. She's like the district manager of First American Credit Union, and she's real smart. She's the only one that ever finished college.

But this is my biggest problem: just being able to, you know . . . (softly:) the plans I make, the goals I set, being able to accomplish them. 'Cause I always think, "God, I'm going to end up back in *here*, I know it. I'm going to end up locked up again."

Why do you think so?

Because I *tell* myself I will. And, you know, my family is like . . . Well, my mom, she's like "Well, you're just a *drug addict*, you're not good for *anything*, you don't do anything *right*, you can just rot in *jail*." I say, "Well, if that's how you want it, that's how it will be." I'll make sure she gets her way.

I think she's afraid me and my brother will wind up *better* than her.

She doesn't like us to know that she's in a financial bind and everything. She'll try to lie to us about it, when we *know!* She doesn't *think* we know, but we do. And like she'll get really upset when we try to bring up, you know, the financial situation and everything. She'll get really, you know, like "Oh, we're doing fine. Don't worry about it. Well, you've got clothes, don't you? We have the house, there's still food, isn't there? OK, then don't worry about it." It's like, well (shakes his head, exasperated), we're losing things slowly but surely. Last week it was the phone, and what's next week? I mean, we'll lose the *water,* the *electricity,* what?

And my brother, he's like "You don't need it, Nicky." He's always telling me, "You don't need it." He said, "You need a job, an apartment." And he said, "You're not going to stay with Mom anymore, you're going to live with *me.* Because you don't need this kind of thing." I got a sister who's thirteen, she doesn't even live with our family. She lives with my stepmother, my dad's wife before he died. She doesn't want anything to do with our family.

I do a lot of that—just getting down on myself, thinking: "You can't do it, you can't even, you know, stay out of *jail.* How are you going to finish high school, finish college?" That's one thing I really want to do, at least finish high school, at least get my high school diploma. I'm not going to take a G.E.D. or anything like that. I want to get my high school diploma, graduate from high school. I've only gotten one D in my whole life in school. It's the lowest grade I've ever got is a D, and the rest of the time, it's all A's, B's, sometimes C's. The only time I get C's it's like history, civics, government. There's nothing to it, really. I mean you don't really learn too much. I mean like civic government, it's real boring. I like history. History's a lot better. I like learning what happened before our time. I don't like to know about our government, whatever. I mean, I kind of understand democracy, republic, and all this stuff, the Democratic Party, voting; I understand all that pretty much. But it's just . . . (searches for the word) bland.

We're talking about why so many Rivertown kids seem to wind up in the Hall—including a lot of Nick's friends. He reflects for a minute.

A lot of people are . . . unfair to society. Like, you know, child molesters, rapists; they're unfair to society. But it seems like society had

to do something to them to make them the way they are. They feel that
society has *done* something to them. It makes me mad that they just like
. . . I don't know how to put it . . . (Hesitates.) Like probation departments.
They're a part of society. They make up a *large* part of society in Rivertown.
They get like a hundred kids, and they just *keep* them kids. They try to
get you to spend two years of your life just being the way they want you
to be. (Intently:) They know it's impossible for you to do it, they *know*
that, and they know they can keep getting you back to where they want
you. They can keep getting you in here where they don't have to *deal*
with you. They leave someone *else* to deal with you. They just have to
come by once a week and say "Hi, 'bye." And I just don't think that's
fair. And it makes me mad.

And . . . I don't know, the way the police—the way they handle things.
A lot of times, they just go out to *look* for people to arrest. Like we drove
past a cop in a car and my brother yells a rude remark to the cop. The
next I know, we're pulled over. It has nothing to do with the rude remark.
It's "Oh, you don't have brake lights," and my brake lights work fine! "No
they don't. You've got a ticket." I mean the brake lights *worked*. I didn't
have a driver's license anyway (laughs), so I just gave them a fake name
and everything and told them my driver's license is at home. He gave me
driving without a license. I don't know who got the ticket, but somebody
by the name of Aaron Goetz got a ticket for it! (Laughs.)

I just think if *they're* going to be unfair, you *know* I'm not going to
be fair to *them*. It's like they come to your house at three in the morning
and search your house. I mean that's a little un*called* for. You stand there
in the middle of the hallway in school putting your books up, and the
next thing you know you're *slammed* up against the locker, two cops got
you spread-eagled, searching you, patting you down, search your locker
and the lockers around it, make sure you didn't throw something in the
next locker.

You're subject to search and seizure at any time, day or night, and
you're subject to urinalysis, blood test, at any time, day or night. They
come in your house and draw blood from you at three o'clock in the
morning, make you pee in a little bottle for them. So they can do just
about anything. (Quiet anger.) They like *control* you. You're *theirs*, you
wear their dog tag. I mean you've got their address and everything stamped
on you. So if you're lost, that's where you get sent to.

And it's like they just keep them same kids over and over. Like if you

come through here, over in the Juvenile Hall, and look at the faces of
these kids, and come back next year, you'll see the *same faces* because
they'll still be on probation, and they're still not (sarcastically) *angels* like
the system wants them to be, so they'll be back *in* there. And like after
the second or third time, they feel like it's society, it's society itself, that's
screwing them, and they start striking back at society with vandalism,
robberies . . . (Pauses.)

A lot of kids that break into places, they're from wealthy families. They
do it just to get back at people for, you know, putting them in jail, locking
them up, getting them on probation and everything, just ruining their
life. We want to get back at them, and that's the only way we know how
to do it.

What do you do when you start feeling that way?

Vandalism, mostly. Like going out in the park, where everybody goes,
society's nice pretty little park, like the picnic table, you know, light it
on fire, start burning the bench, take gas and pour it and write dirty words
on the grass and light it on fire, stuff like that. Just to take money, *society's*
money and everything, the community's money. So they'll have to pay
for it. All this money from the taxpayers is going to have to pay for that
park. And that's a good way to get back at them. And *I'm* not going to
jail, because I'm not getting caught for it. 'Cause it could be any of fifteen,
sixteen thousand kids. And they can't arrest us all.

That's a lot of kids.

There probably are about that many feel that way, because there's fifty-
two or fifty-three thousand people in Rivertown, and most of them are
kids, or at least nineteen and under, say at least twenty thousand of 'em
are. I don't know . . . (Pauses.) I just think that *most* of the kids—'cause
I was in Rivertown for a long time, and I was in different *parts* of Rivertown, I've known a lot of different kids—and almost *all* of 'em feel the
same way. You know, it's like: "Well, why do you want to go rob this
guy's house?" "He *sucks*, man, he put me in jail." "What did he do to
you? Did he *really* put you in jail? That guy right *there* took you down
to the jail and put you there?" "No, man, but all these people, *all* these
people, they've always got something to say." "What do you mean?" "They

say, 'See them kids out there, they're just planning to do something wrong.' "

You see, I'm not for it. I'm not going to stand for this stuff anymore. It's their turn to get theirs. I had to pay for mine, now they can pay for theirs.

If I could be dictator of the United States? A lot of people would say, "Do away with the jail, get rid of the cops." I wouldn't say that, because if I did that, things could get worse. I think that President Reagan is doing a pretty good job right now. I mean, myself, I wouldn't really know what to do until I got the hang of things. I know I wouldn't do away with the arms and everything. 'Cause anytime, Russia could just blow us up. And they're still alive over there, but we're all dead. And so, you know, the only thing that's keeping them from pushing the button is that we got it, too. So I'd keep things like that.

And like people who are doing child molesting, rape, murder? They would get the same treatment. I mean if you molested somebody, you die. Rape somebody, you die. Hurt somebody, you die.

That's how I feel, how I'd change some things. And, you know, try to change the systems, the juvenile systems. A lot. Try to get more money into education, instead of less money into education and more money into arms. I'd try to get more money into education and less into arms.

Does that scare you, all that money for arms?

I think about it a lot, 'cause I spend a lot of time locked up, and I don't want to die in a place like this. You know, if someone pushed the button right now, I wouldn't know what it was like to be out, being able to tell everybody goodbye, and I love them, and everything. I'd just be *dead*, and nobody would know how I felt, what I thought. I think about it. And it scares me, 'cause they could push the button at any time. They could just decide to, right now: "Well, let's blow up America, it's time for everybody to die." So they just start pushing their buttons, turning their keys and everything, and there we go.

Do you think that kids worry about that a lot?

I don't think very many people even think about it. I don't think kids think about it very much at all. Even a lot of kids in here: "Oh, we're going to die? Well, you know, the world's going to end in 'eighty-nine anyway. Let's all just have fun until then." And a lot of kids out there, they don't even *think* about it, they're having fun. (Quietly:) They ain't got anything to worry about. They're not in the situation that I am, where I won't be able to *tell* people. You know, when you hear over the news "The Russians just pushed the button, and we've got about thirty minutes until we all die," it's like "Oh, great!" You can run around saying "Love you, 'bye, love you, 'bye," telling your family you love 'em, cry with them and everything. Here, who are you gonna cry with?

Nobody here really cares about each other. I mean, you have acquaintances, no friends. It's like if the world just started to blow up, everybody'd be feeling sorry for *themselves*. I know I would, too. I'm sure everybody would. I'd go, "Why couldn't I have changed things to not be in here when it happened." But a lot of people wouldn't even think about it. They'd just think, "Oh, God, we're going to die. What can we do? What can we do?" I'd be thinking like "Why didn't I change something when I had a chance?"

"I've seen just about everything in front of my eyes"

Me and my friend Lucinda, and her boyfriend, one day we were
driving around, and this other girl that my home girl's boyfriend
was seeing, we were driving her car. I was the one driving, it was my first
time driving, right? And my home girl's boyfriend went cruising with
another guy and he left me the car. So we were driving around, having
fun, cruising around. We pulled a runner, we filled up the tank with gas,
we didn't even pay for it. My first time doin' it, I was speeding around
corners and everything else. And we picked up a guy, he was driving and
the cops pulled us over because we heard our song—"La Bamba"?—and
we were blasted up and we were swerving around the corners, making
skid marks on the street and stuff, and the cops pulled us over for swerving.
And Rafe, that's the guy's name, he got arrested. He's in here now. We're
really good friends, he writes to me. And he got arrested because he was
driving with an open container of beer, good old Corona! (Laughs.) And
'cause he's a minor and we were out at three o'clock in the morning. And
that's my home girl's boyfriend. She said, "That's it. I want to get arrested.
I love him. I don't want him to go to jail alone." It's the second time
she's been in here. So she came here and I went with her, 'cause I didn't

want her to be alone. I didn't want to look like I'm leaving her hanging. I don't do that to my friends. I don't know why. No matter how bad the situation is, I'll go with them. It's kind of a bad habit.

She's intense, vivacious, quick-tempered, and talks a mile a minute. Heavily involved in the gang scene in the Cherry Grove barrio, she's been thrown out of nearly every public school in Cherry Grove and Rivertown for fighting, using drugs, and cutting class.

I've been shot at, I've been shot in the legs a few times, I've had knife cuts, I've got scars on me, I've seen a lot of bad things, people getting blown to *pieces*, people getting cut *up*, you know. I've seen just about everything in front of my eyes. And I've experienced a lot of stuff with drugs and people and sex and situations, mature situations. If I was any younger, it would have left a scar on me, but now I'm at the age I was able to handle it, you know. And now that I've seen everything, I'm just hoping that my children don't have to go through it.

It's like my father, he's from Spain, and Apache, right? Spanish and Apachian. And they were never able to marry because my grandparents are from Italy, can't marry a Spanish man, you have to marry an Italian, and that's *strict*, right there. Like Jewish have to marry Jewish, you know, all that stuff. And they loved each other a lot but they were never able to marry. And I'm lucky I don't become an addict or something. 'Cause my father was clean for twenty-five years. He was clean off shooting up heroin, and alcohol. And I've tried just about every drug and I'm lucky I haven't become addicted. And I'm planning on *not* becoming addicted. Because if it's in my father's blood, and it's in my blood, then it'll be in my children's blood. The tradition in the blood, I want it to wear off.

I think if *I'm* clean, and my children are clean, maybe my grandchildren won't have it in their blood very strongly.

I was born in Chicago. By Melrose Park? Do you know those whereabouts? We lived around there. I had a cat named after the park—Melrose! (Laughs.) And we moved here when I was six years old. We moved to Cherry Grove, in the brand-new estate called Grey Fox Estates, and I went to a private school, Oates School? I was on the honor roll. I was getting straight A's and stuff. I went there from second grade all the way up to fourth. We had to take French, ballet, all that goopy stuff. And, um, then things started to change.

One night my mom moved out. She decided to move because she was having problems with her husband. He was my legal father, only on paper; he was not my biological father. And just one night, she said, "We're going to move." And I said, "OK," because in a way I really didn't mind, 'cause I knew they were having problems and I was kind of mature for that age. I was ten years old and I didn't have any brothers and sisters or anything, so I kind of knew what was going on. So we moved, it was like two o'clock in the morning and he hadn't come home yet, he told my mom he was going fishing which was always his excuse to go out and drink. And, um, moved into a small, little apartment, got ourselves on housing and stuff, and welfare, my mom got a job, got off welfare. Stayed on housing. It was a real small, ugly apartment. I mean real dingy, in Cherry Grove, a little court called Wayside Court. A little scummy apartment, but we had our pride, 'cause it was our first apartment, just me and my mom. And as the years went by, she started getting better jobs and soon we were up on a hill in a big apartment building called Knightsbridge Apartments. She was the top manager and she was earning sixteen hundred dollars a month.

And then I was a teenager. I got my first D and she hit the roof and I started changing. I started needing her more as a mother and she wasn't able to handle it. So I started *rebelling* against her. And the first time she really noticed problems was after my first D. I went to Cherry Grove Intermediate and I got suspended for having pot in my locker. And never even smoked it! (Grins.) I brought it home and it was in my little Garfield can, right, and my mom was all "Oh, I love the Garfield can, let me see him." And I'm going, "No, no!" Then she got really mad, she got suspicious, and she forced me to give it to her and she opened it and got pissed off and she overreacted and called the school to get the other kids busted. But she didn't know it was going to get *me* busted. So I got suspended for a week. Then after that, I was suspended . . . (she's calculating) in the last two years of seventh and eighth grade, junior high, I got suspended a total of thirty times. For being late a lot, for having too many detentions, for getting into a lot of fights and arguments and stuff, causing a lot of trouble with teachers.

One teacher had a heart attack because of me, because I gave him such a hard time. That's when they expelled me.

I was in class, and it was this special class where there were dumb kids and smart kids. They divided it, so it was like ten kids, and it was like the Breakfast Club! I mean there were a few preppies, a few nerds, stoners, punk rockers, a Chicano surfer boy, chola girls, Chicano girls, you know, just oddball people, everybody was totally different. And it was fun, I enjoyed it. I was always smart mouth and stuff, cussing at people. And I was *bad*. At least I *thought* I was. And one day our teacher walked in, Mr. Watson, and everybody hated him, or they *pretended* they hated him, of course, 'cause you *got* to hate the teacher, right? (Laughs.)

And we were stuck with him all day in that one special class. And he told me to collect the homework. So I collected the homework, I gave it to him, and he said, "Well, where's yours." And I said, "Well, I didn't do it." He said, "Well, I'm going to have to give you a zero for the day." I said, "Well, I really don't give a shit." And he said, "What did you say." I said, "You heard me." And then he said, "Well, I'm going to have to call the office." I said, "If you do that, man, you're going to get in some big trouble." I was being a real bitch, I was smart mouth to him, I was cussin', words I didn't even understand myself, just words I'd heard, right? And next thing I knew he got so mad he started shaking his finger at me and (she puffs up her face) his eyes got real big and all the sudden he started gasping and stuff and clenched his hand around his heart and fell gasping, leaning against the chalkboard, and collapsed, and fainted. I just stood there going, "Whoa, what happened?" And then somebody ran down to the office, the ambulance came, and they said he had a heart attack. He survived, he was back within a year. But I wasn't there, they expelled me for giving my teacher a heart attack.

And then, that's when we moved to Rivertown, 'cause I was going down to Cherry Grove hanging out with cholos and pachucos and stuff. My first boyfriend was from El Salvador and he was nineteen when I was thirteen and I was growing up real fast, and my mom was starting to get a little jealous, starting to envy and starting to feel sorry for herself. Which wasn't her *fault*, she was lonely at the time, I was lonely at the time, when she first got her divorce. We needed more than just a mother-daughter relationship. We needed a friend relationship to hang on, but then after the friend relationship started to depart, there was nothing there. And so she was trying to cope with me growing up and I would try to talk with her on a mature level, mature mother-daughter level, you know, about your *body*, and, you know, about boyfriends, girlfriends, making love and all that. And she would get real jumpy or she would make a snide remark and the rest would just blow up into an argument. She wasn't able to handle it good.

'Cause I was her only child, I'm her baby. (Laughs.) And, um, I'm growing up and she's scared that when her daughter grows up she's going to get old. But I think that's the problem with a lot of parents. She's my mother *and* she's my father, you know, she's all of them combined in one, because my aunts and uncles are all the way out in Spain and Italy and Mexico and all over the place, and I've nobody out here except my legal father David, which they've been divorced now nearly eight years and I don't contact him no more, I don't keep in touch with him, he's an alcoholic, he has problems and stuff. And she doesn't want to grow old. You would agree with that if you saw my mom.

Well, it started with the getting expelled, and after that I went to high school, Cherry Grove. Lasted two weeks. Got jumped by three black girls, one was put in the hospital. But the other two got me pretty bad, and I had bruises and stuff my mom didn't even know about. And by then I was already into gangs and warfare, barrios, turfs and stuff, drugs and all that stuff with cholos and Chicanos and stuff, and I got expelled from *there*.

So I went to Watson High and within two weeks I wasn't even going. I'd just go when I wanted to, 'cause it was easy to cut. I discovered cutting with all my older friends. All my friends were seniors and juniors. Never hung with freshmen. Not that it wasn't cool or anything, it's just they weren't up to my mentality. I'd talk to them and it'd be like (she puts on an exaggerated "surfer" accent) "Whoa, dude!" and "Killer bud!" and all that stuff, you know. I'm not into all that. And so like we'd cut, you know. Go get stoned and stuff. Do drugs. Go to my house. One time me and two girlfriends went to my house, we got stoned and then we got into a big pudding fight and (much laughter) there was pudding all over the walls and I had to clean it up and stuff. Had some good times.

I'd go to school when I *wanted* to. And finally, I wasn't in the school for like three months, and I kept getting notes going, "Your daughter has not attended school," so finally my mom called them up. 'Cause one day we got a letter saying I would have to go in front of the school board. And my mom, she got pissed, even though I was cutting school, I was reading books at home and everything. She got pissed that they would have to make me go up to the school board, because there were *tons* of kids doing worse shit than me and they weren't getting caught for it at school. And she called them up, "You asshole," bitched them out, and then after that we moved again to Rivertown because she found a better job up in Riverwood apartments. And then I went to Rivertown High School and I was there for like three weeks and I stopped going.

I didn't like the people there. It was a totally different atmosphere, you know? Where I hung around before, there was people speaking Spanish and stuff, low riders, it was sort of like East L.A. around there. But when I came to Rivertown, Rivertown High was like—I'm not prejudiced, but like (laughs) honkies and *hill*billies, big four-wheeling trucks and stuff, and country music, rock and roll and stuff. Not that I'm not into it, I just wasn't *used* to it. And I felt on the defensive side because I wasn't familiar with my surroundings. And that's a natural instinct. If you're not familiar with what's around you, you get defensive and you're on alert and you're cautious. And so I was being real cautious and stuff, and finally one day in the girls' locker room—I was there for like two and a half weeks—one white girl came up to me, she said, "Well you think you're hot, don't you?" 'Cause it had been nearly three weeks and I hadn't talked to *any*body there. In the halls nobody talked to me, I didn't talk to them. I was alone in class, did my work, went home, did my thing.

And then she goes, "Well you think you're hot 'cause you don't talk to anybody." I said, "Why don't you leave me alone, man, I got to go home now." She said, "No!" and she grabbed me and grabbed the back of my hair and she threw me up against the wall and we got into a real big fight. And then I got expelled and she got suspended 'cause she had a broken nose and I had bruises and scratches and shit.

They kept keeping me in school because my past record is very good, you know. I have potential, I'm just too lazy to use it. You know, I'll go through periods, spurting periods, a month or two I'll get A's and B's, but then I'll say, "I don't want to do this no more," and I'll start getting D's and F's right away.

My attitude can change real different. And then it's like they put me in Rivertown Continuance High School and I went there. Too easy! It was just too easy for me. I said, "Why should I go to this shit, it's too easy for me." It was stupid going, when I know it all already. 'Cause I have problems in multiplying and division, but I don't have problems in fractions and algebra and negatives and positives. And they were giving me negatives, positives, and computers, and I'm real good at that stuff,

I'm just bad at the stuff like fourth- and fifth-grade division and my times table.

So, they couldn't put me any lower or they'd think I was really stupid, but I'm not. I just missed some parts in my schooling, 'cause when I was younger we used to move a lot 'cause my mom always had different jobs and my father, my legal father, was a carpenter, so we had to move from place to place and I was always changing schools so I never had time to study, and I just didn't go.

And now it's like I was on six months' probation at that time for fighting, hurting . . . well, *assaulting* a girl. (Laughs.) I was put on probation for six months 'cause they found me. I went to Ash Hill School in Cherry Grove one day and this girl was bothering my home girl, her name's Cindy? We were best friends, we've known each other for a real long time, we've been through a lot together. And I just kicked her ass. And I don't know *what* happened to that girl, 'cause I ran. And then they found out about it and they finally found me, they picked me up at home.

And somewhere in between that . . . (a short pause) something got messed up. My first boyfriend I had, he was nineteen, from El Salvador. We were together three months and I was living in Cherry Grove at the time. And one day I ran away because my boyfriend wanted to break up with me for no reason. Two days after my mom let him move into my house! She thought I was mature enough to handle the situation.

She let him move in. Two days later, we broke up. He got back from L.A. and he broke up with me and I ran away. I was really upset. I was on the run. I went down to Iron City, hung out at Twelfth Street and stuff with a girlfriend of mine, and then I went to a place called Mason House? In Rivertown by the K Mart? It's a house where runaways go for the weekend. I stayed there for a week and then I got a phone call from my mama saying Albert—that's my boyfriend's name, Albert—he got in a car accident. So I came home because of him.

Then the next thing I know, my mom was saying, "Albert's been having to sleep with me because I have to wake him up every two hours to give him his pain pills." I said, "OK, Mom," you know. And then it's like I started noticing them flirting and stuff and it really hurt me at first, 'cause I was confused. (Indignant:) I only saw that kind of stuff in *soap operas* and stuff! I was starting to think, "No, man, my mom can't be *that* immature." And sooner or later I found out that they were fucking around behind my back.

I had to face it. I asked 'em. I walked into my mom's bedroom and they were lying in bed together and I hated looking at that, 'cause he was my first infatuation. I wasn't in *love* with him, he was just my first infatuation, puppy love. And I saw that and I said, "Mom, why are you guys doing this to me?" And it stabbed me in the heart because Albert said, "I'm a man, she's a woman, we have needs." Just straight up like that.

I looked at my mom and I go, "Is that true?" She said, "Yeah." And I go, "Okay, I'm gonna go fuck your ex-husband." Right! (A disgusted snort.) And I wouldn't touch him with a ten-foot pole! I was just saying that to hurt her.

And anyway I didn't like saying that 'cause I don't like saying things to hurt my mother. And she just said, (nonchalantly:) "Hey, fine." And I said, "No, *fuck* this," and I started crying, going into the bathroom, and I was crying. Albert came out, and he started talking to me and shit, and he's all "Didn't I tell you one day I was gonna do something that would hurt you for the rest of your life?" I looked at him and said, "You're *cold*." And he goes, (arrogantly:) "What did I tell you." And he was the original latino, stubborn, stuck up. He's the man, there's the woman, the woman stays at home, cooks all day and stuff. I wasn't into that. And so I ran away again.

And that's when my mom kicked out Albert and then I came home again. But she was always talking to him on the phone and always going out with him. She kept telling me, when she would come home after a date with Albert, "I'm never gonna see him again, he's just a little boy" and shit, and (singsong) "Don't worry, I love *you*, you're my daughter" and shit. And the next thing I know, he was moved back in, after three days. And it went back and forth. And I came home one day after I ran away. I had a new boyfriend, he was a nice guy, and he was letting me stay at his house, you know, and I was sleeping with his sister in his sister's bedroom. And I came home one day, I was planning on staying home. And Albert came in with my mom, and he told my mom, "It's either me or her. If you want me to stay, you tell *her* to leave." And she actually told me to leave. And I really couldn't believe it.

I left. I went back to stay with my new boyfriend. And we stayed together for a very long time. I just broke up with him around four months ago.

Nearly a year and two months, a year and three months, me and my new boyfriend were going back and forth. I was going back and forth with my mom, and finally she kicked him out and we moved to Cherry Grove and we were living up on Long Hill Road and just kicking back. This was when I was going through my hard times at Cherry Grove High. And then one day Albert just walks in! Just walks through the door. I didn't say anything. I was hurt. I just went to my room. And then they were in my mom's bedroom talking and I got really crazy. I went into their room and I had a gun in my hand. I said, "Albert, if you stay here tonight, I'm gonna kill you." And he got really spooked. And so he said, "Fuck you." I said, "Yeah, I used to be your girlfriend and you said you loved me." And I was psyching him out, you know. (Earnestly:) I wasn't gonna *kill* him. But I wanted to show that I meant business. That I hated—that I didn't like him. I can never say I hate anybody because that's a sin right there. I don't think you can really hate anybody.

And so he left that night and things went back and forth. Then—now back up to the future—we were in the Riverwood Apartments here in Rivertown. My mom got a new job as manager and she let Albert move back in again. But I was ignoring it. I was getting better with my situation. My attitude was getting all better. My mental state of mind. I was starting to feel more positive about myself. I said to myself, "Fuck *him*. He ain't worth jack *shit*. My mom will understand what she's doing one day." I always forgive her. 'Cause she's my mom.

But I only forgive her to a certain point. And then one night he came home and I was on the phone and—this is like three months ago, four months ago—he said, "Get off the phone." I said, "Fuck you. I'm on the phone. I live here." And he goes, "Yeah, and I don't?" I go, "You won't be living here for that much longer." And he started cussing at me in Spanish and stuff—"Fuck you, puta," and all this—and he pulled the phone out of the wall, and I went to get up and out of the corner of my eye saw him raise his hand, so I turned around and smacked him on the head with the phone! (Laughs.) And he grabbed me and really hurt me bad, you know. He left scratches on my face and stuff. My face was *dripping* with blood. That's happened to me a lot before, but in *fights!* (Laughs.) He did it to me. And I said, "You're *dead*." I went down to see my mom, but my mom was down visiting a tenant living in her building, named Rich, a guy. I went, "Mom, look at my face, look what happened." And the guy, Rich, was just a real good friend. My mom's like me, I can have a lot of male friends 'cause I can talk with them. But

I can't have a lot of female friends, 'cause they're all backstabbers and bitches, you know. *God*, I don't get along with girls! (Laughs) This guy Rich is real mad. He said, "I'm gonna kill him" and stuff, you know.

She said, "No, no, it's none of your business." And she went, "Albert, what did you do?" He was standing there smoking a cigarette and goes, (airily:) "I didn't do nothing." I go, "Albert, *look* at me. Who did this, the Ghostbusters?" (Laughs.)

And he goes, "No." I go, "OK then." And my mom told me to go in my room. I went in my room, and then she called me out like five minutes later and goes, "Well, Albert?" and he looked at me and goes, "I'm sorry." I go like (outraged:) "*Whaaat?!*" And he goes, "I'm sorry." "How can you say you're sorry! Look at me!" I go, "You're lucky I don't get that butcher knife right now and cut you up." I go, "How would you like me to do that to you?" I go, "Because one night maybe I will." And he looks at me and says, "I'm sorry." And "I'm not scared of you," and goes, (sarcastically:) "Oooo, I'm *shaking!*" I go, "You're a fool if you're not scared," and I was talking *hella* shit because I had my pride, right? I don't know if I could of really ever hurt him, but I had some pride. I just stuck up for myself.

And then my mom kicked him out for that night, had the locks changed and everything, called the police. *I* called the police 'cause I started thinking—this is like ten minutes, it all happened within ten minutes—and I was thinking to myself, "Wait a minute, I'm a minor, he's twenty-one now," so I called the police, saying child abuse. And when the police came, he ran. He drove away right before the police came. Shit, and I filed a report, filed charges, and my mom kicked him out, we had everything done, locks changed and everything. And then two days later, he was back!

I was going crazy. It was a game. Jeopardy! (Laughs.) I couldn't stand it. I didn't run away, though, because I wanted to *be* something. I wasn't going to school, but I was having a tutor come and my mom was helping me get as much education as I can. Because I read a whole lot. I'm on the senior level and I'll be a sophomore. I read a whole lot of books.

We moved, 'cause she kicked him out again one night, for some reason. She just kicked him out. He left. I was happy as a lark. I thought, "Hey, this is for *good*, right?" And then we moved into a little dingy apartment, 'cause one night my mom lost her job. She blames it on me! We were getting into a lot of arguments because of Albert. She was yelling, then

I was yelling. She was yelling, Albert was slamming things around. And Louise, that's the main manager, my mom was the assistant manager, the lady fired her, saying that I was making too much noise. My mom came up and started bitching me out. She made me feel real bad. 'Cause I thought it really *was* my fault. We had to move. Now we live in a little apartment down by the Veterans' hospital.

She told him to move and he packed his bags and he left. For a few days after that it was real hard—he was calling, cussing, crying. I don't blame him. My mom's a real intelligent lady. She's smart, she's pretty, she knows her ways, and he was in love with her. (Quietly:) I think that was his first love, I hate to admit it. He fell in love with my mother instead of me. But in a way, I got my pride, because that's my mom and I realize she's pretty, she can get a young man if she wanted to, and she can get a mature, older man if she wanted to. And anyway, I feel sorry for her cause she got stuck with a wetback! (Laughs.) No, I'm not against wetbacks, but I was raised around them since I was ten years old.

But then Albert's gone now. My mom's seeing this man that's *her* age, and they're getting along good. But I keep telling her just to be careful, 'cause she just got over a relationship and she might—this just might be a replay because she's lonely now 'cause Albert's gone, there's nobody to tell her what to do or nothing and in a way she might miss it. I just hope this new relationship doesn't hurt her.

I've been doing good now that Albert's gone. My mom and I get along more maturely. 'Cause Albert was jealous. He didn't like me talking to my mom a lot. She was always in their bedroom. They had a TV, they had a small refrigerator, stereo in there, telephone, they practically *lived* in there! The only thing they needed was a coffee maker and a hot plate! I'm serious. (Laughs.) He never let her talk to me. And we never had a chance to expand our relationship to make it better. Now that he's gone, we do. My mom and I are getting along better.

But I went through a lot of hard times with her. And with myself. In Cherry Grove, there was a lot of warfare going on with turfs and stuff, and I was getting into a lot of fights that my mom didn't even know about. I'd come home with ripped clothes, *blood* and stuff, and she'd say, "What's wrong?" I'd go, "Nothing, I got in a little—me and my home boys was messing around and I fell into bushes or something and got scratched," right!

I think a lot about my future. I want to make something of myself.

I'm in here now 'cause I messed up. And, I hate to say this, I don't regret it. I don't regret a single thing I did. I lived my life on the other side of the tracks. I got thirty-dollar, sixty-dollar shoes and stuff, boots, real high-class boots and everything. Now I'm wearing five-dollar boat shoes that have been through everything. (Laughs.) I *love* these shoes. God! It just drives me crazy, I'm *serious*.

The thing that bothers me is, I don't know *why* I had to go through all this. I don't regret anything, but I don't know why I was picked. Out of all those rich little girls. I mean, we had money, believe me, we were rich. Very comfortable up in Grey Fox Estates Condominiums. I was picked. From all those girls on the other side of the tracks.

Maybe because I was an only child. Maybe it's because when I was younger I was the nerd of the school and stuff. I was always picked on. I never had friends. Because living in Cherry Grove . . . (hesitates) there is white society, *modern* society, and surfers and stuff, and the Spanish people lived in the rundown houses, in the hole-in-the-walls on the side streets and were never really recognized, but I was Spanish and I had nice clothes and everything. I was living in nice white society and I was not recognized, not in a good way. I was looked at bad. So when I started going to Rivertown, I met people of my own type, in my own society, and I was enjoying it. I think that's what did it to me. Feeling lonely and needing to be with my own people. I'm not saying they put me here, I put *myself* here.

I want to go to college real bad. I was thinking about going to State. I was always thinking about going there because I've done a lot of stuff, and I'm planning on getting good grades. Because I'm so good with reading and drawing, I want to combine that. I want to be like "Fame," you know, the TV show "Fame"? Ever since I seen the movie, that's my daydream. I just get infatuated every time I see this TV show "Fame," and see all those people dancing, because I mean they're expressing themselves so good, and perfect, and dancing, and they're from the *streets*, you know. All different people, some are from the streets, some are from *rich* society and stuff, and they're all together dancing, the same movements, expressing themselves with smiles on their face. And a teacher, a black teacher, she's cool and everything. That's my daydream. My mom, when I was like eleven, she called the School of Arts in New York just for me because I was bothering her so much about it. And we've known for a while that I just have to get C's, C-plus to a B-minus, to get in and stuff, and we're still thinking about it, but after this . . . I don't know. Money's real tight.

My mom's trying to save up because I'll be sixteen on November 20 and she wants to have my party at Elks Lodge. It's like a big auditorium, dance hall, and she wants to rent it out for me because I'm gonna be sixteen. And Mom's making a big deal out of it, only kid being sixteen, right? (Laughs.) Sixteen, spoiled. It's pretty fun. Whole thing could be OK. I don't know *where* I'm gonna go from here. The only place to go is up. I'm gonna go up higher. See, that's another thing I like about dancing. It feels so high when you dance. Up and up and up.

"How do straight people have fun?"

I'm a thief. I mean most people put thieves down, but it's an *art*, it really is. It really is an art. You have to be *good* at it, or you're just gonna get caught. I wasn't so good at it, you know, I was just a rookie at it, and I got caught many times. I don't get caught no more. I'm *good* now.

He's a wiry, freckled redhead who could have stepped off a Norman Rockwell painting on the cover of the Saturday Evening Post. *He's open, quick, friendly; he lives with his parents—retired military people—and two sisters in Wildwood Hills, an area of semirural sprawl spotted with new housing developments that have sprung up in the flat farmland and barren rolling hills outside of Rivertown, miles from shopping, schools, or other neighborhoods.*

Well, it's so-so, you know. Like there's not too many things to do, but then there's a *lot* to do, all right?

When I first moved out there, it's like I liked the place, you know? But then after a while I wanted to be next door to someone I *knew* or something, because it took me like an *hour* to walk to my friend's house.

That's basically why I started getting in trouble, man. Because I lived out in the country. Really nothin' to do, so I'd go into town and cause trouble.

Every kid I know out in Wildwood Hills, they all say, "Well, this is boring, let's go find something to do." You'll find that the bus always has more business in Wildwood Hills, 'cause they're taking kids from Wildwood Hills to another city real quick. Like the closest city that's *kind* of exciting, but not too much, but Rivertown, that's kind of the next one in line for us. Cherry Grove, I always go to Cherry Grove or Rivertown. They've got a lot of things going, parties, that's about it, you know. Wildwood's kind of boring.

It's just like . . . *desert* out there. I've been out there two years now, and nothing really exciting's ever *happened*. Except maybe my chickens get killed by the dog next door (laughs), stuff like that.

He's been sent to the Hall five times: originally, for "stealing, mostly," but now "I don't get caught no more. Every time I come in here now, it's for violation of probation." He was first arrested for a burglary when he had just turned eleven.

Stealin'? How'd it start? I don't know—I'm kind of like a kleptomaniac, but not so severe, you know?

I burglarized a railroad car, in Rivertown. You know, there's a railroad track, and a railroad car on it. And me and my friend busted into it, and we're stealin' all *kinds* of stuff (he grins; he's still excited). And the cops pulled up and busted us.

Then I got busted for stealin' bicycles, petty theft from stores, stuff like that.

First time I come in *here*, I burglarized a house. And, um, I ripped off a couple of stores, you know, walked in and stole stuff. And I got drunk in public.

So I pretty well stuck myself in here, now. (A sigh.) Hope I can make something out of myself.

I just didn't hang around with the right friends. It's the older kids that really got me, you know, like kids that'd already been to Juvie before? They're like eighteen or nineteen, running around town, and they're the ones that influenced me. But when I'm around friends my age, I influence *them*, really. I'm the one that comes up with the crazy ideas. You know—"There's a store up there, let's go get some cigarettes!" "That's a nice *car*, right there." (Laughs.)

It's like—when I *want* something, I'll take it. I have a friend of mine, and me and him used to go into stores. And we'd steal *immaterial* things, that we didn't need, and then we'd run out the store with 'em and then *break* 'em, and throw 'em someplace! Didn't need 'em, you know?

The only thing that I really stole that I really *needed*, that'd probably be Pepsis, and cigarettes, maybe a car every once in a while. Not too many cars. I stole about five or six cars in a year, for about three years. So you know, when you hear there's about a million cars missing, you know about thirty of 'em are mine. (Laughs.)

I like driving, though. I think the reason I steal is the adventure. You know, the fact that when you get out of the store and you've gotten away with it, your *heart's* pounding, you know; whaaa! (he's laughing, breathing hard)—that's what I like. You're drivin' down the street in someone else's car, and lookin' around, heart's poundin' away, and when you get away with it and three days later you're—whew! . . .

Relief?

Yeah . . .

Makes the blood flow?

Yeah! It's kind of like . . . adventure.

When you stole the cars, what'd you do with them?

I've *sold* cars before—traded 'em and stuff like that. But [usually] when I'd get a car I'd *wreck* it, or something, you know. Like I wouldn't wreck it like drop it off a *cliff* with me in it or nothing. I'd just, dzh, dzh, (he's pretending to drive, hunched happily over an imaginary steering wheel) skip trees on purpose, and do jumps, and *whoooo!* go through sand real fast, and if it got stuck, I'd wipe off my fingerprints and walk away.

Or like going ninety miles an hour on the sand dunes, then jumping off a *hill* or something like that, you know? Landing, and the car's like *face-up*, and you're crawling out of the car upside *down*, you go, "Wow!

I'm still alive! Come on, let's *go!*" (Laughs.) And that was all fun to me.

Hurt? A couple of times I got hurt, but not really bad. I mean, I *crawled* away a couple of times, but I never really, like, had to sew myself *together* (grins), put a cast on myself.

Certain days I can control the stealing and other days I can't. Like if I saw a red, brand-new Porsche one day, and it had keys in it, and I felt *good* about myself that day, and I knew I was probably gonna go see my grandmom the next day, and she was gonna give me like ten or twenty dollars or something, I probably wouldn't think *twice* about stealin' it. I'd just keep walking. But then say the next day I had a bad day, and I saw those keys in the car, and I'd say, "Damn, forget it, let's go!"

Mood change. (Laughs.)

What would make it change? School—being forced to go to school. Probation, drugs maybe—drugs do influence me. Family problems, like worrying about my sisters, what they're up to, 'cause they do a lot of stupid stuff, too. Let's say I got in an argument with one of my friends, or my parents found out I was cutting school that day—that kind of stuff.

What about this place—does it help you to come in here?

(Quickly:) It really sucks. I mean they can't help you. Everybody here has got a mind of their own. And if you ever change that, you'd be like . . . brainwashed. When you get out, you do it yourself.

I've been paranoid about getting free, you know. Last time I was in for six months and I got out and "Oh, man, what am I gonna do? What am I gonna do if I get in trouble again?"

My problem is I'm spontaneous. Like a kid comes up to me and says, "Oh, man, there's this Porsche down the street with the *keys* in it, man, let's go!" Then I just thought to myself, "I just got out, I can't do nothing like that." The *first* time. But if that kid comes up *again* and says, "Man! This is the first time I've ever seen it! A Porsche parked down the street *again* with the keys in it?" I'd say, "Man! My parents been giving me a bad time, my P.O.'s on my back, I know I'm gonna have a dirty test tomorrow . . . man! OK, let's go!"

Me and my friend'd take off in the car, eeerk! Drive somewhere far maybe, I don't know.

*He's been heavily into drugs since he was twelve or thirteen. He
says the drug scene where he lives is thriving: "Drugs circulate in
Wildwood pretty good. Everybody just about has 'em. Everybody's
lookin', everybody's got 'em."*

Well, it's a crankster, pretty much, town. I pretty much did it
(laughs)—you know, I did a *lot* of it. And I *like* the stuff, actually. My
favorite drug is acid, LSD? And I can go for *days* on acid trips. But crank
is my *second*-favorite, it's my second drug of choice. Cause, uh, it gives
you a high, you know, and . . . it makes you look *bigger*, you know?
Makes you look *big*-time, you know, when you got an eight-ball of crank
in your pocket, and two hundred dollars in your *other* pocket, and you're
walking around town and you've got nice *clothes* on and stuff like that,
and you whip out the eight-ball, you snort a line, and you're all—you
snort a line and your *eyes* get all big, you're running around (he makes
a wild-eyed, goofy face)—waaaah! (Laughs.) It's really fun, it's really cool.
I really like it.

Bigger?

To your friends, and to yourself. If you go up to some dude and he's
just totally nothing but *weed*, he can't even *find* someone who sells crank,
and you come up and you say, "Yeah, I got the connection, I just bought
me an *eight-ball*, and I got two hundred dollars for *another* two eight-
balls," and he says, "*Whoa*, dude," you know? And you're like (proudly:)
"All *right!*" Makes you look bigger, you know, that you've got all these
drugs and stuff like that?
   Some people *brag* about being drug addicts. You know, they brag like
"Oh, *I'm* the biggest drug addict in east River County!" (He laughs de-
risively.) You know—kind of makes me laugh. *I* do drugs, but I don't do
it to an extreme, you know? I *stop* when I know I'm gonna *croak*, you
know? (Laughs.)
   I used to be that way. I used to brag about the things I did. But now
I don't, 'cause I feel *stupid*. Bragging about stupid crimes, bragging about
doing drugs, overdosing, stuff like that. So I don't brag no more. If
somebody asks me, I'll tell 'em.
   Some people *push* it, you know? I *used* to push it. Three years ago I
used to push it to the *edge*. And I just said, "Forget it," you know? I used

to get the bad side effects, so I said, "forget it, I'm not gonna push it no more, just do a little bit."

I'll never say I'm gonna stop doing drugs. They can't stop it. It's like alcohol—like in the twenties, you know? The more it was illegal, the more they drank it.

I started about twelve, thirteen, maybe eleven. Earliest was about eleven. My sisters used to give me cigarettes, and that started it off. I'd walk around town with cigarettes. And then . . . they didn't actually shove a joint in my face and say you're a wimp if you don't do it. I was the type of person who'd say, (whispers) "Lemme try it, lemme try it." It was like adventure, it was fun. I liked it.

I've got this little thing in my head about the difference between a drug *user* and a drug *abuser*? Now a drug user's like me, you know? I can take it for the high, and get the fun out of it, and I don't see how these other people can keep taking drugs, and they know the more they take, the less effect it has on 'em, really. I mean the more bummed out they get.

Like crank: if you do so much crank, sure you're gonna get wired, you know, but it's like when you're doing the drug, you're grinding your *teeth* and your *eyes* are all bulging out and your ears are all hurtin' and your head's poundin' . . . and that's all happening at the same time, and then the aftereffects, when you wake up the next morning? God *damn!* When you wake up and you're coming down, it's like you're a grouch, like you hate the world.

That's the difference, to me. There's just people who can take so much, and then know when to say no, that's enough. And then there's people that just: "Bring it on, bring it on!" (Laughs.)

So I just started slowing down, and things got better. (Proudly:) I'm not *dead!*

His other passion is music. He's a big heavy-metal fan.

MOD, that's Method of Destruction, you ever hear of them? They always talk about sex, drugs, and rock and roll. They always talk about, uh, political things, you know? They always talk about like the government, anarchy, Russia, and stuff like that? And they're always talking about posers—like if somebody doesn't listen to the same music I do, but they claim to, we call 'em a poser? "You ain't nobody, you ain't nobody,

you're a poser!" And they always talk about *parents*. (Laughs.) And they've
got an album cover, if you ever see it, it's really funny—it's a dude surfing,
and his leg's getting bitten off by a shark! And it says "Surfin' MOD."
There's a shark behind him with his leg in his mouth. It's really gross.
It's really funny. I really liked it.

And there's a lot of groups. They always talk about stuff like, ah . . .
satanism, and Jews, and the Holy Cross is coming alive, and . . . (He's
excited.) I've got a lot of Slayer tapes at home, I used to listen to them
all the time. I've been to Slayer concerts, I've been to Venom concerts,
Venom's like satanic rock and roll. Like they have this song called "Buried
Alive"? And it's about this guy who's getting buried alive. And you've got
to buy this tape one day, it's called "Black Metal."

They've got this thing, it says, "Lay down your soul for God's rock
and roll", or, um, "Lay down your soul for the God of rock and roll,"
or something like that. And this song "Buried Alive," in the beginning
he goes—this guy's talking like a preacher's talking, he goes, "We come
into this world with nothing and we leave with nothing. So I commit this
body to the ground. Ashes to ashes, dust to dust." And you can hear the
shovel, dzump, dzump, dirt on top of the grave . . . It's a really cool
song, I like it. Haven't heard it for a while. But it really makes me want
to go home, you know?

It's like some people fiend for drugs, I fiend for rock and roll! I really
like it. You ever hear of Black Sabbath? They're like my favorite of all
groups. I really thrive on Black Sabbath. I got all the old Black Sabbath
tapes. I got that at home—man, I wish I had that here right now! (Ex-
citedly:) Man! I'd love it. I mean—I could handle living without Slayer,
I could handle that. If they just brought some Jimi Hendrix in, or some
Doors . . . I can sing along with any Jim Morrison, Jimi Hendrix song
you've got. I really like those groups, those old groups.

The music talks to you in a way that makes sense then.

Yeah! They say things that I really—I mean I don't really take it to
the *fullest*, don't get me wrong, I'm not saying that if they say (stage
whispers) "Go kill your mom!" I'm gonna go out there and kill my mom.
"Steal your mom's car!" "EEEark!" Really, I'm not that type. But they
say like . . . (hesitates:) parents are wrong, because of this and that, you

know, stuff like that. And I'll say, "Yeah, you know, you're right," you know?

I mean music is . . . really the part of my life that really makes me function. If there was no more rock—if there was no more music, I think we'd *all* be in here! (Laughs.) I'd go crazy. I mean I can't handle a life without music.

Like many other kids in the Hall, he's headed for a group home after a string of repeated incarcerations and violations of proba-tion. "I've been in just about every institution they've got around here, and group home is about the end of the line. (Quietly:) 'Cause I'm almost to the age where it's too late, you know, to . . . like . . . finish high school. 'Cause I'm getting kind of older." But he doesn't really want to go to a group home: "If I had my way, I'd be home right now"—and he doesn't think they'll be able to keep him.

The fear that they have right now is me packin' up and going. 'Cause . . . I'm a runner. They can't keep me in one place for more than six months. (Proudly:) They've never done it before.

Sounds like you're pretty proud of that.

I am, yeah. I am. I've got a pretty good reputation there. Actually, badder reputations—some kids *like* bad reputations. They really thrive on it. People lookin' at 'em, saying "Ooh, man, he's *bad!*" You know, "I'm cool, I'm cool."

His granddad was in the army, his dad's recently retired from the service, and he thinks he wants to go in the military, too, if he can get two felony convictions cleared from his record.

Then I'm just gonna finish high school and do whatever I'm gonna do after that. So—you know . . . (He pauses, stares quietly at his hands.)

I hate school. I mean kids'll *say* they hate school, but I *hate* school, OK? I *really* hate school. I mean, not to a point where I'll burn it down (laughs), but I just . . .

I guess it's because the authority's there. People telling me what to do and how to do it. I mean I don't think there's anybody in the *world* smarter than anybody. And they're all equal. Some people just don't know as much, that's what I figure, you know?

You see, everybody's been telling me that I'm smarter than the rest of the kids they know. And when somebody's trying to teach me something I already *know*, or something like that, and I tell 'em that I already know it . . . Like here, 'cause in the school here, they just teach you the *same thing* over and over, you know? So I just don't like school.

He liked going to school "when I was in like second or third grade,"
but things went downhill when he started junior high.

I went to that school, and I went for about *three days* out of the year, and the rest of the time I was out gallivantin' somewhere. (A big grin.)

Did the school try to figure out where you were, to find out
what was wrong?

Well, not really. They've got a program there, if you call in school and say "I need a ride," they might come out and pick you up. But if you don't bother to call the school, they don't bother calling you, or nothing.

The *cops* don't even bother you. They *used* to bother you. If you like sat in the park, the cops'd come by and pick you up, take you to school or whatever. But if you're just like . . . nowadays it's just like you sit in the park all *day*, smoke cigarettes, whatever, go hang out somewhere.

Now what the kids do is they get on the bus, and they ride over to Rivertown and go out in Rivertown and walk around Rivertown. Cops don't bother you over there!

I just cut school 'cause I wanted to. You know. I cut school 'cause I thought I *knew* too much! I really didn't think about it that I needed the education, one day I'd be regretting it. Like *today!* (Laughs.)

They should do something that'd strike the kids as *interesting*, you know? Like things on drugs, more studies on drugs and stuff. Chemistry classes. Making things. (Laughs.) Not making *drugs!* Go in there and make PCP or something! Just to go in there, find something, make something. I feel like I can make things. I used to like to make things. Or drawing class, something like that. English and mathematics should be worked into that, too, you know? Like a drawing class with English in it, you know? Yeah, while you're drawing, or reading mixed into something else? They don't do that now. It's just "Here's your classes, pick 'em, and if there's too many kids in that class, you can go to the next one," you know. They had *some* good classes there. Like they had photo, where you take pictures, and develop 'em. We had video, where you walk around with a video camera and stuff? But then you're stuck reading a *book* again. (Laughs.)

School'd call up like once a month and say, "Your son's missed so many days." And I'd come home, my parents'd scream at me.

They couldn't control me. The only thing they could use against me was my probation officer. "I'm gonna call your P.O." That'd sometimes work, sometimes it didn't. If they threatened to call my P.O., I'd just chh, chh, chh. (He's pretending to climb out a window and run away.) I'd be gone for a couple of days.

Did they come after you?

My parents? They used to. They used to, but not anymore. And they're pretty disappointed in me. 'Cause they went through it with my two sisters and me. I got two older sisters that are the same way. They've never been in here before, they've never been in really serious trouble like I have, but they were always like cutting school, making my parents disappointed—all the other stuff, so I was like the last in line. So . . . they decided not to come after us no more. Unless we called 'em, said we needed, you know, help. They'd get in the car and come get us.

When it first started out, my dad'd ground us for bad grades. Like I'd come home with straight F's. Throw 'em on the table. He'd say, "You're grounded until the next semester!" And I took that like "Well, you ain't gonna be able to control me no more. Watch me." And I'd go in my room and I'd sit on the bed, wait till they're asleep, I'd crawl out the window, go to my friends' house, party all day, and come back: "Where've *you* been?"

We used to be grounded to the yard: "Don't leave the yard." We'd do it anyway.

And after a while, there was no way in the *world* they could control me. I could've made up my *own* mind to control *myself*. But no NA meetings, no AA meetings, no therapists, no psychiatrists, no P.O., no teachers, no parents, no neighbors, no*body*, could convince me to stop doing what I was doing. I mean not even—if the *president* come over to my house and gave me a million dollars and said "Stop doin' what you're doin'," I'd probably *think* about it, but I'd (laughs)—I probably couldn't do it, I really couldn't.

It's *hard* to behave. It's the peer pressure, and for the adventure, and the fun . . . (He's thoughtful for a minute.)

I never—I never really thought a straight person could have *fun!* Really! Seriously! (Laughs.) I—all my life—every time I do drugs, I'll be sitting back, and me and my friends'll be *laughing* about that! We'll wonder, it'll almost *kill* us, how do straight people have fun?

I mean, if you never gonna do *any drugs*, if you never have any *sex* unless you use condoms, or maybe once a year with your *wife*, I don't know, but (laughs)—you know, the straight people don't do drugs or drink or do nothing but go to *work?* What makes them *tick*, you know? What makes them laugh and have fun, what makes them *drive* straight, what makes them get up for *work* every morning? *That's* what I wonder. That must be tough on them.

That's a tough chore for *me*, that's for sure.

"I like violence—that's my problem"

She could be a rock star, or an actress. She's part Hispanic, part Anglo, vibrant and animated, with great masses of dark hair and an easy smile. A tattoo on her upper arm reads "Loca"; a smaller one, between thumb and forefinger, identifies her as a hard-core member of one of the most visible youth gangs in River County. She turned herself in to the Cherry Grove police to face charges of drug sales, and assault.

At the end of eighth grade, I became into this gang war kind of stuff. I was into this group that was called BGS, Barrio Grove Sur? And I loved the way they were, because they were always *laughing*, they were always get-up-and-go, you know? And it was just something I thought I wanted. But it turned out I didn't, but I really *thought* it was what I wanted. 'Cause, you know, we would start fights all the time, or get *into* fights, and I'd always get my drugs free; they always had it. You know, they would sell it, but the money wasn't really an object to them, it was more as we were like a *family* together. Nobody would trespass against us, nobody would mess with us, nobody would touch anything of us, nobody would disrespect us or anything; it was just like, you know, we were just all close together and just have a good time. And that was our own little world.

And as it progressed, I was lying a lot more, running away from home, and going on so-called missions, going from each little city, and meeting people and partying with them, in barrios. So it started progressing like that, and then when I became in like the middle of my high school years, about tenth grade, I dropped out of high school. I really wasn't *going* to school, though. You know. I would go to school, but I wouldn't go to class. (Laughs.) I would go off-campus, I would go there to meet my friends and we'd go off-campus and we'd just party, anyplace that we could go, we'd go party.

That was my daily routine. Getting up, not even getting out of bed, smoking a joint. Making the guy that I lived with, that we lived together, making him breakfast. Smoking joints all through that morning. Waiting for my friend to come over, we started drinking forty-O's of Old English. And then we would smoke a lot *more* joints! (Laughs.) Visit some schools, you know, sell some joints. Go pick up a carload of friends. Go cruise around for a while, but while all this, drinking tequila, José Cuervo. And just drinking Old English and smoking a lot of joints and KJ, that's the four main things, really, that I would do.

KJ? That's PCP. When I heard it, I thought it was coke and a joint! (Laughs.) But then I found out it was PCP when I first smoked it, 'cause it kind of tasted funny, didn't taste like coke and a joint. They just told me, "Call it KJ," so I did. KJ! What was the other word for it? "Frajo," but that's kind of different. It was opium with PCP in it, or a "bomba" (smiles)—it bombed your head, that's my definition for that.

Well, by nighttime we would be maintained, drunk, wired, stoned, everything you could possibly be. But by nighttime that means we're almost to the belligerent where, you know, nothing matters, somebody walks across your path, you're into a fight. Mostly every *night* we were into a fight. So that was mostly our daily routine . . . Then we'd sit down after a while and party some more and talk about "Oh, I could've done *this*, I could've done *that*"; "Should've flipped him over like *this*"; and "I should've stabbed him like *this*," and that was our daily routine. But it was always fun because . . . (Hesitates, smiles.) I like violence—that's my problem. I don't know why. I guess because it's a habit. A habit of getting into fights . . . (Puzzled:) I don't know why.

Did you get scared doing this?

Getting into fights? Yes. But . . . some of my friends, they were involved into a martial arts called chi? Have you heard of that? Kind of a brain muscle, or whatever you call it? But they kind of taught me how to control my mind. (Softly:) And I would turn over my scaredness and sadness and every kind of feeling that I had, I would turn it over to anger. And that's how I got my name, Loca. I would get really crazy (laughs) and after a while they tattooed me. See, "Loca." (She's pointing to the tattoos along her arm.) And I've got these, see, and I've got this, for 13 . . . but soon as I get my act together, I'm gonna have them taken off. I was gonna burn them off, but that's too painful.

That's one thing I can't stand, the sight of my *own* blood. I don't mind anybody else's unless it's really, really *gory*, but . . . (Laughs.)

I've been stabbed here, and I've been stabbed *here*, and broke a lot of bones. I've broken my ribs twice, from chains mostly, getting dragged by a chain, like in gang wars? And broken arms, I don't know *how* many times I broke my arms, missing and hitting a car! (Laughs.) Those kind of things. My leg's been broken a lot. I've had my head cut open back here. That was from a car accident. Well, I wasn't *in* a car, I just kind of got run over. I don't know how I survived out there, I really don't.

But all I remember is I was laying there for a minute and all of a sudden I see a whole bunch of people fighting and I get up and start fighting! I mean, blood's gushing out of my head and I don't care! That's insane! (Laughs.)

OK. I'll explain to you what happened. Me and this other kid, guy named Wino, that was with me—they used to call me "Winess" 'cause I used to drink, I *consumed*, a lot of Old English, let's say. But we were walking down from this party, just taking a walk just to get out to get some cool air, and along comes a lot of drunk guys, grown men, driving, and they hit me and they hit my little friend Wino. And he messed up his leg a lot, and I just kind of cracked my head open on one of those speed bumps. And all my friends heard it, 'cause, you know, I *screamed* when I fell, but then I was kind of knocked out. And then when I woke up, they were all fighting and he was still laying on the ground, 'cause he couldn't move his leg 'cause his *bone* was all messed up, and that got me mad 'cause me and him were really close.

He was the only person I ever talked emotionally to. Like I would talk to him—wasn't *that* often, though, because I was too busy fighting or getting drunk, doing something, but I'd talk to him about missing my family, you know, and stuff like that. I really did, but I kind of covered it up by drinking Old English.

I woke up and I seen him there and *boom!* I started fighting, and then I finally realized there were *seven* of them, grown *men*, drunk, belligerent, and there was only three of us, and one was lying on the ground already messed up, and I was a *girl* (laughs), and there was two guys there. One guy left, and I was getting slammed on the ground, but I was keeping up pretty much . . . And he came back with a gun and shot off one guy's leg and said he was gonna blow somebody's *head* off if he didn't leave us alone. (Pauses, laughs.) He was my old man. And he was a little bit more *loca* than *me!* And so they stopped, and he said, "If you ever touch my lady like that again," and all this stuff like that, and they stopped, and they said, you know, "We're sorry" and stuff, but I was still mad 'cause one of my good friends is still *laying* there, and then I finally realized that I fell and I bumped my head and I reached back, and I'm like "Oh my *God!*" and I started fighting them all again, 'cause I was mad because they hurt me and they hurt one of my friends . . . but you know, I got hurt a little bit more, 'cause, you know, seven on me, it didn't work!

But that night kind of ended pretty rationally because the other guy that was there too, he got hit over the head with a forty-ounce bottle and had a big piece of glass about *that* big stuck in his head. (Thoughtfully:) We never went to the hospital, though. I never figured that out, how we survived. Because he was bleeding pretty badly. So I kind of bandaged him up, but I didn't do too good a job because I was kind of dizzy myself.

That's why people liked me, I was smart . . . I mean I knew a lot of things, what to do, you know. Especially like stealing. I would plan things out instead of just going in there and getting it. You know? I was a planner.

Then I started getting into a lot of fights. And then we started getting into a lot of gang wars, from different barrios to barrios, and getting into a lot of PCP and KJ and acid and 'shrooms and peyote and so forth. I did pretty much anything besides shoot up. I'm really scared of needles.

That's one thing, I love to travel. I'd say I've been to most of the cities around here. I love traveling. I mean going to each city, finding out new things, about partying, new ways how to smoke pot, new ways how to snort this . . . (Laughs.) It was a trip, I mean it was fun. Those were missions. Out of the blue: "Let's go on a mission, let's go on a mission!"

And on our missions we'd go and we'd stay out maybe three weeks just traveling . . . One night we'd be in Hillview, one night we'd be in Valley City . . . Valley City was a hip place. Winston Boulevard? It would take four hours to get down one side of the street, that's how *booming* it was. All it was was just Mexicans from all different barrios would get together, you know, just cruise around, stop and party with *this* gang, stop and party with *that* gang . . . That's the way it was, it was cruising the boulevard.

And then when I started getting into that, I really liked it more, because . . . you know . . . (Hesitates, thoughtful.) I felt in *control*, that nobody wanted to mess with me, 'cause, you know, I'm *bad*. You know: I can beat you up, I'm *down* enough to beat you up, I'm down enough to go into that store and steal a case of Old English. You know? And so, I don't know, I felt really good about myself then. But I really didn't. (Laughs.) But I thought I did.

They would call me the heart of the club, you know, the heart of the group, because I was bold enough to do anything that sounded illegal, or sounded a threat to society. And you know, that's what I *wanted*.

How come?

I was mad at the world because . . . (Scratches her head.) I don't *know* why! But I was mad. I haven't found that out yet. I'm working on that. (Laughs.) I don't know who I was mad at, I was mad at myself.

Your parents?

I was pretty much mad at them, too, because, you know, they weren't there when I needed them and I didn't know how to express to them that I needed help. The only way I did that was disrespectful . . . and didn't really work, until later on in the years.

I don't remember too much of my childhood, you know, when I was really little. But I do remember I started stealing and lying when I was about in second grade. And then we moved on to Arizona, 'cause my dad was traveling a lot so we had to move to Arizona. And there I did pretty OK, you know, not lying and stealing, all that. And we only stayed there for six months, and then we moved again out here.

And by that time, I was in third grade. Stealing. Stealing became my priority then. I was stealing *little* things, you know, like candy and money from my parents to go get candy. And I was always lying. That's when I think I started my whole life, right there, down the drain.

And it was in my elementary years that I first started the taste of beer and alcohol. I think I was in fourth grade when I started drinking alcohol. And I liked it 'cause I'd see my parents drink sometimes when they were at home together. They'd drink a couple wines and stuff, and I don't know, I was "How come *I* can't drink that?" So I was a curious little kid. And by the time I was in sixth grade, I started smoking pot. Actually, it was *fifth* grade. And I was stealing jewelry by that time, jewelry and candy, little knickknack things.

Sixth grade, that's when it *started*. (Laughs.)

First time, I stole my mom's car and drove around. While in the meantime I was stealing a lot of alcohol from my parents, bringing it to school, sharing it with my friends. And at that time my sister—she's older than me, she's twenty-one—and me and her kind of were really close together in our childhood, but then I kind of got jealous of her 'cause she had a lot of friends that were always *laughing*, and I wondered, why are they always laughing? She was really a partyer. And I found these little pills in her room one day. And I thought they were candy! You know, I mean I never thought a little thing like that could get you all wooooo! . . . (Laughs.) So I just tried that, and I liked that. Because I just sat in my room for a long period of time, when my mom worked nights and my dad was out of town, and just *laughed*, you know, all by myself! And I thought that was funny! So I laughed some more! (Laughs.) And so I started stealing those from her and she started to notice that they were gone, you know, missing some of them. And, you know, I denied it.

But then by the time I was in seventh grade, I had my own connections of weed, and then I started getting into crank and coke, and like Quaaludes and reds and (laughs)—and on and on and on!

But then in seventh grade I started a fire in my school. Just for a laugh, you know. I don't know, in between my sixth grade and my seventh grade I was gaining a lot of weight. And that depressed me, but I also started getting real conscious of myself in between that time. And my mom was going to school, my dad was always out of town, so there wasn't really anybody there for me to talk to. And when my mom was finished with school, you know, I just kind of felt like well, I don't know how to talk to her, so I just would leave it alone. So I was getting more heavy into drugs. And a lot more like violence and stuff, you know.

Like when I was in seventh grade, I hit up the walls, you know? I started hanging out with Mexicans. And after I started the fire, I started forging checks. We had a candy run at our school and I used to forge checks so I could win a hundred dollars. I had big plans, yeah! (Laughs.)

And that went on for a couple of years.

And I was running away between all this. I remember one time that I came home, I don't know *how* I got home, though, but I remember how I was about ten miles away from my home and I'd been out for about a week or so and I was on a lot of drugs all at the same time. And I remember walking toward my house, but I don't remember how I got there. And I remember going to the door and *sitting* there for a minute and then finally ringing the doorbell. And I said, "Mom, take me to the hospital, I think I'm gonna die." And my mom hospitalized me for that night and then she took me to a rehab. And I stayed there for a week, and I ran. (Laughs.) After the drugs flushed out of me and I started detoxing. I was pretty much detoxing pretty bad. And so I ran with another friend that I made in there, or I should call acquaintance, rather than a friend. And I ran and I stayed out there for a week and I used all the same drugs and came back thinking I was gonna die *again*. And I was having a real bad trip and everything.

So I came back to the rehab, I finished off that program. I thought I was being honest back then, but I really wasn't, and it was just a whole game, that whole rehab was a game to me. You know, I could beat the system, which I did. I graduated from there, I stayed sober for about two weeks! Then I kind of kept it undercover for about three months. I'd go out, say I'm going to an AA meeting or something, and I would not go. I would go out, meet my friends, and go party.

When I was living at home, I'd get up every morning, smoke pot out of my window, and I'd get ready for school and I'd go to school.

I went to Truman High School. That was the main drug school in Cherry Grove. You could get any kind of drugs there. And I would go there and I would buy about an eighth a day, and that was just for the school time. And I'd go to school, me and my friends, smoke pot. And I'd go to this one class which was my so-called favorite teacher, because he would do coke, you know, in the classroom. He was really a cocaine fiend. There's a lot of teachers there that drink in the classrooms too. It's a really bad school. (Laughs.) Don't ever send your kid there, if you have any.

The teacher was snorting coke in the classroom?

Yeah, he did a *lot* of cocaine in there. And I found that out after I was his T.A. [teaching assistant]. 'Cause I would start off good, you know, and I wouldn't do any drugs and everything, and I would go to school for about two weeks. And be teacher's pet. But then I became *his* teacher's pet, but he would always talk about partying. So one day I looked in his drawer, you know, to get some files out to correct some papers. And I seen a mirror. And a *razor* in there. I mean, what are you gonna do with a mirror and a *razor?* (Laughs.) You know?

So I just kept it to myself for a while. And one day I came to school, I mean really *out* of it. I walked in there and I remember him just sitting there and closing the drawer really fast. And I said, "Aha!" And I walked up to him, and I sat down, and I said, "You wanta smoke a joint?" And I just boldly handed it out to him. And then I kind of caught myself and I said, "I'm just kidding, it's just a cigarette." And he goes, "No it's not, I can smell it on you every day." I said, "You can? How come you didn't say anything?" But a lot of the teachers there aren't really the kind of people to tell on you, because we wouldn't have a population of the school, you know? (Laughs.) 'Cause I only know two kids, really, that went to that school who didn't smoke pot.

And we started talking about drugs every day and stuff, and I asked him if he does coke one day, and he told me yes he does. And we went out to lunch one day and I seen a couple of my friends, that they came in there and they gave me some coke, and everything, you know, on the *table*, they thought that maybe he was a drug dealer or something, but he was my *teacher!* And he goes, "Well, that looks like some good stuff." And I was just shocked out of my mind! I said, "I thought you were gonna *tell* on me or something," because, you know, they're *giving* it to me. And then after that, we started lighting each other up. And then it got kind of boring, you know, 'cause I wasn't really a coke sniffer. I'd rather smoke it, you know . . . So I kind of got out of that scene. And I wouldn't go to his class anymore. But I'd always go to that school, and sometimes I'd say "Hi" to him. 'Cause I'd always be there getting into fights and selling my drugs and doing everything else.

But there's other teachers there, too, that I would kind of share brandy with. I didn't really like it, just to get high . . .

It's really not a good school. Not at all. I mean I thought it was the *best* school when I went there, 'cause I mean, God! "You sell this, you sell this? Wait! I never *heard* of this!" (Much laughter.) You know? It was really a trip.

When I got to that school, I was just doubly shocked. I said, "Whoa! All these *drugs!*" But I loved it. And then I met a lot more Mexicans there. That's when I got into that heavy violence thing. But most of the time during school, I would stay at home, drink forty-O's. But when I'd visit school, on the way back, because I lived by the [train] station? We had to cross through the parking lot to get to the school. So we'd go to school, on the way back, stop by, pick up a couple Kenwoods, you know, stereos out of cars.

But I think I did learn a lot. Mostly math, I liked math. I was always wired in there, 'cause, you know, he gave it to me free! So it was like I would do the work, I was always the first one to do my math. And I would always say "Math is so *easy.*" But what I really did was I picked out the easy stuff, you know, but actually I knew a lot of harder stuff than I really did. But I did learn a lot, like algebra and calculus, sometimes, and study those things when I went to class . . . (quietly:) and felt good about myself, I mean really good about myself, had a natural high, and I wanted to learn something that day, and I would study it, so I did learn. But I think people can learn from school *if* they want to. You can go to class, do the work, "Aw, this ain't teaching me anything," you know, but later on when you realize you still want to learn, that stuff will still be in your mind. I mean I still remember calculus . . . (Laughs.) I'm surprised, I mean, from all these *drugs* . . . (Shakes her head.) I *miss* school.

But after a while, it kind of got worse, and I noticed it progressed a lot and I started doing a *lot* more KJ, PCP, and more acid and drinking a lot more alcohol, and then came the Mexicans again! (Laughs.) And I was back to the same old thing, except that progressed, too. The gang wars that we were having then were involved with knives and guns and chains and stuff like that, and that went on for maybe a year.

And, you know, driving crazy on the street. That's what scares me. (Shudders.) I can't *stand* cars anymore, 'cause I remember the last time that I was *completely* out of it, but I knew what was happening, and we're driving down the freeway with no *lights* on in the opposite direction in the middle of the night! And *that* scared me. Yeah, I still have dreams about that, and I think that's keeping me not going out there. And I didn't get in a car again unless we were not partying. So I was kind of being precautious, but I was still doing the same things. Besides for just getting into cars, because that scared me.

But I was still, you know, shooting off guns and getting into a lot of fights. And I'd been to jail a couple of times. Me and a couple friends went to L.A. for a gang war out there and got caught. We had a fake ID because we would go to bars all the time. Had a fake ID on us, they'd bring us in, being overage we went to jail, and got to know people in there and became so-called hard-core, you know. And I really *liked* that, you know? Because like, being in *jail* . . . (Grins.) Hey, I'm *bad*, you know? I'm not even eighteen yet! (Laughs.)

And then I started getting my own apartments. And what I remember now, which I really didn't even notice, is I was paranoid of everything. I mean I *knew* it, but I wasn't really responding to it as though, why am I so paranoid? I would sleep in one position, you know, with a knife just like *this* crossed over me, (arms across her chest) and I mean that's *crazy!* 'Cause I was selling drugs then, I was selling cocaine in large amounts of quantities, and I was selling a large amount of quantities of marijuana, too, and I don't know, it was paranoia! (Laughs.)

But I started stealing a lot more. I would steal about three to four hundred dollars' worth of clothes, or like we'd go on a run and we would steal a lot of jewelry from a lot of stores, and sometimes we'd steal from houses, which was progressing a lot. And then I kind of cut back on that and let other people do it.

I never got caught except in third grade. I almost got caught, though, in Cherry Grove Mall. OK, I was stealing a stereo, a disk player, out of Cherry Grove Mall. I didn't know that those wires, if you cut them, they had an alarm on them. Stupid me! (Laughs.) They did! So I took it anyway, though. And it was me and another person I call my road dog, a good friend of mine, and another person, they were both my good *rucas.** So we each had two bags filled with clothes and jewelry and all that stuff, and we all had trenches on. So I had these wire cutters right here, and slipped 'em on this stereo and boom! (Laughs.) Alarm went off! And I said "Oh, no," and I already had the stereo, so might as well run,

---

* Pals.

right? And we planned this out, though, of course! Me! And I had somebody waiting . . . at the *other* end of the mall! (Great laughter.) All the
way at the other end! And so it was pretty embarrassing, because I seen
a lot of my neighbors in there, from my parents' house . . . Running
down, like this, in a trench coat, all hard-cored out, with two bags, with
a whole bunch of security men following me and my friend, too, I mean
just *running* down the mall—"Move out of the wayyy!" (Laughs.) I mean,
I was jumping over little *kids* and stuff, it was crazy! But I never got
caught. We jumped in the back of the truck, we all had this call whistle,
you know (whistles) and whistled really loud and luckily they heard us
'cause they started the engine, they were starting to go slow, we just threw
the bags in, we jumped in, and that was it. Got away! But I thought I
was really lucky then . . . I mean, that was a *lotta* clothes that we had.

One thing I do laugh about is, though, one of my other friends, her
name is Shy Girl, she's really shy, but she had on pumps with a trench
on so she lost one of her pumps, and that little thing . . . I always laugh
at that.

It sounds like you guys took care of each other.

Yeah. It's always been like that. I mean like somebody would disrespect
somebody in that barrio and I mean they were just *out*, I mean they were
just gonna regret that for a *long* time. A lot of people went to *hospitals*,
you know . . . (A long pause.) It really hasn't hit me too much, though,
right now . . . I don't know why, but it hasn't. I mean there's a lot of
people that I know that went to the hospital, you know, from *us* . . .
(Hesitantly:) I mean I could just imagine from *their* point of view, you
know: "I didn't know they were so hard-core and all that stuff, I didn't
know they were crazy like that!" But I don't know, it really hasn't hit me
yet, you know, the fact that I've broken *collarbones* and stuff, of people,
just because they named something off at me, or something, calling me
a female dog or something? And me wrecking their *collar*bone . . . I can't
believe that I even liked that . . . did that . . . today. I don't know *what*
I am, how I'm gonna be, but I'm finding myself out.

The last time I went to jail was in Valley City, and we had had a gang
war out there. And I remember I went into jail but I really didn't want
to go that night, because there were a lot of 14's in there; I claim 13, the
southside, and 14's northside. And there was a lot of 14's in there. And

that means war! (Laughs.) So I really didn't want to go in there. But all I remember is I was really out of it, had just got done fighting, cops pulled me in, and boom, got in a fight as soon as I got in there. They took me out and put me in another cell and I stayed there for a while, about two days, and then we had a gang war in *there*, 13's against 14's. Well, it got broken up, nobody really won, except a couple of people got stabbed.

Badly?

No, not really. I mean you can't really stab too many people, you know, unless in the eye with a toothbrush.

So that happened. And while I was in jail, I really started thinking about my life. And I really didn't want this anymore because that night, you know, too many guns were fired at my way. And it started scaring me just like the car did. And I said to myself, "Alright, when I get out of here, I'm calling my parents and I'm gonna go turn myself in," 'cause I had a lot of warrants out on me, and I turned myself in and they were kind of shocked that I did because, you know, it was right before I turned eighteen. 'Cause I didn't want to go back to jail, because I have enemies in there now, too.

And so I did it unknowingly to my barrio, my gang, because if they knew that I was in here, they would contact me and I knew I wouldn't want to change. So I'm keeping that kind of cool.

But I'm gonna take my G.E.D. and I'm gonna go to college. And I'm gonna go in the restaurant business. I've always wanted to own my own restaurant. (Smiles.) French! 'Cause I love to cook French food. And I've always wanted to be a chef, too. I loved to cook, ever since I was a little kid. I'm surprised I kept that with me though. You know, being in the restaurant business. Ever since I was a little kid, I wanted to be a chef. Just kind of didn't work out that way.

And that's pretty much my life story.

James L.

"That's what it's about—respect"

He's almost painfully slight, but his chiseled features and abundant dreadlocks make him look both vaguely regal and quite fierce. He's been sent to the Hall for a minor theft in Iron City, a charge he denies with convincing contempt. He thinks the real reason he's behind bars is his reputation as a leader in a rash of recent youth gang wars in Iron City. It's rumored that, despite his youth, he is not only a major player in the local cocaine trade—having taken over a turf formerly held by his older brother, recently hospitalized with gunshot wounds—but a main gang "shooter" who has put several rivals in the hospital in his own right. The day after we spoke, in the worst gang violence in the city's recent history, a carload of youths from his neighborhood, Manorville, opened fire with shotguns and machine pistols on a group of young people from a rival turf, Bay Ridge, killing two and injuring several more.

He chooses his words carefully; guarded at first, he becomes increasingly warm and reflective as we talk.

My brother got shot up in Iron City, he got shot in the face with a twelve-gauge. He lost his eye, some teeth, and they was talking about it was all over a *gang* and all that. His name Leon? And they say he the Manorville gang leader, talking all that stuff, they trying to say he a gang leader, it was over a drug deal.

They been trying to say that my brother was a big-time gang leader and I was a *little*-time gang leader, I'm taking over his drug business and all that type of stuff like this. (Scornfully:) I'm in a *gang* and all this, I'm a big shot and all type of stuff like that.

But it wasn't nothing like that! It was just like, you know, we all be hanging out together, we be hangin' in Manorville, 'cause one of my grandmothers stay in Manorville and one stay a few blocks away. So we all be hanging together like, and then these other dudes, we be going to parties and then they be talkin' all this, like, you know, "Y'all can't come over here," and all this. And we be like "We just coming to the *party!*" and we just start *fighting* and all that. And then they brought guns into it, and they start shooting and all that.

And like we was all out in Manorville one time and they was gonna come shoot us up like, you know, 'cause we was all out there having fun, there was about maybe forty or fifty of us out there, right? And my brother he seen them, so he chased them out of there, and when he was driving, they started shooting at him and he was the only one that got hit. So like he really saved a few people' lives, taking that twelve-gauge to the face.

He lived, though, he all right. He was in the hospital for about a month and a half or two, he was in critical condition for a week, they had to do all type of surgery and all, to get the things out. Then he stay in the hospital for a month and a half. So I was just like up in the City, running wild like, and then I just got caught up in some stuff and got busted.

It's gettin' kind of *dangerous* out there. 'Cause my mother just came up here and told me that one of my cousins *he* got shot, he *dead* now, his name Richard Sims? They had it all in the news and stuff, they saying *he* was the Manorville gang leader! (Laughs.) See, they don't know, they just saying that he got shot over gangs and drugs and all this. But it was like he was just driving in the car with my other buddy, and the dudes, the same dudes that shot my brother, they shot *him*. Same dudes. And I know they ain't like—they ain't nobody, they just like, see, when they come to fighting they don't *fight*, they want to use guns and all that, you know what I'm saying?

But it seem like everytime when somebody get shot over there from *they* side, the police they be in Manorville trying to find out who did it and all this, investigating, but then when somebody from *our* side get shot, they just like "Ha-ha," *laugh!* They say, "Oh, one of your guys got shot," then they *laughin'* and stuff.

With your relatives getting shot, do you feel scared out there on the street?

Naw . . . not really. I don't be scared. They don't be coming through where *we* be at with guns. Only like they might come through some time at night, or something. But I really don't even be *out* there at nighttime. It ain't like—you know, they just like . . . (pauses) they like *us*, but they just . . . I guess they got they time to get us, like.

You know.

Every time, if it be gangs, they always say they fighting over *dope*. 'Cause one turf want to sell they dope over here and they ain't gone let 'em. (Earnestly:) But that ain't what it be over! It's just over—like, you know, you from Manorville, you from Bay Ridge, so they gone fight! *That's* what its over! Like this been going on for years! I remember one time, it was about maybe a year ago, we used to be *hanging* with the Bay Ridge dudes! We used to go up there and be up there where they be, you know, chilling with them, hanging with them and stuff, having fun . . . you know?

And then like, something happened. One time they—like the *old* ones that's about twenty-five and stuff? They be like "Yeah, a long time ago we didn't used to be like that, we used to be *fighting* them Manorville niggers," saying all *this* type of stuff, so that get the little young ones that's our age, they try to get, you know, all *tough*, thinking about it . . . So then that's how it got started, like. And then ever since then, we ain't been cool with them, we just be cool with the Harrison district and Manorville, we just be together like. And then Bay Ridge, they just be with Richfield and a bunch of other turfs, and all that.

But that seems too bad, you know . . . these guys are really just like you—young guys, living in the neighborhoods— . . . Kind of sad, that you're shooting at each other . . .

Yeah . . . (Softly:) It ain't no end to it, though, I guess. I know they just gone be like that, since two people got shot already, it ain't gone be like . . . that easy. A few of *they* people up there got shot too! One dude lost his eye up there, too. Another dude he got *paralyzed*, all *type* of stuff. I don't know.

And then the police was trying to say, they was trying to get *me* on some of the shootings that happened up there, trying to say *I* did it, like I'm the main shooter. Like one time they jack me and they had the *news* cameras and all that out there, right, put me on the news saying that I'm known as one of the main shooters, the one most likely to be carrying a gun on me and, you know, telling who my *brother* was, and all this, and I go home and my grandmother she was *cryin'* and all type of stuff, she crying 'cause she's sitting right there and it was on the news, when I came in the house it was on the news. And (he's looking at the floor) she was crying, and all type of stuff.

Made me like—I put my hand on the Bible, told her I was gonna stay out of it and all that. Then I *was* stayin' out of it, wasn't gettin' in no trouble, just comin' in the house, doin' what she said, like. She was telling me like to quit being with my brother so much, 'cause he *older* than me, *much* older than me, he twenty. And she was saying, quit being with him, just hang with my friends. And I was just hanging with my friends.

All it really is, it ain't over no drugs, it's just over who want to have the most *respect*, with the girls and all that, you know what I'm saying? That's what it's about—respect. They just want to be known the most to the girls, you know, to the boys that's just going to school and all that, you know? 'Cause like now the *girls* they ain't no good neither! (Laughs.) They just want you, like, if you got money, or if you have a fresh car . . . Not *all* the girls, but I'm just saying *most* of 'em is like that, they want you 'cause you got a fresh car, or you got money, or you *known*, like everybody *know* you. So they just want to be, you know, known as your girlfriend, like. That's all it really is.

The girls don't be in this game, they don't be in none of this gang stuff. They just watch. They just watch so they can gossip, and tell who won and what happened, and you know. That's all they do.

Do you have a girlfriend you hang out with a lot?

I don't be with her *all* the time. 'Cause if I be with her all the time, you be with a girl every day, you be liable to break up with her pretty soon. If you just see your girlfriend like three or four times a week, you know, not saying you got to *do* nothing everytime you see her, just like *be* with her, that's cool. So you know you won't be arguing that much and all that. 'Cause if you bein' with each other every day, you gonna get on your nerves! (Grins.) It's just like you hangin' with your best friend every day? You just gone start arguing, think y'all both know so much about one another, and all this . . .

Today she was talking about should she have my baby and all this. You know, don't rush nothing (laughs), you better like ax your *mother* like! 'Cause you know, she only sixteen, right? And just what her mother gone be *thinking?* Her mother might start hatin' *me*, you know, 'cause I got her pregnant and all this. You know mothers don't want their girls having daughters *this* early. So I wrote her back today like, telling her like "Don't rush nothing, you planning on that, you better ax your mother, talk to your mother first." 'Cause her mother nice to me. You know. She let me come over. Come over eat dinner, she be inviting me to dinner all the time and stuff. I just be going over there, talking to her, I know her grandmother and like her uncles, I know all them, they just cool with me.

Would a guy lose respect with a girl if he said, "Hey, I'm not going to do this anymore, not going to fight"?

If she just like you for who you is and all that and what you *got*, maybe she would. But the type of girl I got, she ain't like that. Like when I used to be taking her out, I used to be like "Is you want something to eat?" and all this, and then she's like telling me "No!" And I'm like, I *know* she hungry, why she ain't eatin'? And she told me the reason that she didn't used to want to eat or nothing, 'cause she didn't want me to think that she just wanted me for my money! She used to *never* eat, you know? I'll be eating and like "Man, you ain't gone eat nothin'?" She'll be "No, I don't want nothing." (Laughs.) I'm going, "Man, what's going on?"

He moved into an apartment with his brother, until the brother was arrested for selling cocaine: "My brother don't have his apartment no more. Police took it. He going to jail for a while, for about five years maybe. One of his friends set him up, planted some stuff on him and snitched on him to the police. But this dude, he was supposed to be getting about ten years, and then he got out in two weeks! And he ain't been coming around no more. (Laughs.) I was telling my brother, 'cause the dude seemed kind of funny to me anyway, I didn't ever trust him, like. But my brother, like that was his best friend, and you can't tell him nothin'. Like he going, 'Uh-uh, he cool,' 'cause he did so much stuff for my brother, know what I'm saying?"

I'm not saying your brother was into this, but you know a lot of people who're out there dealing drugs—why are they into that if there's such a danger of being set up, of going to prison?

Most people need the money, they can't get no job, most of 'em like messed *up*, cuttin' school and all this, and all that, you can't get no job. If you *do* get a job, you gone have to *wait* a while, then what you gone do (laughs), you *broke*, ain't got no money . . . Then when you *do* get a job, you ain't gettin' paid that much, you might get a job at McDonald's or something like that, four sixty-five a hour, and that ain't nothin'! When people be out there making thousands! In just one day! You know most people just take the fast money, they just want they fast money so they can like, you know, help they *mother* out, or maybe buy they mother something . . . (Softly:) Some people' mothers on drugs . . . So they can't, like, they ain't got nothing else to do . . . Some of 'em ain't got no in*tell*igence, so they don't know, they just do it to make their money.

I hear that a lot, about guys helping their mothers out, with the rent and everything.

Yeah . . . 'Cause most of the mothers be on drugs! And if you got little brothers and sisters, then, you know, you don't want to see them all *dirty* and all that, you gonna make money any way you could, even if you *do* have to go to jail. (Quietly:) At least they'll have some money or something. And they won't be starvin' or nothin'.

'Cause I be out there seein' a *lot* of little kids, they all *dirty* and stuff, don't be dressin' all right and stuff? I know when I was out there I used to take a lot of little kids to the store, buy 'em little stuff, and I didn't even *know* 'em, like. Like all the little kids used to know *me*, calling my *name* and stuff when I walked past, talking to me and stuff, little kids like about four or five! (Laughs, shakes his head.) You know, I'd just be giving 'em money and stuff, "Here, go buy you something to eat!" You know, just like—coming through, taking care of little kids, like. 'Cause I know I wouldn't want *my* little kids to be like that.

There's a lot of little kids like that where you live?

They's a *lot* of 'em. I remember on Christmas I was going out there giving little kids money, 'cause like on Christmas, you know, I used to see little kids playing with all they toys and remote controls, and little girls carrying dolls, and all type of stuff? And like when I went out there, I was just looking around, me and some of my buddies, seeing how many kids, you know, *got* stuff, like. And like hardly none of the little kids *had* nothing. And I'm like—you know, me and my friends, *we* got *everything*! It's like we was taking they parents' money and stuff, we taking *they* money! So that's why I just, like, give the little kids money, 'cause you know, if it wasn't for me and my friends taking they *parents'* money, they would *have* something. Not saying they parents ain't gone go to somebody *else* and get it, but I used to just, you know, be feelin' kinda *bad* like, 'cause *I'm* having a good Christmas, but what about the little kids?

When I was little, I had *all* good Christmases, all *my* Christmases was good. And I'm just thinking like, man, they don't *have* nothin'! I got all they money, *he* got all they money, so . . . All my friends, we havin' fresh clothes and all like this, while *they* ain't got nothing for Christmas. I was just like givin' the little kids five, ten dollars. Tellin' my buddies, "Give the little boy some money," and stuff, you know? Like little kids they'll come up, they'll ax you, they'll see you counting your money or something: "Could I get a dollar, could I get two dollars?" You know, *little* kids like! They shouldn't even really *know* nothing about money! (Laughs, amazed.) You know, they shouldn't know nothing about money, or what you can buy with it! They out there hustlin' already, and they *that* little, axing for money. You know, I didn't use to turn 'em down.

'Cause part of the money *I* got was maybe from they parents or maybe from somebody in they family or something.

He dropped out of school a few months ago.

I'm 'spose to be in eleventh, next year 'spose to be my last year of school. But I was just cuttin', wasn't going to school. 'Cause I *was* getting good grades in class and all of that. In math, I got all the way up to Algebra I—I passed that. Then when I got to Algebra II it was like gettin' kind of difficult . . . Then I was just like cutting class: "Forget it, I ain't gonna go," 'cause it wasn't nothing but like *Chinamens*, Chinese in this class! You know, they all *smart*, they all smart in math, I'm feeling like "Man! I don't know *what's* going on!" (Laughs.) So then I'm just like "Forget it, I ain't gone go to this class." I was just cuttin' and stuff.

Did you ask the teacher to help you out when you didn't know what was going on?

I was axing 'em *some*times. But, you know, I didn't want to ax every time . . . You be axing questions and everybody *looking* at you like, all in your *face* and stuff . . . The teachers be helping, they helped.

I know when I get out I'm planning on graduating from regular school, high school. When I get out, I'm just gonna move up to Rivertown with my mother, cause its *slow* out there. I won't hurt nobody. And then just finish school, and all of that. I want to just go to college, and then go to cooking school and become a chef. That's what I want to be—a chef.

'Cause when I was little—I been like cooking ever since I was about nine or ten. My mother used to give us all a chance, like, to cook dinner, like me and my brothers? She'll be right there, and you know, just have us cook up a meal like steak and potatoes, vegetables and everything, you know, garlic bread, all type of stuff, just watch us cook. (Smiles.) And then she's going, "You should be a chef when you get older!" 'Cause I was the youngest *one* and I used be cooking the best! You know, they be burning they stuff up and all that (laughs), and I used to be cooking the best. And ever since then, I just wanted to be a chef. Like I be cooking my own meals sometimes. Not that my mother won't do it for me, but I just like, you know, "Lemme cook my stuff", and just watch her, and she show me how to do it, you know, how to put the right amount of seasoning in there and all that? She just showed me that.

And then when I started messin' up, she was like *mad!* Like my grandmother wrote me a letter the other day, up here? Wrote me a letter telling me that I need to get going because I got a lot of intelligence, and I'm *smart*, and all this, and that I need to, instead of just being nobody, like messing around out there, I should become *some*body. And I was just thinking about, you know, that's *right*, 'cause I just be lettin' it go to waste! 'Cause the schoolwork and all that, it don't be nothin', I'll be getting through it—if the teacher *explain* it, I understand it! And get through it, and just be finished like. Seem like up here, every day in class, I be like the first one finished with my work, and just be sitting around, just thinking.

See, I wanted to be a construction worker, but I was talking to this man, and he said that you only get to work eight months out of the year because four months is the rainy season, like. So you got to have another job, too. I was just thinking about maybe I'd be a construction worker *and* a chef, or something like that, 'cause they make good money. These counselors up here, they be making good money, too. Some of 'em, twenty-five dollars a hour if they work double time, overtime I mean? Like this counselor Steve out there, he be working sixteen hours some-times, a day. And I just be imagining how much he be making if he make at least maybe sixteen, twenty dollars a hour, that's *still* good. That's good money. I know if I could get a good-paying job I'd get a job . . . (hesitates) instead. That'd be better.

Do you think a lot of guys your age feel pretty much the same way—if they could get a good job, they wouldn't be . . . you know . . . messing up, dealing stuff?

Some of 'em. Some of my friends probably do. But some of 'em just don't care. They just want they money right *now*, they not even thinking about the future really, they just thinking about day by day.

'Cause I know since I been in here I been just like *thinking* a lot. I'm just thinking how many times I could be *dead* and all this, maybe gotten shot, you know, just thinking that God just put me in here to let me know. Just slow me down, so I won't get in no trouble or nothing. Maybe that would've been *me* who got shot instead of my cousin, if I would've been out. That's why I just be thinking, I'm glad God *did* put me in here. Slow me down so I could get in touch with Him, like.

You know, at first, when I was out, I would pray every now and then, but the only time I would *really* pray or talk to God is when I really *needed* Him like. And then, you know, maybe He help me and maybe He won't. But like now I just pray and talk to God every night, every day. (Softly:) Talk to Him.

Was your family pretty religious? Go to church a lot?

Not really. We used to go to church. I used to go to church with my mother and them. My father's side of the family, they go to church every Sunday. But like I don't even talk to them—I *talk* to 'em, but I don't mess with them, 'cause I ain't seen my father ever since I was . . . eleven years old, I think, ten or eleven, I haven't seen him ever since then. He live in Boston somewhere now, I think. I don't even know if he still *alive.* 'Cause when my grandfather died, his father, he didn't come to the funeral. 'Cause I think he on probation or parole out there, or something, you know, you can't leave the state. Maybe if my father was there, you know, I'd be going over and visiting them and talking to that side of the family. But it's just like . . . it just don't feel right with them.

But it sounds like you got along real well with your mom.

I got along with her for a while. And then she got on the drugs. And then I just stopped talking to her, just started living with my grandmother. My grandmother's like, she's been my—I been calling my grandmother "mama" and calling my mother "mom," calling her mama ever since I was little. You know, I just look at them like *they* my mother and father. 'Cause I really never had no father, like. I lived with my father for like maybe four years, five years, something like that. That was when I was from a baby till I was about in kindergarten. Then after that, I just started to see him—'cause he was a merchant seaman—off and on I'd see him, you know. He'd pop up maybe three times, four times a year, something like that, sometime I'd go stay with him, he had a little apartment, I'd stay with him for the weekend. But then after that, I ain't seen him for a *while*, like.

That must've been hard, when your mom started on the drugs.

At first, it was like we was a real, like . . . regular family. Like we used to go to the movies, and do all *type* of stuff. And then when she first started off, one of her friends that she grew up with, she was on drugs like real bad. And then I guess somehow she just got my mother to try it. And like on Friday night—my mother worked through the week, she wouldn't do no drugs all through the week or nothing like that. But when Friday night come, they started drinking, and then they'd start doin' they drugs. (Softly:) And I could tell . . . when she was doin' 'em, like . . . you know, she *changed*, like, 'cause I *knew* her, you know? I just could tell when she was doing 'em. And then my brothers and them, they was tellin' me—I'm like the littlest one, and I wouldn't believe 'em, right, and I just be *cryin'*, and then I'd go tell her what they were sayin' and all that. And then *they* would get mad at me 'cause she be mad at *them*, right? (Laughs.) Then they wouldn't be talking to me, so I was like "Damn!" Then I just be callin' my grandmother and talking to her. And then just go and stay at my grandmother's for a while.

She just like—at first, she used to buy us like about eight pair of pants, like for school? You know, when you first go to school? She'd get us like eight pair of pants, eight shirts, you know, about three pair of shoes apiece, stuff like that, and then, you know, it just started getting *lower*, like. She'd get us like maybe five pair of pants, one for each day of the week. Sometime maybe four, and then she'd just like get us a pair of shoes, and it just started going *down*, like.

And so my older brother started making his *own* money, and he was sellin' weed, to make his own money. And she used to take his weed and stuff, 'cause she didn't want him sellin' it. So she'd find it, she'd take his weed, take his money. But then he moved with my grandmother. Then he was living with her, then *he* got in the fast life, and then *he* got on drugs. (Sighs.) And then my other brother, the one that's in jail now, it was just me and him. And then *he* start goin' to Juvenile . . .

I remember we used to come up here and visit him—I was only about twelve. I was going, "Man, I'm not *never* coming here." And then I remember when he was at the Farm, and we used to be going up there, visiting him and stuff, and he used to be out there working, in the fields with all them *cows* and stuff? And I used to be thinking like "Man, I'm following right in his footsteps." Then I went to Hillview [Juvenile Hall], was up there for about thirty-five days, just like he was, and then I came down here, I been here for a month, maybe I be here for two months, and *he* was here for a while. But then I'm thinking, now he going to the penitentiary . . . (Shakes his head.) I just want to change before I follow that step and end up going to the penitentiary. 'Cause that's the next thing, you know, I don't want to do that . . . I'm just trying to change, like . . .

Do you want to have kids of your own when you get older?

I want to get married. I want to have kids. I think I'm gonna have a kid by the time I'm eighteen! (Grins.) That's two more years, I think I might have a kid by *that* time! But I know when I have my kid I'm not gone be . . . you know . . . like my father—I'm gone be a *real* father to my kid. You know. I want my kids to have a real father and real mother, like. And grow *up* right. You know? And they really could *be* somebody, you know, make good money and stuff. (He's quiet for a minute, looks at his hands.)

'Cause it just seem like most of the blacks is just goin' down the drain. They killin' off each *other*, like. They put the drugs in they own—in the ghettos, like. That's where most of the drugs be. In the ghettos. And they give 'em them little welfare checks and *know* they gonna spend it on drugs, so the white man gettin' the money right back anyway! They makin' the money right *back*, the big man, whoever that is, they gettin' the money back anyway. So they don't really care. Like they should have more little job centers in the ghettos or something, you know, *helping* people. You know, helping people get jobs and all type of stuff like that, so they can take care of they *kids*, and all this.

That's what I was saying before—it's sad, young black guys killing each other—they're not the enemy . . .

Yeah, killing off each other. A long time ago like, I wasn't around then, but when heroin was out, when they used to sell heroin on the streets, right, like they sell hubbas? And then when it started getting into the white neighborhoods, to the rich people, and *they* kids was doing it, you see, they put a stop to that, they got it off the streets. Where you could just go—you know, you couldn't buy it off the streets no more, you could just buy it like if you *know* somebody connect you up, and you could get it from him. And now they put the crack out in the black areas. Now when *that* start gettin' to the rich white people and all that, *they* sons and all that, and *they* start doin' it, losin' they money, then they gone—that's why they trying to put a stop to that real bad now. 'Cause at first, when it first came out, they wasn't too worried about it, they just do they little raids maybe twice a week, you know. They just see you sellin' it, they don't care. Unless there's a *lot* of 'em or something, they'll come out.

And then like around election year, you know, for the mayor and all type of stuff like that? That's when they *really* be raiding, trying to get people, they start coming out there with the *motor*cycles and *dirt* bikes coming through, with stun guns and all that type of stuff, and then the news cameras, puttin' it on the news, trying to make it like that's the worst place and all that? That's when they start doin' that, around election time. And then after about a month, they don't do nothin'.

They don't be caring. They see you with your cars and all that, most of the time they be *mad*, they be jealous 'cause you makin' more money than them! (Laughs.) So they be jealous, taking your money and stuff. Like when I got caught, I had five hundred dollars on me. And when I went to court, they didn't mention nothin' *about* that! They didn't say nothing about my five hundred dollars. I had some Gazelle glasses, they took them, they didn't say nothing about *them*.

*I just heard Jesse Jackson talking about this—about respect—
saying black people ought to stop turning on each other.*

Yeah . . . (Slowly:) I just be thinking, like Martin Luther King went through all this to get black people equal rights and all that, and now we fightin' each *other*, just killing off each other. I just be knowin' he turning over in his grave thinking about all this! How he did all that, gave up his life, he wasn't using no violence or none of that, he gave up his life so we could like really get equal rights, you know, be treated the same. Now *we* fightin' each other, killing each other off . . . That's stupid! But you tell somebody that . . . (Pauses.) They don't think like that. They just thinking what they gone do tomorrow or next week, and all that. They don't think about is they gone *live* tomorrow, is they still gone be *alive* tomorrow, they don't think about nothing like that. You know, people just gotta stop and think! They moving too *fast*, like!

But I know when I get out, a lot of my friends will say I changed, maybe be saying I'm a *square* now, and all this. But it's just that I ain't gone be doin' the things I was doing at first. And I just, like, had time to think about it.

Afterword

I

White, black, Chicana—what most unites the young people in this book is how thoroughly the collapse or abdication of adult systems of support and care have forced them to make do on their own, with few resources and limited options. "You for your own, and, you know, your self only," Shaniqa says; and that discovery comes to most of them sooner or later. By the time they are well into their teens, most have come to accept the parameters of the Darwinian, "sink or swim" world that surrounds them, and much of their energy is devoted to making their way intact within that world.

As these stories make clear, that world has become increasingly chaotic, dangerous, ungenerous, and unhelpful not just for the urban "underclass" but for a much wider spectrum of the American young. In the past few years, during the time I was talking with youth in the Hall, there was growing national concern about what was often called a "generation at risk," and a flood of warnings that our neglect of the problems of the young would bring dire consequences. But that rhetorical concern hasn't been translated into much tangible help for kids like Shaniqa, Lucifer, Saffron, or Rocket Queen. If anything, we have retreated even further from a serious commitment to address their needs, and that continuing failure is painfully apparent in their stories. Over and over, the clearest message that comes through in their accounts of their own lives is how little that is constructive ever happens to them. Mostly, they are shuttled back and forth between their inadequate, exploitative, or nonexistent families, the "street," and the formal youth control system, which at best, in the post-Reagan era, is typically passive and reactive, rarely preventive or supportive.

With some exceptions, most of them are mired in the juvenile justice system (and the ancillary public systems of child welfare and mental health), not because anyone has any serious expectation that being there will do them any good, but because there is nowhere else to put them.

As growing numbers of families in River County have disintegrated or become dangerously dysfunctional, more and more adolescents have come to need help of various kinds and, often, a safe and dignified place to be outside the home. But the same policies that have undermined families and communities in the first place have also gutted the options for doing much beyond bouncing them back and forth from one part of the youth control and child welfare systems to another.

Nationally, according to statistics compiled by the House Select Committee on Children, Youth, and Families, despite rising numbers of youth in trouble, federal funds for delinquency prevention dropped by half in real terms over the 1980s, funds for substance abuse and mental health services by 30 percent. Federal funds for services to children and youth under the Title XX Social Services Block Grant were no higher at the end of the eighties than at the beginning, despite substantial rises in the number of young people and families needing help and sharp increases in reports of child neglect and abuse. "Regardless of the system," the committee notes, "the lament is the same: where services exist, they are generally ineffective, inappropriate, or inefficient . . . Needy children and families get attention and services only after the fact—after abuse has occurred, after a crime has been committed, or after a child has died." River County is not different; and what makes this especially troubling is that River County is not an exceptionally hard-pressed region, measured against the rest of America. It has substantial areas of harsh poverty, in Iron City and elsewhere, but it is a predominantly "middle-American", generally prosperous county. What you see in River County, then, is only a hint of the erosion of services for the young that has taken place in poorer, harder-pressed communities across the United States.

Yet as these stories suggest, here, too, there has been a severe deterioration of public social services that could intervene constructively in the lives of these young people, and that helps account for the depressing recycling of many of them from one youth institution to another and back out to the family—such as it is—or the street. Over a quarter of the youth in the Hall at any given point are there awaiting "placement" to a group home, foster care, or a residential drug-rehabilitation program; the proportion reaches up closer to half during periods when the Hall is seriously overcrowded. They are waiting both because there are only a handful of such programs anywhere in the county or in the surrounding area, and because the placement staff of the youth probation department is stretched so thin that it often takes weeks or months to match up the kids with the places that do exist. Increasingly, River County's troubled young who do not go on from the Hall to fill the state's swollen youth prison system or to the street are being sent to families or programs *out* of the state because of the shortage of adequate placements in the state itself.

The decline of more *preventive* programs—what in the jargon of the child welfare system are called "front end" services—has been the most dramatic. As in the country as a whole, the pattern in River County has been for the money to dry up for all but the most reactive and crisis-oriented services; the juvenile authorities have consequently been forced to target what resources they have on kids who have already reached the stage of serious lawbreaking or who are in immediate need of out-of-home placement. As in some other parts of the country, there are now some small-scale programs in River County that work with troubled families to try to prevent conditions from escalating to the point where institution-alization or foster care is necessary, but those efforts have been miniscule in comparison to the growing need. Even the most immediate emergency-care services have also been hit brutally hard by the cutback of public services in River County, in the face of rapidly rising numbers of children and adolescents without adequate food or shelter, many of them fleeing life-threatening conditions at home. The county had a total of six beds in emergency shelters for runaways, "throwaways," and severely abused children at the time I was interviewing in the Hall; dozens of kids applying for shelter were rejected every week because there simply was no space for them.

What is surprising is how well many of them are able to take care of themselves when no one else is willing or able to do so. They are especially adept at building networks of supportive relationships with friends, siblings, or the occasional helpful adult: many talk about creating makeshift "fam-ilies" to provide what their original families cannot or will not. "We actually were like a little family," says Kathy of her arrangement with her male friend Juster and "old Fred". "We were just all close together," Loca says of her gang, "and that was our own little world." Even the street drug business is described in family terms: "We was all like brothers and sisters," says Latasha, "we all stuck together." Teresa's old lady, Dawn's twenty-three-year-old soldier, Rocket Queen's friend Ray—these connec-tions are like lifeboats for many of the young people who move through places like the Hall. Without them, many would be truly on their own, and the prospect is frightening. "Right now I've got all these people out there that I know and that love me," Kathy says, but they could be gone when she gets out, and "I don't know what happens to you if you went to start over."

The perils are especially intense for young women. Girls trying to make their way outside the boundaries of their families face all the threats of exploitation and neglect that young men do, but also must contend with the pervasive risk of exploitation by men—in relationships and on the street. For Ginny, Saffron, Shaniqa, and Kathy, daily life involves complex negotiations with men who sometimes offer the prospect of support, protection, and partnership, but more often present immediate threats of sexual and economic exploitation and violence. It's hard enough for a sixteen-year-old boy to make his way alone and unscathed in the increasingly risky social world that is America in the final years of the twentieth century; it is even harder for sixteen- (or fourteen-) year-old girls. The ability of very young kids like Kathy or Ginny to cope with the constant threat of male abuse and violence is impressive; but it's also an indictment of our failure to provide reliable sources of help or shelter for more than the short term, so that these young women wouldn't need to live in constant danger or enter into potentially life-threatening alliances with men in order to get by. For many of them, the only accessible sources of protection are personal friends—like Kathy's solicitous bikers—or the juvenile justice system, which by locking them in also usefully locks their men out.

II

As this suggests, the shrinking of preventive and emergency services for the young has meant that the juvenile justice system has increasingly become a kind of all-purpose social service agency in River County, at least for the children of the less affluent. If nothing else, the Hall offers some basics that are decreasingly available to youth outside—a roof over their heads, protection against predators or abusive parents and guardians, three decent meals, regular showers, and basic medical attention. The savvier kids understand this function perfectly well, and consciously make use of the juvenile system as a periodic respite from life "on the outs." "They're like a hotel, or something," says Ginny Swenson; "if it gets to be terrible, then I come to them." Teresa Watson, fighting a losing battle with cocaine, "got so tired of being on the street *that I got in trouble and I got sent to the Hall.*" For Saffron Bailey, it was the constant threat of abuse from men that made the Hall look good by contrast: "I *wanted* to get caught, because I didn't feel too safe being out on the street." In this context, well-intentioned police or probation workers will sometimes "re-label" youths as delinquent in order to ensure that they can get at least the rudimentary services offered by incarceration in the Hall or the County Farm. "Relabeling" presents little problem in most cases, because it is very difficult to be underage and out of the home for long without breaking some sort of law, whether it's "defrauding an innkeeper"—which might mean walking out of a hamburger place without paying for your french fries—or getting caught with a bottle of vodka, a joint, or a forty-O of Old English.

The authorities who practice this sort of "relabeling" are aware that they're going against the spirit of the federal Delinquency Prevention Act of the 1970s, which sought to reduce the use of juvenile institutions to house young people who were not seriously delinquent—the so-called "status offenders" and the simply thrown away and exploited. But they are also keenly aware of the grimness of the alternatives, in an era when the promise of "deinstitutionalizing" troubled youth has been canceled by our unwillingness to provide other agencies of care and opportunity *outside* the youth confinement system. "Lucky I stole my Mom's car and wrecked it," says Cindi, "because otherwise I wouldn't have gotten the help I'm getting now." And that about sums up the state of things in the youth welfare system in River County today.

But though under current conditions using the juvenile justice system as a catch-all social service agency for youth may often seem the only humane thing to do, no one believes it is the *rational* thing to do. Even on the barest economic level, it is hugely, self-defeatingly expensive. In this state, it costs, at a conservative estimate, between $25,000 and $30,000 a year to keep one teenager in secure custody; in some states it's much higher—over $50,000, according to a recent study, in New York. Every-one, from state legislators on down to the probation worker on the street, understands that it would be far cheaper to keep the adolescent out of the institutions in the first place; but that universal understanding, here as elsewhere, has barely affected the drift of public policy. And so the state, following the lead of a rudderless federal government, continues to pour increasing sums into the incarceration of youth while steadily slashing less expensive programs to prevent delinquency and family disintegration. Nationally, while we were busily shrinking the already Lilliputian budget for delinquency prevention (only a little over $100 million at the start of the eighties), we nearly doubled our spending on youth correctional institutions, to almost $1.7 billion by 1989 (for operating expenses alone, not to mention construction).

That we now spend over twenty times more to operate holding pens for youth than for programs to *prevent* delinquency would, in a more reasonable world, seem utterly nonsensical on economic grounds alone; but more than economics is involved. The economic irrationality of our current approach to troubled youth reflects our continuing adherence to the ideological conviction that it is *wrong* to spend money to help undeserving children or the dubious families from which they come; so preventive services are viewed as frills at best, coddling at worst. That attitude runs very deep in American culture, and it strongly influences the political climate. No politician in memory in this state has ever been swept into office on a rising tide of public demands for social services for children and adolescents at risk; many have been catapulted from well-deserved obscurity by promising to get tougher on juvenile thugs. That goes a long way toward explaining why in River County, as elsewhere in the state and the nation, we continue to spend great sums to isolate or punish children *after* they have hurt someone or been seriously injured themselves, physically or emotionally, rather than spend *less* to prevent those tragedies from taking place.

The same attitude helps to shape what goes on or, better, does not go on, inside the youth institutions themselves. There are many fine and conscientious people working in the juvenile justice system in River County—probation officers, judges, counselors—but their capacity to help has been frustrated by the corrupting lack of sufficient resources and by the operating ideology of the system, which insists that it is both too costly and morally counterproductive to do much for kids in trouble.

Resources for counseling and aftercare for troubled or addicted youths, and for effective education and job-training programs shrank or remained level in the last decade, while the caseloads of juvenile probation agencies in many places shot upward. Again, River County's troubles are fairly minor set against those of big cities, such as New York or Los Angeles, where probation officers' caseloads can run in the hundreds and where the proportion of seriously violent or emotionally disturbed youth in the system is usually greater. But increasingly, during the lives of the young people in this book, the erosion of resources has meant that the juvenile justice system has become reduced to a crisis-response operation, providing little for its wards other than a secure bed, adequate food and medical care, and a modicum of physical exercise. And even that slim provision is being slowly chipped away as the fiscal disintegration of even relatively prosperous places like River County continues to deepen. Not long after I finished these interviews, one of the Units of the Hall that held many of the young men with more serious problems—"Blaster," Nick, and "Lucifer" among them—was abolished in a cost-cutting measure necessitated in part, by the expense of building a gleaming, new, and already severely overcrowded county jail for *adults*, a facility to which some of those young men will almost certainly make their way soon enough.

But again, the forces behind the stripping-down of the functions of the juvenile justice system are not only economic: they also reflect a deep ideological shift in the way the system has chosen to define its purposes. In this state, as in most others, juvenile justice (following the lead of the adult criminal justice system) formally retreated during the late 1970s and 1980s from its earlier concern with dealing with the "whole child" and working to reintegrate troubled kids into the community. Before then, it had been widely agreed that incarcerating youths ought to be a last resort because of its destructive and well-documented effects on their morale and their chances in the future. If we *had* to place young people in secure care, we should try to help them develop the skills that could lead to a productive life in society. By the eighties that assumption was rarely to be encountered in most juvenile systems in the United States. (Massachusetts' system was a humane exception.) In part, that shift reflected the popular view that little *could* be done with delinquents, even if we wanted to; that "nothing worked," since most were presumably too hardened to change by the time they reached adolescence. It was also another manifestation of the spread of self-righteously punitive attitudes toward the disadvantaged generally in the eighties. Like others who hadn't "made it" in America, youth in trouble were said to have failed because of a lack of individual responsibility, which would only be exacerbated by offering them serious help. And so by the 1980s, the juvenile justice system in River County, as in much of the country, had come to resemble a small version of the adult prison system, shorn of any mission beyond removing the dangerous from the community and providing minimum shelter for vulnerable youth with nowhere else to go.

III

Clearly, the young people in this book—and the hundreds of thousands like them across the United States—deserve a better deal. Some of the most urgent needs stand out clearly from the stories in this book.

First, we need to reverse the current perverse policy of starving preventive services for children and families—services that might help keep some youth from reaching the state arrived at by Latasha or Teresa or Rocket Queen in the first place. Increasingly, we have a fairly good idea of what many families in trouble—especially low-income families—need; where we fail is in implementing what we know on a substantial enough scale to make a difference. Family support programs that offer comprehensive help for families with multiple problems—including training in more tolerant and effective child-rearing, help with financial troubles, advocacy around problems with housing or the schools—are especially promising, and we have encouraging evidence that they can be successful. They could have helped some of the kids in this book: we need more of them.

More fundamentally, these stories make it all too clear that even the most basic material needs of children are routinely unmet in many American communities today. That is true even for children who still have families; for the growing numbers living by their wits on their own, things are much worse. It shouldn't even need to be said that no child should have to get herself committed to a juvenile institution in order to receive elementary medical care and shelter. It's time to insist on the principle that young people, whether or not they are living in families, have an inalienable *right* to basic health care, safe and dignified shelter, and access to respectful counseling and assistance with drug and alcohol problems and threatening relationships. We might begin by establishing a network of "user-friendly" community health centers that adopt a nonstigmatizing, supportive attitude toward adolescents, offering both curative and preventive health services and help with emotional problems and substance abuse, and which are committed to reaching out to the young in the schools, at home, and on the street.

Beyond assuring basic care, we need to aim higher, toward building a system of support for adolescents that builds on the positive strengths they possess and that is designed to prepare them for an independent and contributive role in society. This means rethinking some of the assumptions that characterize, even at best, our current systems of youth welfare and juvenile justice.

The issue is not only about money. It is about how we define adolescents and their problems in the context of the realities of American society in the 1990s. Even a system of well-financed services for the young might not appropriately address their needs or help them move toward what I would call contributive independence; our existing approach for more affluent youth bears troubling witness to that. All too often, we are quick to find reasons to place youth in "secure care" in closed psychiatric or drug-treatment facilities with little evidence that they need it. Indeed, as the University of Michigan researcher Ira Schwartz has shown, the growth of questionable institutionalization of troubled young people has become a real scandal in recent years—a scandal driven by the desire of too many affluent parents for a quick-fix solution to teenage troubles or rebellion, and by the easy availability of third-party insurance to cover increasingly expensive "treatment" of dubious effectiveness. Today, indeed, we have a curious dual system of youth control in which no one wins. For those of the young whose parents (or their insurance carriers) can afford it, there is a growing trend toward overinstitutionalization and over-"treatment"; for the rest, as we've seen, there is little help at all.

We do not, in short, simply need more of the *same* services and institutions for youth that we now have. We need a different approach —one that takes account of changes in the surrounding society and in the family, and that also takes adolescence itself more seriously as a time of positive change and growth.

The system of services and institutions for adolescents in America is mostly a poorly fitting extension of the *child* welfare system. But adolescents are very different from children, and that helps explain why the system is failing them today.

Adolescents occupy an ambiguous place in modern "postindustrial" societies. No one really mistakes them for children, but we have steadily lengthened the period of formal dependence before they are considered quite adults. Ideally, that period of dependence is experienced within the context of a stable family and a successful passage through the formal institutions of socialization outside the family, especially the school. The dilemma appears when, as is increasingly the case, those institutions function badly or fail to function at all.

Adolescents who fall, or are pushed, out of that "normal" trajectory are plunged into limbo. There is no established role for them as independent contributors to the larger society; at the same time, they are too old (and often too streetwise) to fit well in a system of foster care and group homes designed for younger children.

Experts in child welfare are increasingly aware of that disjunction, and there is considerable sentiment in favor of doing everything possible to return troubled adolescents to their families, often under the rubric of "family preservation". In many cases, especially for younger children, that's surely a worthy goal. Even for some of the older adolescents in this book, the more innovative programs designed to head off "placement" in the formal justice or child welfare systems seem promising. A program like that in Hennepin County, Minnesota, for example, which works with troubled families to deal with crises *before* the child must be removed from the home, by offering everything from family counseling to paying the rent, has had success with some teenagers otherwise headed for the youth control system; and it could be a useful model for some of those who, like Sean O'Farrell, have basically solid and functioning relationships with a parent.

But many cannot, or should not, go back to their original families. For "Lucifer" and tens of thousands of kids like him, it's probably too late for family preservation; even if it were realistic to expect a significant change in his father's alcoholism and relentless violence, it's not clear that much in the family is by now worth preserving, or that "Lucifer" would be better off it it *were* preserved. It's our failure to provide real options *outside* either the family or the formal youth control system, in fact, that keeps "Lucifer" stuck in the depressing cycle that ensnares him: being returned over and over again to an intolerable family situation from which he must recurrently escape—through drugs, suicidal gestures, and/ or another stint in the Hall. For kids like Dawn Olivetti or Saffron Bailey or Ginny Swenson—and there are growing numbers of them—family preservation is also clearly too late, for there is really no family left to preserve. If ever family intervention might have been helpful, it was a very long time ago, before the parents collapsed or left. And so the question of what to do with those kids here and now won't go away.

We are becoming numbingly familiar with the statistics on the wide-spread disintegration of American families, especially at the lower end of the income scale; but we have not yet really incorporated that awareness into our policies for children and youth. To a large extent, those policies still reflect an earlier, less chaotic time, when intact families were still the norm and our main worry was about the spread of *single-parent* families. Today, in most of the communities that routinely send kids to places like the Hall, the intact family is a rapidly diminishing species and even the stable, well-functioning single-parent family is often replaced by the "no-parent" family, or the threateningly dysfunctional family. I don't want to exaggerate here, or to tar all the families of poor and working-class Americans with the brush of "pathology." But for a big proportion of the young people who enter the public juvenile justice or child welfare systems, the assumption that the family of origin is even *present*, much less fixable, can no longer be automatically held.

At the same time, the forces that have combined to undermine the family in these communities have also made things tougher for the traditional alternatives to it; the foster care and group home systems. Just as the need for foster care has risen, fewer families have the time or resources to be able to provide quality care, especially given the trend toward deeper problems among children needing to be placed. Today children may be shuttled between half a dozen or more foster homes before landing in a stable one—if that happens at all. Group homes, in the current climate of fiscal meanness, have too often become little more than small-scale versions of the large juvenile institutions—temporary holding grounds for youngsters who have exhausted other alternatives—from which many (as we've seen) will routinely run away.

A more comprehensive strategy for youth, then, though it should surely work to improve family functioning where it can, should also confront the reality that some families are so inadequate, neglectful, or dangerous that many youth need permanent alternatives. And those alternatives should be based on the recognition that most of these young people have a variety of strengths that we can nurture and enhance—a recognition that leaps out from many of the accounts in this book.

Most of them work hard at what they do. Whether it's piecing together a complex system of shelter and support on the street without adult help, or sustaining, at fourteen or fifteen, a successful drug business in a brutal and competitive industry, they demonstrate extraordinary initiative and creativity. Often this goes along with a slightly skewed (but in an increasingly rapacious economy, *only* slightly skewed) expression of the traditional American work ethic. "If I'm gonna sell," declares Blaster, "I'm gonna be a *good* one." The ethic of industry, of technological mastery, that Erik Erikson describes as part of the developmental stage of adolescence generally is evident in many ways, only some of them illegal. Most of the kids I interviewed are good at a lot of things. Some are good at cooking; many are good at sports or are gifted with their hands; others can take apart a motorcycle or a Camaro and put it back together with care and ease. Some are especially skilled at caring for those younger, weaker, or less resilient than themselves. (A surprising number, when I asked them what they wanted to do in later life, said *first* that they'd like to get a job working with kids like themselves.)

We can appreciate these capacities without romanticizing them. Some of these young people are truly self-destructive, others disturbingly unconcerned with the lives of other people. Many have a history of tripping over themselves and systematically fouling up their best chances to do things differently. Some need deep psychological help; a few need secure confinement, at least for a while. But to view the growing population of delinquent and discarded youth in the "system" today as simply a collection of the damaged and destructive is terribly misleading—and probably self-confirming.

IV

That many "delinquent" youths have considerable skills and abilities is not an original observation, but it needs reaffirming because it is rarely taken into account in devising strategies to deal with them. (There are some alternative programs that do so, but I am speaking here of the formal systems of child welfare and juvenile justice.) Instead, most of what we do with the young and troubled is rooted in one or another variant of what I would call a "deficiency model" of delinquency; we assume that the adolescent's problems stem from some deficit, some lack, within them, and our strategy is accordingly to correct that lack, to fill the lacunae in the youth's development. Obviously, there are times when both the diagnosis and the prescription are accurate. But, as often, the deficiency model prevents us from making the most of what the young person has to offer.

The deficiency model can take many forms. At worst, the delinquent is defined as biologically inadequate or intractably "antisocial," and those definitions are used to justify either systematic neglect or the overuse of institutionalization (complete with excessive "medication"), or both.

But there is also a subtler variant, generally well-meaning, which, in overstressing "damage" and "vulnerability," can also mask the multiple strengths the youth possesses and lead to inappropriate strategies of intervention. It leads us to overemphasize "fixing" the individual adolescent while ignoring the evidence that we need to alter the institutional structures that have helped to cause the damage and place the youth at "risk" in the first place, and which profoundly constrain the adolescent's realistic chances for a richer and more secure life. The deficiency model focuses on the kids' problems, not their potentials; and it locates the source of those problems too much inside the individual (at best, inside the family) and not enough in the shrinking opportunities available in our society to put that potential to use. It focuses, for example, on a kid's apparent incapacity to learn, while ignoring the revelation that what he does with his spare time is work on his *computer*. It scrutinizes the psychological deficits of a boy who steals cars and wrecks them for fun—and fails to ask what *else* he might do with his energies, if he wasn't stuck, alone and bored to desperation, in a bleak and isolated community where the main legitimate diversion is taking the bus to someplace else.

The alternative is what I will call an "opportunity model." The opportunity model acknowledges that the young person may have suffered a great deal of emotional and psychological trauma, but does not conclude from that that he or she is helpless or irrevocably damaged. It acknowledges that some have behaved destructively and selfishly and may have become hardened to the well-being of others, but it does not automatically discard them as thugs incapable of change. It assumes that what adolescents in trouble—like all *other* adolescents—most need is assistance in growing toward increasing competence, responsibility, autonomy, and capacity to care—and tangible opportunities to translate that growth into action in the real world. The opportunity model has many implications for our strategies for the young—both outside the juvenile justice system and inside it, both for those who do not really need to be in the youth control system and for those who do.

For many of those whose problems are less severe, it seems obvious that most of their difficulties—with family, school, the law—have less to do with intrinsic deficiencies or damage than to the narrowness of the legitimate options available to them. That problem, clearly, cannot be addressed effectively through the existing youth control system. For what is most glaringly missing in the various parts of that system—group homes, foster care, shelters, the juvenile institutions—is any context for challenge or any real opportunity for growth. Again, in many cases we put young people in these places because we cannot figure out anything better to do with them, at least until the army or marriage or prison takes them off our hands, or the magic age eighteen arrives to relieve us of formal, quasi-parental responsibility for them. The worst consequences are painfully, bleakly obvious: the depressing cycle of shunting kids from one temporary holding ground to another, the pattern of "running" from foster care or group home to the street, the resulting threat of exploitation, violence, and chemical abuse that lies in wait outside. The longer-run consequences are less visible but equally depressing; caught in the typically neglectful and often inappropriate youth control system, most are denied real opportunities to learn much that is useful or necessary in the adult world of work and responsibility, or to grow in maturity and capacity, so that even if they manage to escape the violence and exploitation and the most obvious kinds of self-destruction, many simply fade into the swelling ranks of the economically and socially marginal, the alienated, and the hopeless. That's a fate many are clear-eyed enough to see looming before them; it is one reason why so many, like Shaniqa Brown, talk about being afraid of getting older.

The opportunity model suggests an alternative to that common but destructive scenario. First, and most important, it would provide new kinds of settings—both residential and nonresidential—in which young people could engage in serious alternative education and challenging, useful work. Interestingly, the need for these alternatives was understood better in the 1930s than it is today. The Depression stimulated a truly large-scale public effort to develop alternative ways of sheltering, teaching, and nurturing adolescents and of putting them to important work in their communities. Today we are most familiar with the Civilian Conservation Corps (CCC), which put several hundred thousand young people to work in the thirties and which has more recent (but much smaller) incarnations in several states today. That model remains useful, and such evidence as we have tells us that it can work for many youths if given half a chance. But a still more intriguing effort, much less known, was the National

Youth Administration, NYA. Until its funding was eliminated at the start
of the 1940s, the NYA housed, clothed, fed, schooled, and employed
hundreds of thousands of youths who otherwise would have been un-
employed or terribly impoverished—some of them homeless, malnour-
ished, and in poor health. Many of them would have been classified, in
today's jargon, as "high-risk" youth—and many would, like their counterparts today, have wound up in institutions, on the street, or on the
road.

Much of NYA's work took place in "resident centers" where, as a
contemporary account tells it, "young people, both boys and girls, live
together, work and study, learn useful skills, and experience group life on
a civilized plane." These centers bore little resemblance to the modern
"group home" for adolescents. NYA did not view youths as overgrown
children needing the restraint of a quasi-family environment, but as potentially competent citizens who could be expected to make a real contribution to the larger community if they were offered the institutional
means to do so. Consequently, no stigma was attached to belonging to
NYA, no sense that it was an inadequate but necessary replacement for
a failed family life.

And NYA did indeed enable the young to contribute. There are few
areas in the United States that do not today bear the marks of some NYA
project begun more than half a century ago. During one year alone—
fiscal year 1939–40—NYA youth, among many other things, built 324
schools and rehabilitated 3,872 others; produced, in their own workshops,
over 8 million articles of medical and hospital supplies; served over 25
million school lunches, mainly to low-income children; built or improved
23,000 public parks; planted 7 million trees, stocked 137 million fish,
and produced 3 million pounds of food, some of which was used for their
own consumption, the rest distributed in low-income communities. NYA,
in short, put the young to work doing vital and useful public tasks that
otherwise would not have been done, which cushioned the harsh effects
of the Depression on many Americans, and which often remain visible
today in our public infrastructure, both urban and rural. NYA was also
remarkably "cost-effective," in the timid language of the eighties. It always
tried to make the best use of the meager materials at hand in the
Depression—turning old buildings, like churches or abandoned schools,
into dormitories and workshops, for example, creating integrated public
spaces where young people could live, learn, and work.

We don't need to follow the exact lines of the NYA model, or any other, to do something similar today. But the experience of NYA does suggest some useful guidelines, especially the basic concept of creating nonstigmatizing living, schooling, and working arrangements for youth who would benefit from options outside of the home and the formal systems of child welfare and youth control. A main attraction of this approach is that it kills two birds with one stone. We create challenging and supportive environments for young people who otherwise would have far more limited possibilities at best, and at worst would remain trapped in dangerous or abusive environments; and we accomplish important social tasks that the young could do well and which are now *not* done, or are done poorly and skimpily. There are scattered examples of community-based youth programs that do something similar, and some of them are very good. But we will need a commitment to these principles on the national level, with real resources to match, or we will not be able to create meaningful roles in the community for the vast numbers of young people now consigned to the dead-end institutions of the youth system or to the street or some combination of both. *With* that broad national commitment of resources, we could begin to build a culture of youth contribution and opportunity in place of the culture of consumerism and predatory individualism that now grips so many of the young (including several in this book) as it grips the larger society.

That commitment is especially urgent in the face of key changes in the opportunities that will be available to the American young in the future. The military, for example, once absorbed many of the Jeremy McClures and Lucifers of America; if, as we hope, we will before long see a smaller role for the military in American life and the American economy, we will need new kinds of civilian counterparts of the opportunities for work, training, and housing the military once offered. It was only World War Two that absorbed the youth displaced from the NYA and the CCC after the thirties; the long postwar economic boom pulled many into the industrial jobs that built places like Iron City and Rivertown and provided solid opportunities for the broad mass of young people. Today we cannot expect simple economic growth alone to do the same. Jeremy McClure sees that, even if some in Washington or in the universities do not; soon even construction jobs for kids who're strong and good with their hands may disappear—instead of building houses the old way, they'll just "connect bolts." So our alternatives are either to accept passively the ever greater abandonment of many youth to the economic marginality and desperation that has accompanied the decline of the old industries, or to build publicly supported alternatives in job creation and training to make the best use of what they can offer.

We have some current examples, including the Job Corps, that have repeatedly proven successful in training young men and women for useful work, keeping them out of crime, and avoiding futile and expensive incarceration. But the Job Corps and similar programs have been "targeted" to the *most* disadvantaged and delinquent kids; in the typical American pattern, you have to be really hard-core before you can get government assistance in becoming a more productive member of society. That is foolish, and many of the youth in this book illustrate the consequences. The vast majority of young people who move through the youth welfare and juvenile justice systems are not hard-core in this sense, and as a result they may actually have fewer options than those who *are*. What we need now is a support and opportunity system for the young that is broadly available to all who can benefit from it. That kind of system would have the supreme advantage of not concentrating our resources solely on youth *after* they have suffered the worst neglect and done the most damage. And by making broader opportunities for youth universal across the society, it would also avoid the stigma often attached to conventional youth-serving agencies, which diminishes their appeal to youth and simultaneously ensures that they will be given second-class treatment by legislatures and the public.

V

To be sure, some troubled kids will need to spend time in formal youth detention institutions even in the best of alternative worlds: a few of those in this book may be among them. But for them, too, we should apply the more hopeful and less wasteful principles of the opportunity model.

That we need to move beyond the traditional approaches is painfully apparent from the dismal statistics, both national and local, showing that most kids who wind up in places like the Hall or in group homes or drug "rehabs" have been somewhere in that "system" *before*, probably more than once. Indeed, River County's figures show a much faster increase in the category of those "readmitted" to the Hall than in first admissions. And the kids are keenly aware that they are recirculated over and over in the system. "Last time I was here, two years ago, come back, see the same faces," says Blaster. "They get about a hundred kids," Nick Barone complains, "and they just *keep* them kids." The bone-deep sense that nothing is happening in any part of the "system" to deflect the course of their lives is a persistent refrain for most of them. The really tough kids, like "James L.," who come from neighborhoods where the state penitentiary looms large over daily life, are all too aware that it is a very likely future for them, as it has been for their fathers, brothers, uncles, or friends, and that no one outside of themselves and a handful of dedicated friends, lovers, or relatives stands willing and ready to step in to deflect that trajectory. For the drugged-out "children of the air," the despairing sense that with no one to help them they may not be able to fend off the pull of ever more destructive drug use runs like a red thread through their stories; for them, the Hall appears as little more than a short respite, a momentary halt to what they fear will be a long downward slide.

We need to return to the more serious and humane notion that the juvenile justice system ought to help those who pass through it to live more productive and more contributive lives. Twenty-five years ago, we believed, at least on the level of official rhetoric, that the purpose of that system was to change lives, to return the young offender to the community in better shape than before. The idea of a rehabilitative juvenile justice system was much more promise than reality even then, and some of what went on under the rubric of "helping" kids should not have gone on at all. But today we've largely abandoned even the rhetoric of constructive change—as, not coincidentally, the communities to which young offenders must return have become decreasingly viable places, economically and socially.

But unless we are simply declaring that we wish to give up altogether on kids like James L., Loca, or Nick, part of a revised strategy for the troubled young must be a rethinking and upgrading of the mission of juvenile justice. We can begin by assuring that the youth confined in that system are granted the same rights to essential care and basic needs as youth outside. In some juvenile systems today—not in River County's—some or all of these basics are routinely unmet; in a few states, children inside are left to languish in brutal and unsafe conditions, at the mercy of predatory staff and of the most violent wards. Even in better systems, there is a tendency to let the quality of staff and of educational programs slide, and to overuse psychotropic drugs to calm and control kids in place of serious efforts to deal with the roots of their problems.

The notion is disturbingly pervasive in many youth control systems that kids who have broken the law are by definition unworthy of help, that indeed it is society's overindulgence of their needs and whims that has gotten them into trouble in the first place. What is striking, in fact, when you spend much time in the juvenile justice system, is how wildly the operating ideology of many staff people diverges from the reality of the lives that most of their charges have actually lived. You will hear over and over again that the real problem with the kids is that they have been coddled and given everything and that they must learn to accept some "limits" and to take some individual responsibility for their lives. Yet virtually every account given by the kids themselves tells of lives sharply constricted by routine brutality and exploitation at worst, and at the very least of having been forced too early to make do on their own: lives often hobbled by both material and emotional poverty. And those accounts can be easily backed up by evidence from less partisan sources. In this systematic and self-serving myopia lies part of the reason for the failure of even the best juvenile systems to prepare youth for better lives outside.

Beyond insisting on minimum standards, we should aim higher: the original purpose of juvenile justice should be not only affirmed but much enhanced. For those of the troubled young who do need secure care, we need to ensure that the time they are in care be used constructively—to make a frontal and serious attack on the illiteracy, innumeracy, lack of formal skills, and emotional problems many bring with them. To be sure, that's not an easy job. But it can bring returns that make the effort eminently worthwhile.

As a beginning, we should put in place high-quality education, serious training for useful work, and substance-abuse programs. We should add good aftercare once young people leave the system; perhaps most importantly, by providing them with reliable advocates who will help them negotiate the difficult road to a good job, a dignified place to live, and a set of strong and sustaining relationships with others.

To accomplish these things, we will need more and better-qualified staff in the juvenile institutions. Within River County's system, there is no shortage of qualified probation workers on the higher levels; the same cannot be said for some of those who staff the institutions to which the county consigns kids in trouble. Once when I was killing time in the Hall in between interviews, I was reading a manual, put out by the state, that describes the laws and regulations governing the youth system, its wards and staff, and sets out the philosophy that is supposed to underlie their work. A counselor, looking over my shoulder, asked if it was a book I had written; it was clear that he'd never seen it before and was unaware that it existed. On my first day in the Hall, I was called to one of the units to see if I could calm a sixteen-year-old who was crying uncontrollably and threatening to hurt himself in his room; it was rumored that I was "someone who talks to kids," and as such was deemed the most qualified person available in the institution to work with a kid who was freaking out. As it turned out, the boy was frightened that he would lose contact with his girlfriend while he was inside and no one could, or would, tell him whether she was allowed to visit (she wasn't). I don't mean to impugn the character of the frontline staff people in the institutions; I can't remember meeting anyone who wasn't trying, on the whole, to do the best they could. But too often the best they could wasn't good enough—not for the tough job someone needed to do. And the situation is much, much worse in many youth systems outside of River County. In those systems, most staff have been taught little or nothing about the developmental or social issues presented by delinquent or discarded youth; in some of them, the staff seem deliberately selected from those least able to empathize with, or care seriously about, young people.

My modest proposal here is that we reverse the current pattern; instead of putting the least qualified teachers and counselors to work with the most difficult kids, let's put the best, most skilled, most initiating, most flexible, most empathic at working with the young, to work with those who need that skilled and empathic engagement the most. The quickest way to make that shift is by substantially and rapidly upgrading both the qualifications and the rewards for this work.

We talk much these days about youth being our nation's future, and about the tragic and costly consequences, both social and economic, if we do not nurture, train, and teach them better. But it's one thing to talk about these issues in the abstract, another to commit ourselves to sustained efforts to help the young black woman with no formal skills languishing in a group home because her family has disappeared into the nightmare world of rock cocaine, or the poor-white kid who has been brought to the

Hall after poaching his brain with gasoline fumes and who is desperately afraid he won't be able to handle his drug problem by himself on the "outs." The young men and women who move in and out of the youth systems are viscerally aware of this contradiction between rhetoric and reality: "You don't learn nothing here, not one thing." "Thing to do is be quiet. If you're quiet, you'll do good." "They never set me to go out there and do better." "I stayed seven months in this motherfucker and I didn't learn *nothin'*, man. Only thing I learned, how to break into houses more, how to hot-wire, how to kill somebody and get away with it." "I ain't set no goals for myself. I'ma do the same fucking thing."

That we do not seriously address these needs reflects, in part, the dismally predictable fiscal starvation of public agencies in general and youth services in particular. But beyond that, the systematic neglect of the kids inside betrays our pervasive belief that most of them are undeserving or expendable or both. "They can keep getting you in here where they don't have to deal with you," Nick says, and he cannot be altogether wrong. There is a part of our national psyche that would rather put a boy in prison for not going to school than make a serious effort to teach him how to spell. That mentality governs too much of our policies toward youth today, and it is one reason why it is so difficult for kids like Jeremy or Nick to extricate themselves from the youth control system once they're caught in it.

There is a better way, and its basic principles aren't difficult to grasp. "They should work with each kid and find him at his level," Jeremy proposes, "see what he can do." And he's exactly right. We should certainly do no less. Indeed, we can't *afford* to do less. By failing to do what Jeremy suggests, we are steadily swelling the ranks of young people whose potential is being systematically wasted (or stolen); who are consequently forced to cope on their own and at a sharp disadvantage by whatever strategies, legal or otherwise, they can devise; and who, perhaps most tragically, may increasingly come to regard that condition as the natural state of things. If, as a result, some seem less and less capable of maintaining enduring connections with others, a motivating hope for the future, an allegiance to purposes larger than daily survival, or a reliable concern for the welfare of others, we shouldn't pretend surprise. "Children have never been very good at listening to their elders", James Baldwin wrote a generation ago. "But they have never failed to imitate them. . . .

That is exactly what our children are doing. They are imitating our immorality, our disrespect for the pain of others." Fortunately, not *all* of them are doing so; as many in this book testify, there are extraordinary expressions of solidarity, of keen social awareness, and of undiminished hope for the future. If we listen, we can learn from those sentiments; and if we are willing, we can build on them.

About the Author

ELLIOTT CURRIE is the author of *Confronting Crime: An American Challenge* (Pantheon Books, 1985); *America's Problems: Social Issues and Public Policy* (with Jerome Skolnick); as well as other works on crime, delinquency, and social policy. He is currently a research associate at the Institute for the Study of Social Change, and a lecturer in the Legal Studies Program at the University of California, Berkeley. He has taught sociology and criminology at Yale University and the University of California.

A graduate of Chicago's Roosevelt University, he holds a doctorate in sociology from the University of California, Berkeley. He is vice-chair of the Eisenhower Foundation in Washington, D.C., which supports innovative delinquency and drug-abuse prevention programs in the inner city, and co-author of the foundation's recent report, *Youth Investment and Community Reconstruction: Street Lessons on Drugs and Crime for the Nineties*. He has served as a consultant to a wide range of organizations, including the National Council on Crime and Delinquency, the National Advisory Council on Economic Opportunity, the California Governor's Task Force on Civil Rights, the Correctional Association of New York, and the Home Office of Great Britain.

In 1988, he received the first Donald R. Cressey Award from the National Council on Crime and Delinquency, and in 1990, the Paul Tappan Award of the Western Society of Criminology and an award for Dedicated Service in the Field of Prison Research from the Prisoners' Rights Union.